Web3 Development using Hyperledger Fabric Framework

Build, deploy, and scale your blockchain applications using Hyperledger Fabric chaincodes

Marcos Sarres
Samuel Venzi

www.bpbonline.com

First Edition 2025

ISBN: 978-93-6589-989-4

LIMITS OF LIABILITY AND DISCLAIMER OF WARRANTY

To View Complete BPB Publications Catalogue Scan the QR Code:

www.bpbonline.com

Dedicated to

My brother and first blockchain teacher ***Rafa****, my sister* ***Simone****,*
my girlfriend ***Joana****, my father* ***Luiz***
and my mother ***Mamy's Helena***

- Marcos Sarres

My wife ***Fernanda****,*
and my family, ***Roberto****,* ***Chirlene****, and* ***Pedro***

- Samuel Venzi

About the Authors

- **Marcos Sarres** stands as a pioneering figure in the realm of permissioned blockchain technology and smart contract development. With over 20 years of experience as CEO and CTO in innovation startups, he has led groundbreaking projects in the blockchain industry. As a leader of the Hyperledger Blockchain Brazilian community for two years, Marcos has played a crucial role in fostering the adoption and development of blockchain solutions in Brazil. He has also contributed to academia by teaching blockchain classes for developers in Brazilian universities. Recognized for his expertise, Marcos was nominated among the top three blockchain professionals in Brazil in 2020 (Prêmio Digitalks). His influence extends globally as a well-known speaker and panelist at blockchain and tokenization events worldwide. Passionate about blockchain technology, he actively participates in the Brazilian technical group of the ISO/TC 307 discussions on blockchain and distributed ledger technologies, shaping the future of decentralized systems.

- **Samuel Venzi** is a CTO and blockchain developer with extensive experience in enterprise blockchain solutions, including Hyperledger Fabric and Besu. Samuel is proficient in many programming languages and frameworks as well as planning, designing and implementing blockchain solutions for complex business requirements. Samuel is certified by the Linux Foundation as Certified Hyperledger Fabric Administrator (CHFA), Hyperledger Fabric Certified Practitioner (HFCP) and Besu Certified Professional (BCP), the last two accomplished by integrating the Exam Developer team responsible for creating the certifications, reinforcing his role as a Subject-Matter Expert in the field. He has delivered over 20 blockchain projects to public and private companies. He contributes to the Hyperledger Fabric Admin SDK codebase and, most notably, is a core maintainer of the Hyperledger Labs CC-Tools project. Samuel also is a mentor in the mentorship project Hyperledger Fabric CC-Tools Support for Fabric Private Chaincode funded and promoted by the Linux Foundation. Finally, Samuel has been a speaker in multiple blockchain events including Blockchain Rio and the Hyperledger Member Summit in San Francisco and Tokyo.

About the Reviewers

- **Pulkit Saraf** is a highly skilled software engineer with an extensive background in blockchain technology. He earned his master's degree in Computer Applications from Vellore Institute of Technology. With professional experiences at AKEO, IBM, and Settlemint India, Pulkit has significantly contributed to projects across finance, digital currencies, and automation sectors.

  Pulkit's expertise encompasses Hyperledger Fabric, Ethereum, Kubernetes, and Docker, focusing on designing secure and scalable decentralized systems. He has also shared his knowledge through blogs on blockchain deployment and security. Beyond his professional pursuits, Pulkit enjoys traveling, participating in outdoor sports, and delving into new technological advancements. Driven by a passion for innovation, he is dedicated to advancing decentralized solutions and fostering real-world blockchain adoption.

- **Sophielily Weinstein** is a fiscal engineer and Econimiteician who is the CEO and co-founder of Numeraire Group. In the fall of 2017, Sophielily was asked to write and advice Fintech and banking regulations for the EU's Economic and Financial Affairs Council. In summer of 2020, she gained membership to the WTO's Strategic Intelligence Committee which she is not on the Expert Council of. The same year, she was invited to act as a liaison between Banking for International Settlements' Payment, and Market Infrastructure Committee and their innovative hubs. In 2023, Sophielily started acting as an advisor to the General Council of the World Trade Organization.

Acknowledgements

We are very grateful to everyone who has contributed to the existence of this book.

We would like to thank our families and friends who have supported us during the writing of this book. We could not have done this without their words of motivation and love.

We also extend our profound thanks to our colleagues at GoLedger, who contribute to our technical growth every day. Thank you for all the work that you do in pushing the boundaries of blockchain further every day. We would also like to thank our fellow maintainers and contributors of the CC-Tools project, who voluntarily chose to help create a tool that can be used freely by anyone.

We would like to thank the Linux Foundation Decentralized Trust. Without its efforts, projects like Hyperledger Fabric would not be possible. We are immensely grateful for being able to contribute to such a wonderful community. A special thanks to LFDT Chapter Brazil, an outstanding group of experts, developers, and blockchain enthusiasts who continuously drive the community forward, fostering innovation and collaboration.

We are very grateful to BPB Publications for trusting us with this book. Thank you for your guidance and support in every step of writing this book.

We also would like to acknowledge the reviewers, technical experts and editors who helped shape the book into its final form. Your insights and expertise have undoubtedly enhanced the quality of this book.

Preface

Understanding blockchain technology is increasingly important in today's world. It impacts many aspects of society, from financial services to supply chain. This book Hyperledger Fabric Chaincode, from Development to Cloud Production Mode prepares developers for the new age of computing.

The book comprises 13 chapters, covering all topics necessary for understanding and being able to develop blockchain-based solutions. The book starts with the history of the blockchain, discussing how humans have valued assets in the past and present. We then move into blockchain concepts and introduction to Hyperledger Fabric, providing the basic understanding of how these systems function. Fabric Concepts and Components dives deeper into the details.

Chapter 5 explains the Transaction Flow, the core process of achieving data integrity in Hyperledger Fabric. In Chapter 6, the reader is presented with Deploying Your First Chaincode, a practical chapter designed to give the reader hands-on experience.

In Chapter 7, Introduction to CC-Tools library, the reader gains even more insight on how blockchain applications can be created. More details are given on asset, data types, transaction and in custom transactions, giving the reader the toolset to develop complete applications.

Chapter 10 details how applications can be interacted with, providing explanations on API integration between systems and the blockchain network, a core part of real-world applications. Chapter 11 details the important topic of data privacy, explaining how to achieve the desired level of privacy depending on the use case.

In Production Networks the reader is presented with best practices and options for deploying production-grade networks. Lastly, Chapter 13 sheds light on how this technology impacts our society.

This book is designed to cater to technically-oriented students from various backgrounds and programming levels. Prior knowledge of blockchain is not needed, however readers with blockchain knowledge will find this a great resource for learning new tools to bring their applications to fruition.

Chapter 1: History of the Blockchain - This chapter provides a historical overview of record-keeping systems humans used across time. It covers how societies have assigned value to objects and resources, from ancient examples like rai stones to modern ones like NFTs. The chapter, then exemplifies many iterations of ledgers such as clay tables, scrolls and the revolutionary double-entry bookkeeping system. Finally, it explains how that culminated in the creation of Bitcoin and Ethereum, introducing protocols to ensure trust and unequivocally execution of business rules.

Chapter 2: Blockchain Concepts - This chapter serves as an introduction to the core concepts of blockchain technology, outlining differences from traditional databases and introducing essential components. It introduces the main characteristics of the technology such as decentralization, immutability, consensus and smart contracts. The chapter provides a thought experiment guiding the reader through solving an issue of tracking borrowing and lending money in a digital manner while introducing concepts like digital signatures, unique identification and linking data to ensure integrity. The chapter compares different blockchain implementations, giving the reader a bird's eye view of the types of blockchain available.

Chapter 3: Introduction to Hyperledger Fabric - This is an introductory chapter on Hyperledger Fabric. It details the origins of the framework and how it became the most used permissioned blockchain platform in the world. The chapter sheds light on how previous solutions had trouble adhering to the standards of the enterprise world and how Hyperledger Fabric was able to do so. The chapter guides the reader through key questions to ask when deciding if Hyperledger Fabric is the right choice for a particular project. Finally, it introduces the core components of the framework and highlights its open-source community.

Chapter 4: Fabric Concepts and Components - The chapter provides a detailed explanation of Hyperledger Fabric. It outlines the principles of the framework and explains each component in detail, including CAs, peers, orderers, channels and chaincodes. It then provides a comprehensive overview of a complete business network that integrates every component introduced before.

Chapter 5: Transaction Flow - This chapter describes the process which every transaction goes through in Hyperledger Fabric, the transaction flow. It details how this mode differs from other blockchain system's transaction validations. Each subtopic explores one of the stages of the transaction flow, detailing the roles of each component in this process.

Chapter 6: Deploying Your First Chaincode - Readers will gain practical knowledge during the course of this chapter. They will be guided through the configuration and deployment of a Hyperledger Fabric network complete with a chaincode. They will be introduced to the sample code provided by the official Hyperledger Fabric guides. They will have firsthand contact with a smart contract, allowing them to experiment with changes to the code while understanding core principles that allow chaincodes to register data.

Chapter 7: Introduction to CC-Tools Library - This chapter will introduce the CC-Tools open-source project. It starts explaining the origins of the project and why it exists. The reader will learn that CC-Tools provides a framework for fast chaincode development, a process that can otherwise be repetitive and long. The chapter details the feature set available in CC-Tools, such as a structured framework for defining asset types, data types and transactions. This framework is then compared to the standard way of developing chaincodes.

Chapter 8: Asset, Data Types, and Transactions - This chapter builds on the previous one, detailing in full detail how to define asset types, data types and use the built-in transactions to register data to the blockchain. The chapter explains the anatomy of an asset, moving through all fields that must be defined such as the asset's tag and label, and its associated properties. Such properties can use standard data type, however the reader will learn to define their own custom data types, with validation that takes place automatically during execution. Then the reader will explore all the transactions already implemented in CC-Tools by default, focusing on transactions that allow for creation, reading, updating and deletion of assets.

Chapter 9: Custom Transactions - This chapter explains how to implement custom transactions within the CC-Tools framework, allowing developers to create applications for any use-case. It details the anatomy of a transaction definition, explaining how to define arguments, how to use each CC-Tools resource to create write functions and read functions and finally how to properly test the developed transaction with automated testing.

Chapter 10: Understanding the API - This chapter explains an essential part of blockchain applications which is how to interact with it. It explains the use of Hyperledger Fabric SDKs and their roles in building APIs that allow for programmatic access to chaincode interaction. This chapter explains the built-in API provided by the CC-Tools project, the CCAPI. It details its endpoints giving the reader the necessary knowledge to interact with the applications they have built.

Chapter 11: Using Private Data Collections - This chapter introduces a more complex feature of chaincodes in Hyperledger Fabric, which is modeling collections that serve as a structure for maintaining privacy of data when needed. The chapter details the theory behind it, so readers understand it. It then moves on to exploring use-cases that may require private data and all the features that PDCs support. Finally, it explains how to implement private data within the CC-Tools framework.

Chapter 12: Production Networks - This chapter introduces the end-goal of developing blockchain applications which is having a real-world network running and solving real world problems. This chapter details important characteristics of production networks, providing a good starting point for readers who may want to take their development further. It explores tools that make production deployments easier for various levels of expertise. It also details best practices for Hyperledger Fabric configurations in such a scenario.

Chapter 13: Web3 Society - This closing chapter explores the broader scenario of the blockchain's role in our society. It discusses the importance of the Web3 revolution, and the characteristics achieved by this new paradigm. This chapter details the gains in efficiency and security provided by blockchain technology. It also discusses how this new paradigm differs from traditional application development and how this is shaping solutions in many different areas: financial, healthcare, cloud computing, manufacturing and others.

Code Bundle and Coloured Images

Please follow the link to download the
Code Bundle and the ***Coloured Images*** of the book:

https://rebrand.ly/av9w0tb

The code bundle for the book is also hosted on GitHub at **https://github.com/bpbpublications/Web3-Development-using-Hyperledger-Fabric-Framework**. In case there's an update to the code, it will be updated on the existing GitHub repository.

We have code bundles from our rich catalogue of books and videos available at **https://github.com/bpbpublications**. Check them out!

Errata

We take immense pride in our work at BPB Publications and follow best practices to ensure the accuracy of our content to provide with an indulging reading experience to our subscribers. Our readers are our mirrors, and we use their inputs to reflect and improve upon human errors, if any, that may have occurred during the publishing processes involved. To let us maintain the quality and help us reach out to any readers who might be having difficulties due to any unforeseen errors, please write to us at :

errata@bpbonline.com

Your support, suggestions and feedbacks are highly appreciated by the BPB Publications' Family.

Piracy

If you come across any illegal copies of our works in any form on the internet, we would be grateful if you would provide us with the location address or website name. Please contact us at **business@bpbonline.com** with a link to the material.

If you are interested in becoming an author

If there is a topic that you have expertise in, and you are interested in either writing or contributing to a book, please visit **www.bpbonline.com**. We have worked with thousands of developers and tech professionals, just like you, to help them share their insights with the global tech community. You can make a general application, apply for a specific hot topic that we are recruiting an author for, or submit your own idea.

Reviews

Please leave a review. Once you have read and used this book, why not leave a review on the site that you purchased it from? Potential readers can then see and use your unbiased opinion to make purchase decisions. We at BPB can understand what you think about our products, and our authors can see your feedback on their book. Thank you!

For more information about BPB, please visit **www.bpbonline.com**.

Join our book's Discord space

Join the book's Discord Workspace for Latest updates, Offers, Tech happenings around the world, New Release and Sessions with the Authors:

https://discord.bpbonline.com

Table of Contents

Chapter 1
History of the Blockchain

Introduction

This chapter of the book will delve into the fascinating origins and rich history of blockchain technology. To fully grasp the significance of blockchain, we must first explore how societies have tracked trade and valued various goods over countless millennia. It is intriguing to observe that human beings have attributed value to objects that possess no inherent worth. This intriguing concept lays the groundwork for understanding the correlation between these historical practices and the emergence of **Non-Fungible Tokens** (**NFTs**).

Continuing our exploration, we will delve into the concept of ledgers, tracing their origins back to ancient systems of accountability. By examining the evolution of these ledgers, we will uncover their connection to blockchain technology. This examination will provide valuable insights into how a blockchain functions and how it can be effectively applied.

As we delve deeper, we will shed light on the problems that blockchain technology successfully addressed during its initial implementation by Bitcoin. This groundbreaking application paved the way for subsequent advancements, including the influential Ethereum blockchain. Moreover, we will explore the emergence of permissioned blockchains such as Hyperledger Fabric, showcasing their unique features and contributions to the broader blockchain ecosystem.

By charting the historical trajectory of blockchain, from its ancient roots to its modern-day applications, this chapter aims to provide readers with a comprehensive understanding of this transformative technology.

Structure

The chapter covers the following topics:

- Trade and ancient societies
- Historical and modern representations of value
- History of Ledger
- Bitcoin and the emergence of trust protocols
- Ethereum and introduction of smart contracts

Objectives

By the end of this chapter, readers will gain a comprehensive understanding of the origins of blockchain and its transformative potential in addressing age-old challenges. Delving into the topic, you will discover the diverse types of blockchain that exist, their shared characteristics, and the remarkable advancements made to enhance the technology's efficacy across a wide range of applications. You will be introduced to concepts that will be further explained such as consensus, smart contracts and actual structure that give blockchain its name.

Trade and ancient societies

Before we discuss blockchain details, let us go back in time to discuss some basic principles of our society.

Thousands of years ago society was dependent on carrying all their properties and belongings with themselves. The notion of property was restricted to the condition of protecting their food, clothing, or other valuable objects necessary for their survival and wealth.

As humans settled, trade and property disputes became a growing issue. Establishing a systematic method to register their assets was crucial for the advancement of society, ensuring clear ownership rights and facilitating trade both within their own community and with other societies.

Various cultures had their own forms of tracking trade and ownership. In ancient Egypt, scrolls were used to record harvests, land ownership, and tax payments, while in China, wooden sticks were carved to serve as contracts. Innovations like this not only helped commerce but also laid the foundation for more complex financial systems. With the advancement of civilizations, trade became broader than the local interaction, necessitating other methods of record-keeping.

In present-day Iraq, archaeologists unearthed the earliest documented ledgers, shedding light on trade activities in ancient Mesopotamia approximately 7,000 years ago. These clay tablets served as records, meticulously detailing expenses, received goods, and traded items. These records were maintained by temple priests or government officials, trusted intermediaries that were a fundamental aspect of commerce.

Historical and modern representations of value

Civilizations have had the need for tracking ownership rights for thousands of years, whether it is land, livestock, food, or any other possessions that carry subjective value to society. One example of such possession are rai stones of Micronesia.

Refer to *Figure 1.1*:

***Figure 1.1**: Rai stone located in Micronesia*

Rai stones are stone discs that originated in Micronesia around the 12th century and served as a form of currency. While the use of currency is not unique to Micronesia, what sets rai stones apart is their exceptional size and weight, ranging from 3.5 centimeters to over 3 meters and weighing up to 4,000kg.

Despite their enormous size, rai stones held value due to their scarcity and cultural significance. They were commonly exchanged as ceremonial gifts and symbolized wealth and status. Interestingly, rai stones did not need to be physically transported or accessed to be transferred. In one remarkable story, a stone being transported by canoe sank to the ocean floor, yet it continued to be transacted normally because its existence was collectively acknowledged.

Modern-day NFTs, much like rai stones, rely on the idea of representing ownership of uniquely defined assets. These digital tokens, powered by blockchain technology, serve as proof of ownership for one-of-a-kind assets. While rai stones symbolized value and cultural significance, NFTs have emerged as a modern manifestation of ownership, revolutionizing the digital space. Whether it is digital art, collectibles, or virtual real estate, NFTs enable creators to authenticate and monetize their unique creations in an unprecedented way, much like the significance bestowed upon rai stones in the past.

Refer to *Figure 1.2*:

***Figure 1.2**: The first 5000 days, by Mike Winkelmann, an NFT sold for $69M*

The ownership and accountability of goods historically takes advantage of the ledger.

History of Ledger

This concept is very important, and it will be revisited several times in the following chapters of this book. The use of ledgers in civilization is essential when contemplating the evolution of humankind; it is virtually impossible to discuss this evolution without acknowledging their significance.

Many examples can be found in our day-to-day lives, and contrary to what you might think they are not financial. One such example is a basketball game score.

Refer to *Table 1.1*:

Time	Points made	Team
00:00:21	2 points	Bulls
00:00:38	2 points	Lakers
00:01:04	3 points	Bulls
00:01:18	2 points	Lakers
00:01:51	3 points	Lakers
00:02:08	1 point	Bulls
Current Score	6 Bulls x 7 Lakers	-

***Table 1.1**: Representation of point events in a basketball game*

It is not that hard to think about other examples that might be hidden in our daily lives, like our bank accounts, product stock control and hotel check-ins and check-outs.

For thousands of years this concept has permeated society. Clay tablets were used in Mesopotamia to record financial transactions. In Egypt, scribes used papyrus scrolls for their accounting needs. By the time the Renaissance rolled around, *Luca Pacioli* created the double-entry accounting system, laying the foundation for the modern ledger for accounting.

The ledger is most used in accounting services and banking operations. For example, the statement of a bank account is mainly a list of several transactions of deposits and withdrawals since the account creation.

Refer to *Table 1.2*:

Account 0001	Value	Type of operation
2023-01-20	10.00	Credit
2023-01-21	15.00	Credit
2023-01-22	7.00	Debit
2023-01-23	8.00	Debit
2023-01-24	20.00	Credit
2023-01-24	30.00	Account balance

***Table 1.2**: Representation of financial operations in a bank account*

Most people are usually only concerned with their account balance, but they do not bother checking if deposits and withdrawals add up to the correct amount informed by their bank. Trusting that the financial institution will show the correct information is at the center of the experience of owning a bank account. Something breaking this trust can have significant consequences.

Bitcoin and emergence of trust protocols

Bitcoin, an influential digital currency, has achieved widespread recognition and media coverage, whether for its societal value or its portrayal as a speculative gamble. However, the journey of Bitcoin has been far from its current household name. In its early days, Bitcoin was an enigma understood only by a select group of cypherpunks. The mastermind behind this groundbreaking concept, *Satoshi Nakamoto*, unveiled the Bitcoin whitepaper in 2008, outlining an electronic cash system that would eventually revolutionize the perception of currency itself. This visionary document provided intricate technical insights into the inner workings of a trustless system where transactions could be conducted without the need for intermediaries.

Nakamoto ingeniously combined existing technologies, weaving them into a unique application that challenged the status quo of the financial ecosystem. The concept of cryptographically chaining blocks of data had been proposed as early as 1982, while the notion of a proof-of-work system was first conceived in 1999 and further refined in 2004 by *Hal Finney*, the recipient of the inaugural Bitcoin transaction.

Refer to *Figure 1.3*:

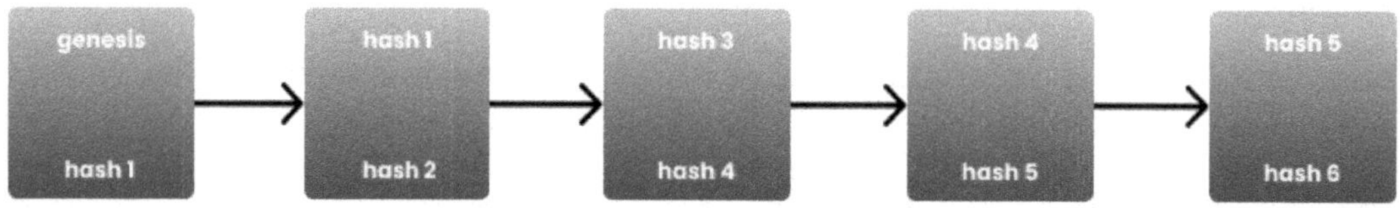

***Figure 1.3**: The structure that gives blockchain its name*

At its inception, the trajectory of the Bitcoin project and its potential were far from evident. However, a significant turning point occurred in 2010, when *Laszlo Hanyecz* immortalized himself in Bitcoin lore by famously purchasing two pizzas for a staggering 10,000 Bitcoins. This landmark transaction represented the first real-world exchange where Bitcoin functioned as a medium of value transfer. Henceforth, Bitcoin Pizza Day became an annual event eagerly marked on the calendars of Bitcoin enthusiasts worldwide.

Bitcoin's unique characteristic of eliminating intermediaries quickly attracted attention, leading to both noble and nefarious applications. Its popularity surged on platforms like Silk Road in the depths of the deep web, where the decentralized nature of Bitcoin allowed transactions to occur beyond the grasp of central entities capable of blocking traditional wire transfers.

Bitcoin has earned the moniker *the protocol of trust* due to its innovative design and decentralized nature, which fundamentally transforms the traditional trust paradigm. Unlike traditional financial systems that rely on intermediaries such as banks or governments to facilitate transactions and ensure trust, Bitcoin operates on a peer-to-peer network secured by cryptographic protocols. Through its decentralized technology, Bitcoin removes the need for a central authority and enables participants to engage in trustless transactions. The protocol's transparency, immutability, and incorruptible nature foster a new level of trust among users, as every transaction is publicly recorded and verifiable by anyone. With Bitcoin, trust is no longer a matter of faith in institutions but rather a result of the robust and transparent protocols that underpin its operation, revolutionizing the concept of trust in the digital age.

Over the years, Bitcoin has experienced multiple cycles of meteoric rises and precipitous falls in value. Despite facing proclamations of its demise with each crash, the remarkable feature of Bitcoin lies in its blockchain, a ledger recording the complete history of transactions since its inception. This permanent and tamper-resistant ledger obviates the need for intermediaries to verify the validity of transactions, providing an immutable record of financial activity.

Bitcoin's journey has made a big impact on the world. It remains an enigmatic and polarizing asset, captivating both seasoned investors and curious newcomers. Its decentralized nature, coupled with robust security measures, continues to inspire fascination and scrutiny. Its main contribution, however, in the context of this book are the foundations it laid for the blockchain to become its own living thing and inspire the next generation of applications of the new era of the internet, the Web 3.

Ethereum and introduction of smart contracts

The Bitcoin protocol sparked a revolutionary transformation in the financial asset exchange, enabling users to transact without relying on a trusted intermediary while ensuring verifiability and consensus within the entire ecosystem. This groundbreaking approach to tracking ownership in a peer-to-peer network gave rise to numerous potential applications beyond mere currency exchange. Notably, applications emerged for registering unique name ownership (Namecoin), website domains, and even alternative currencies (Colored coins). These applications either utilized separate blockchains with the same protocol or were integrated directly into the Bitcoin blockchain.

However, the Bitcoin blockchain presented challenges when it came to expanding the scope of these applications. One of the key obstacles was the absence of a Turing-complete scripting language, which would allow for the development of fully functional applications. The scripting language employed by Bitcoin lacked features like loops, necessitating the replication of code lines for iterative operations. Other limitations were its lack of transaction processing capacity which was limited by average block reaction time of 10 minutes, its lack of statefulness, blindness to external information, and even blindness to the blockchain itself, meaning that the coin transfer logic was decoupled from the blockchain layer.

In response to these limitations, *Vitalik Buterin*, a Russian programmer, conceived the Ethereum blockchain in 2013. In his whitepaper, *Buterin* expounded on the accomplishments of Bitcoin while addressing its crucial shortcomings. The Ethereum protocol proposed a paradigm shift by enabling a new generation of blockchain-powered applications, incorporating significant improvements. Most notably, Ethereum introduced smart contracts designed to operate within a Turing-complete environment.

The term **smart contract**, coined by *Nick Szabo*, refers to a set of instructions or business rules that are executed deterministically. In other words, for a given set of inputs and a specific system state, the outputs are always predictable and consistent. Smart contracts play a central role in this book as we embark on the journey of developing blockchain-powered applications.

By leveraging a Turing-complete environment, smart contracts on Ethereum empower limitless applications and offer the same computational complexity as any other system. This remarkable capability has unleashed a wave of innovative ideas never conceived, ultimately defining the foundation of the Web 3 era and shaping the trajectory of the new internet.

In 2014, Ethereum conducted one of the most significant events in its history, the **Initial Coin Offering** (**ICO**). The Ethereum team sought to raise funds to finance the development of the platform and its ecosystem. During the ICO, individuals and investors had the opportunity to purchase **Ether** (**ETH**), the native cryptocurrency of the Ethereum network. The ICO proved to be a resounding success, raising over 31,000 BTC (equivalent to approximately $18 million at the time). This influx of capital provided the necessary resources to further advance Ethereum's development and solidify its position as a leading blockchain platform.

Over the years, Ethereum has undergone several notable protocol upgrades that have introduced substantial changes to the network's rules and features. One of the most significant hard forks occurred in July 2016 when the Ethereum community decided to execute a hard fork in response to the infamous **Decentralized Autonomous Organization** (**DAO**) hack. This hard fork resulted in the creation of two separate chains: Ethereum and Ethereum Classic. The Ethereum chain continued with the updated protocol, while Ethereum Classic maintained the original blockchain. Since then, Ethereum has undergone subsequent hard forks to improve scalability, security, and functionality.

Ethereum has become the leading platform for the explosive growth of **Decentralized Finance** (**DeFi**). DeFi refers to a broad range of financial applications built on blockchain technology that aim to provide open and permissionless alternatives to traditional financial services. Ethereum's programmable smart contracts and its vibrant ecosystem of developers and projects have facilitated the creation of various DeFi applications, including decentralized exchanges, lending, and borrowing platforms, stablecoins, yield farming, and more. The surge in DeFi has not only showcased the versatility and potential of Ethereum but has also revolutionized how individuals can access and participate in financial services in a decentralized and inclusive manner.

Refer to *Figure 1.4*:

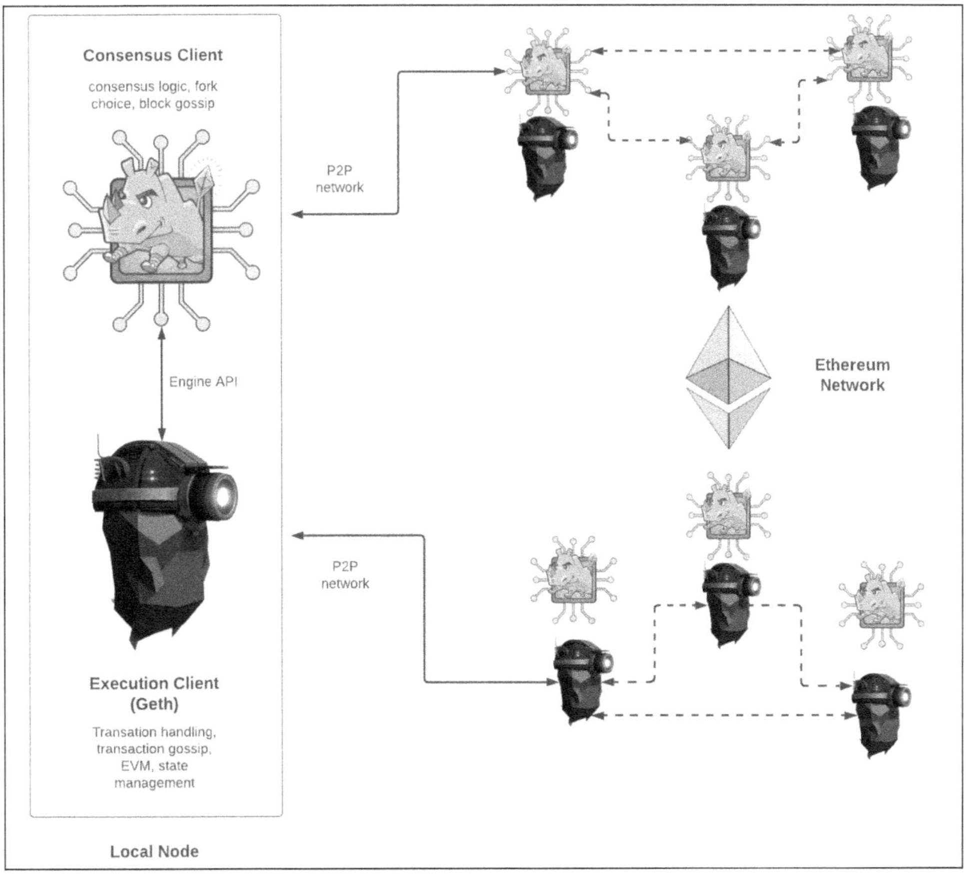

***Figure 1.4**: The current official architecture of Ethereum, with an execution client and a consensus client*

These new applications expanded the usage of blockchain beyond just the cryptocurrency realm, including its negative association with platforms like the Silk Road. Eventually, businesses recognized the potential of utilizing blockchain technology within their own operations to address challenges related to integration, auditing, and traceability. However, there was a crucial difference: Ethereum operated on a permissionless model, while corporations dealt with highly sensitive data that could not be accessed by unauthorized parties. As a result, the demand for a permissioned blockchain became imminent.

Hyperledger Fabric and introduction of permissioned blockchain

The Hyperledger project, established in 2015 under the Linux Foundation, has been instrumental in promoting the development of blockchain technology in various forms. Initially composed of ten companies, including IBM, the project aimed to foster innovation and collaboration within the blockchain community. One of the significant contributions made by IBM was the codebase that formed the foundation of Hyperledger Fabric, the most widely adopted private blockchain framework.

Hyperledger Fabric emerged from the open blockchain project at IBM, where it was initially developed before being released as an open-source project. By redefining traditional structures found in public blockchains, Fabric introduced a scalable and performant framework while prioritizing privacy and security.

From its inception until July 2017, Fabric underwent an iterative development process, gradually introducing and refining core features before reaching the milestone of its production release, version 1.0. One of the key architectural advancements brought by Fabric was its modular design, enabling independent maintenance of components and facilitating plug-and-play functionality. This flexibility empowered businesses to tailor the blockchain architecture to suit their specific needs and use cases.

Refer to *Figure 1.5*:

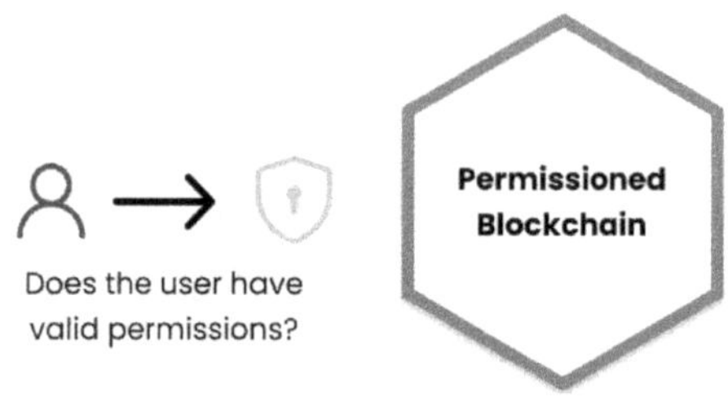

***Figure 1.5**: In Hyperledger Fabric, users need permissions to transact*

Furthermore, Fabric extended the capabilities of smart contracts beyond what was established by the Ethereum protocol. While previous blockchain protocols relied on specific programming languages like Solidity, Fabric introduced the concept of chaincodes, which allowed the use of general-purpose programming languages such as Go, JavaScript, and Java. This innovation significantly enhanced adoption by enabling developers to leverage existing libraries and programming knowledge to build smart contracts on the Fabric platform.

Moreover, Fabric introduced a modular and adaptable consensus mechanism known as the ordering service. Responsible for ordering transactions in a deterministic manner, it provided the flexibility to choose consensus protocols and even upgrade them independently. Initially composed of a single node or a Kafka node cluster, the ordering service has since evolved to utilize the Raft consensus protocol, with plans to release a Byzantine Fault Tolerant version in the upcoming v3.0 release.

Throughout this book, a comprehensive exploration of these concepts will be undertaken, commencing in *Chapter 3, Introduction to Hyperledger Fabric,* readers will gain a deeper understanding of the inner workings of Hyperledger Fabric, empowering them to leverage its features and capabilities effectively.

By leveraging Hyperledger Fabric, organizations have been able to enhance both their internal and external processes, leveraging its capabilities to increase efficiency in integration with business partners. The platform offers trust in data through immutability and transparency, allowing businesses to track all alterations made to the information stored on the blockchain. As a result, Hyperledger Fabric has emerged as a powerful tool for enterprises seeking to improve their operations and streamline their workflows.

Before we talk more about Fabric, we will talk about general blockchain concepts that will permeate the work we will do with Fabric during the course of this book.

Conclusion

This chapter explored the origins of blockchain and its potential for transformation. We discussed how ancient societies used ledgers for tracking ownership and facilitating trade, citing examples such as clay tablets and rai stones. We then highlighted the historical importance of ledgers in accounting, sports, and banking. Bitcoin was introduced as a protocol of trust, challenging traditional finance with its decentralized nature. Ethereum expanded on Bitcoin's capabilities with smart contracts, enabling limitless applications. Hyperledger Fabric was introduced as a permissioned blockchain framework addressing privacy and security in enterprise settings.

In the next chapter, we will dive deeper into the technical concepts of blockchain, including consensus mechanisms, smart contracts, and different types of blockchain architectures.

CHAPTER 2
Blockchain Concepts

Introduction

In this chapter, we will discuss the technical concepts that make blockchain technology incredibly valuable. Here, we will unravel the foundations of blockchain and explore how it differs from traditional databases. By the end, you will have a solid grasp of the fundamental elements underpinning blockchain's power.

Let us start by understanding how the core characteristics of a blockchain can be achieved with an example that will take us from a rudimentary money-tracking system into something more sophisticated.

We cannot forget about consensus: the cornerstone of any distributed system. We will dive into the concept of consensus and explain how it enables the execution of business rules across different nodes, bringing alignment and trust to the decentralized world.

We will also explore the growth of blockchains through the addition of new blocks and how this mechanism ensures the integrity and immutability of data over time. This is where the true power of blockchain lies: maintaining a trustworthy and transparent ledger that is resistant to tampering or manipulation.

Then, we will delve into the core components of blockchain: transactions, blocks, and nodes. Understanding how these building blocks fit together is crucial to comprehend the inner workings of a blockchain network. We will walk you through each element, shedding light on their roles and interactions, so you can see the big picture.

By the end of this chapter, you will have a solid technical foundation that will empower you to understand the intricacies of blockchain.

Structure

The chapter covers the following topics:

- Understanding blockchain technology
- Ensuring agreement and trust in distributed systems
- Adding new blocks for data integrity
- Pillars of blockchain technology
- Exploring smart contracts

Objectives

By the end of this chapter, you will understand the individual components common to every blockchain. You will be able to conceptualize a blockchain from scratch and understand the technical details that underlie it, with a firm grasp of the concepts explored in further chapters. Additionally, you can identify how its technical characteristics, such as connecting blocks with hashes, smart contract execution, and consensus, provide tremendous business value. With this knowledge, you will gain insights into where blockchain can be applied to solve real problems and learn the necessary steps to transition a project from the conceptual stage to implementation. Grasping the fundamental components and technical intricacies of blockchain, you will be well-prepared to evaluate various blockchain solutions in the market and harness their potential for practical applications.

Understanding blockchain technology

In *Chapter 1, History of the Blockchain,* we explored the origins of blockchain technology and how it actually was a combination of many other well-established concepts such as distributed systems, connecting blocks of data cryptographically, and coding business rules into something called smart contracts. Now, we will explore deeply the core concepts of the technology.

Blockchain is essentially a digital ledger structured in a particular way that reflects its name. Its primary purpose is to securely record data, capturing the current state of the world, such as the balance of your bank account or a series of historical records that can be utilized in the future, like a company's expenses. However, let us find out how that differs from traditional databases.

Blockchain and traditional databases differ significantly in several key aspects. Traditional databases are typically centralized and controlled by a single entity, while blockchain operates in a decentralized manner, involving multiple participants. Blockchain utilizes consensus mechanisms to achieve agreement on data validity, while traditional databases rely on a central authority. Data stored in a blockchain is immutable, ensuring its security and integrity, whereas traditional databases allow for easier data modification. Additionally, blockchain enables the use of smart contracts, automating processes and eliminating the need for intermediaries. These fundamental differences make blockchain a unique and powerful technology with applications in various industries, offering transparency, security, and decentralized trust.

The technology behind blockchain consists of various components that come together to form one of the most innovative technologies available today. The fundamental concept revolves around blocks of data interconnected in a chain. Each piece of information is stored within a data block, forming a list of transactions. Whenever a transaction occurs, it is grouped with others to create a block. Every block has its own unique content, including transactions, timestamps, and digital signatures. Consequently, each block can be represented by a distinct string of bits known as a hash. Typically, a hash is 256 bits long and generated using the SHA256 algorithm, although other algorithms exist. The blocks are linked together through their unique hashes, with each new block referencing the hash of the previous block.

One fundamental characteristic of blockchain is its decentralization. This means that there is no need for a central authority or intermediary to control and validate transactions. Instead, the network operates in a peer-to-peer manner, where multiple participants, known as nodes, have a copy of the entire blockchain. This decentralized nature enhances transparency, security, and resilience by eliminating a single point of failure. It is important, however, to understand how a decentralized system can agree on the state of the information.

Consensus mechanisms are crucial in blockchain networks to ensure agreement among participants regarding transaction validity and the order in which they are added to the blockchain. Various consensus mechanisms, such as **Proof of Work** (**PoW**) and **Proof of Stake** (**PoS**), employ different algorithms and incentives to maintain the integrity and reliability of the blockchain. These mechanisms enable the network to reach a consensus without relying on a central authority.

Smart contracts are another powerful feature of blockchain technology. These are self-executing contracts with predefined rules and conditions encoded within the blockchain. When specific conditions are met, smart contracts automatically execute actions and transactions. This eliminates the need for intermediaries and manual intervention, providing automation, trust, and enforceability. Smart contracts have broad applications beyond value exchange, including decentralized finance, supply chain management, and **decentralized applications** (**dApps**).

Combining decentralization, consensus mechanisms, and smart contracts, blockchain technology has the potential to revolutionize various industries and sectors. Its transparent, secure, and efficient nature opens the door to innovative solutions, disrupting traditional practices and fostering trust in the digital realm.

Conceptual blockchain from scratch

To grasp how blockchain can help us solve that and many other problems, let us exercise a situation to help us understand the technology.

Imagine a simple scenario where four friends frequently exchange money among themselves. However, they have grown tired of constantly dealing with physical cash whenever they go out together. To simplify things, they have come up with a system where if one person pays for a meal or activity, the others keep a record of the payments they owe to that person. At the end of each month, they can review the amounts owed and settle their debts. Their main goal is to make this process as reliable as possible.

In this example, *Alice, Bob, Charlie,* and *Vinnie* will record all their payments in chronological order on a public board available to all of them. In other words, they will make use of a public ledger.

Refer to *Figure 2.1*:

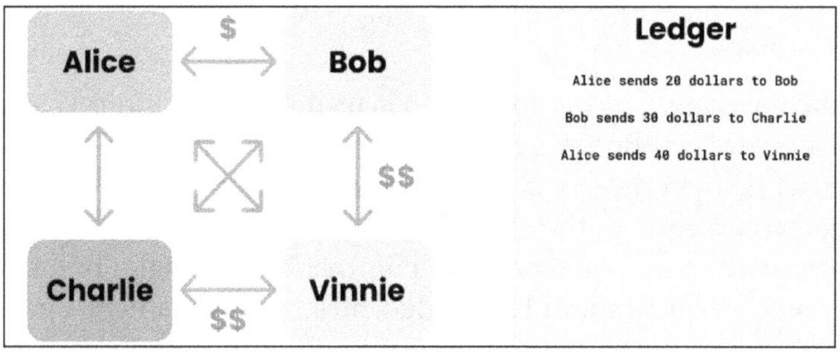

***Figure 2.1**: Ledger shared by participants to send and receive money*

This public ledger can be thought of as a website, a shared cloud document, or even a physical board placed somewhere they can all access. The participants, initially, will be able to read and write anything to the board, such as new transactions coming in.

New information can be written by any of them which poses flaws to the system. For example, *Bob* could become a bad actor and fake a transaction saying that *Alice* sent him a big amount of money. To avoid this kind of tampering, certain measures should be taken.

Refer to *Figure 2.2*:

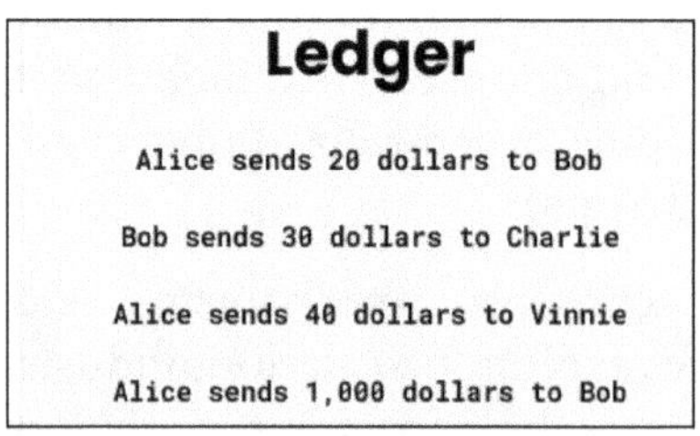

***Figure 2.2**: Bob adds a fraudulent line saying Alice sends him money*

To address this situation, a solution is implemented by incorporating a signature into each transaction. Similar to a contract requiring signatures from both parties involved, the sender of money now adds their signature to the transaction. While a physical board may involve a simple pen-written signature, a digital solution offers a more sophisticated and dependable alternative to a traditional physical signature.

Digital signatures rely on the utilization of an asymmetric cryptographic key pair consisting of a private key for signing and a public key for identification.

This approach encompasses two key functions, as follows:

- **Signing**: The process involves signing the data using the private key:

  ```
  sign(data, privateKey) => signature
  ```

- **Verification**: The process entails verifying the integrity of the data using the public key and the corresponding signature:

  ```
  verify(data, signature, publicKey) => yes/no
  ```

Employing these functions, the digital signature ensures the authenticity and integrity of the data in a secure and efficient manner.

Refer to *Figure 2.3*:

***Figure 2.3**: Digital signatures are unique for a particular key and content*

Requiring that the person sending the money signs the transaction prevents other parties from adding fraudulent transactions benefiting themselves. This makes the payment process much more reliable, as anyone may verify who actually registered each line.

Refer to *Figure 2.4*:

Ledger

transaction	*signature*
Alice sends 20 dollars to Bob	*b58ad3...*
Bob sends 30 dollars to Charlie	*f5ea32...*
Alice sends 40 dollars to Vinnie	*6feb23...*

***Figure 2.4**: Digital signatures appended to each transaction can be verified*

There is still, however, a possible fraud, as someone may still copy one valid line with the signature included and paste it.

Refer to *Figure 2.5*:

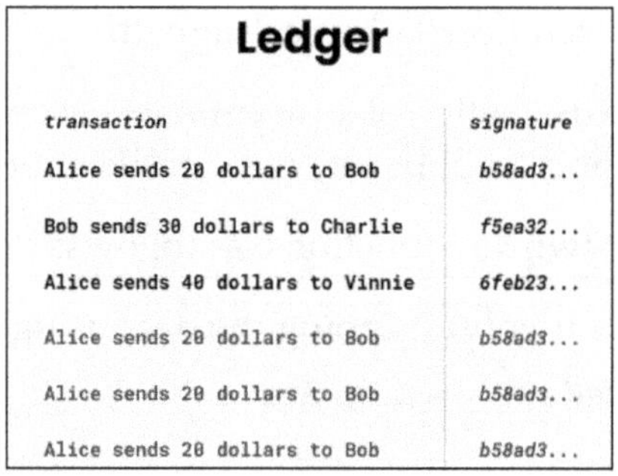

***Figure 2.5**: Signatures do not solve the entire problem as transactions can be copied and pasted*

To address this situation, a straightforward solution is to assign a unique **Identifier (ID)** to each transaction. Incorporating this ID along with the data to be signed, the mathematical algorithm utilized for signing requires the use of the private key, thereby preventing any unauthorized individual from registering a new line with the included ID. This approach ensures the integrity and security of the transaction process. In Ethereum, this concept is applied to the blocks with a nonce (number used once), and transactions also have an ID. In Hyperledger Fabric, each transaction has a **Transaction ID (txid)**.

Refer to *Figure 2.6*:

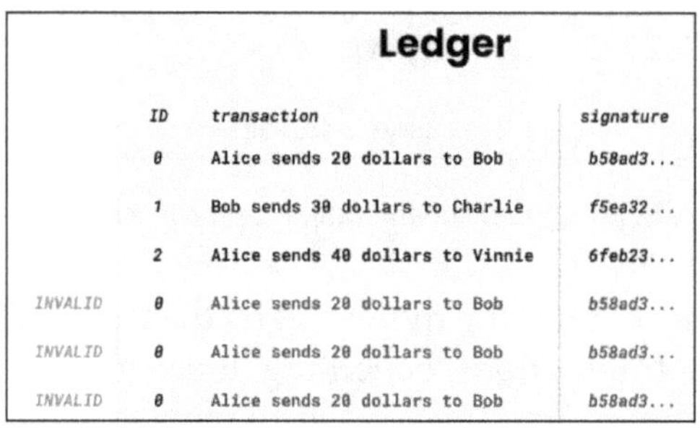

***Figure 2.6**: Repeated IDs are marked invalid and unique IDs generate a unique signature*

Our protocol so far relies on the following process:

- The lines are included in chronological order.
- *Alice, Bob, Charlie,* and *Vinnie* can add lines to the ledger.
- Everyone can read the ledger.
- Only signed transactions with unique IDs are considered valid.
- The ledger is centralized.

Storing the ledger in a single location presents a significant vulnerability, leading to various potential issues, are as follows:

- **Destruction of the transaction board**: If the physical or digital transaction board is destroyed, all the transaction records could be lost, making it difficult to track and settle debts accurately.
- **Replacement of the transaction board**: In the event of the transaction board being replaced, the original records may be tampered with or completely replaced, resulting in a loss of transparency and trust in the system.
- **Unequal access among actors**: If one of the individuals involved in the transactions has greater access or control over the transaction board than the others, it can create an imbalanced power dynamic, potentially leading to manipulation or misuse of the recorded transactions.

By recognizing these potential pitfalls, it becomes evident that relying solely on a single location for storing the ledger introduces significant risks and compromises the reliability and fairness of the system.

A viable solution is to distribute the ledger information among all the participants, namely *Alice*, *Bob*, *Charlie*, and *Vinnie*. Each individual maintains a shared copy of the ledger by exchanging messages containing the transactions as they occur.

For instance, when *Bob* records a new payment, he promptly sends a signed message to all three others, enabling them to update their own ledger copies. This ensures that everyone possesses an identical version of the ledger.

This ongoing process involves multiple ledgers that are continuously updated through the exchange of messages among the participants. This approach forms the foundation of **distributed ledger technology** (**DLT**). By implementing a DLT, the participants achieve a decentralized and synchronized ledger system, promoting transparency and consistency across all copies of the ledger.

Ensuring agreement and trust in distributed systems

Due to the mismanagement of the foundations of financial trust, people have witnessed entire economies crumble and collapse. In 2008 a great part of the world was shaken after discovering that an important part of the American credit market was very unhealthy.

In situations like this, it is normal to discover that the financial books and ledgers that were supposed to control, audit, and prevent crashes like this were not used the way they should have been. It is also in moments like these that people question what would be necessary to prevent it from happening again.

The harsh truth, however, is that it is not easy to avoid fraud, especially when millions of transactions happen in a short period of time. Auditing processes are known to be time-consuming, and the problem is even greater when the information sources are distributed.

As mentioned above, a ledger is a set of transactions registered in order to represent an event, like a financial exchange or property ownership. In our modern world, some guarantees are required to successfully complete a transaction.

For example, if a close family member asks to borrow your car for a two-day road trip, you could say, for example, that the decision would be tied to them returning the car clean and with a full tank. Now, if a colleague from work asks for the same thing, you would probably require much more information for the decision, such as where this person is going, if they have a valid license, and you would think twice before lending the car.

When the trust between parties is low or nonexistent, here comes the role of a third party in good faith. The third party is an entity known by the actors of a transaction. It brings trust into the deal so both genuinely believe they are participating in a reliable exchange. Many institutions in our societies provide trust between parties. Companies like banks, justice, government, title companies, and notary shops are some examples. These institutions work with different ledgers to register information necessary for future audits. Book accounting is a strong part of auditing processes, and ledgers need to be revised, sometimes by specialized departments or companies hired solely to check each transaction and analyze if they respect internal processes, regulations, or government laws. When one of these known institutions fails in their auditing processes, certain consequences arise.

It is not uncommon to watch news about fraud happening in important companies. After the origin of the fraud is discovered, the transaction books are revisited in chronological order to understand the causes and search for the possible culprits for the misbehavior. After an investigation is done and everybody understands the actions that caused the fraud, the market wonders what could have been done to prevent it.

The answer to this question usually is a better auditing process. Real-time auditing, however, is not easy with traditional tools, some of these processes contain several different organizations or entities that are allowed to register new transactions, some of which are distributed in several databases and legacy systems, and that makes it hard to track.

Creating a single point of auditing is difficult because the databases may differ from each other, and the same information is often duplicated in several different systems and storage. Worse than that, some processes use spreadsheets to share data and are usually sent and received manually by teams that need to analyze several batches of information and add them to another database.

In other words, traditional auditing has several points of failure, a high chance of error, and a high chance of tampering due to the distributed (but desynchronized) nature of the data.

The DLT is widely used in several areas to increase trust and decrease the chance of fraud around processes. It is a common misconception that this is a new technology. Many people think that the DLT was created along with the blockchain itself, but the truth is that the concept of a distributed ledger can be traced back centuries ago.

Throughout history, humans have sought to prevent tampering, particularly with regard to registers that hold financial information or establish power dynamics among multiple parties. It is a common practice for these parties to create multiple copies of important documents, typically following these steps:

1. Record a series of transactions in a ledger.
2. Create multiple identical copies of the ledger.
3. Sign each individual ledger.
4. Distribute each ledger copy to different locations.
5. In the event of a dispute, gather the ledgers and compare them.

By following these steps, the parties ensure the integrity and accuracy of the ledger information. This approach allows for verification and resolution of any discrepancies by comparing the multiple copies of the ledger. Take a good look at these steps, as they will provide an important analogy for the understanding of the Hyperledger Fabric transaction flow later in this book.

Since the time of the Roman Empire, DLT has been employed as a means to prevent money embezzlement in distant regions under Roman governance. Similarly, ancient Chinese banks utilized DLT to facilitate cash exchange between their branches.

To enhance security and deter counterfeiting, various primitive anti-counterfeiting measures were employed, such as distinctive handwriting and special ledger materials. However, despite these techniques, a fundamental issue remains unanswered, that of what happens when the documents are brought back, and one or more of them are different from the others.

Facing this situation, it is important to analyze the possibilities that can result in data being different when they were all expected to be the same. The possibilities could be one of the following:

- The transaction was replaced before arriving at its destination.
- The transaction was replaced before returning for comparison.
- The transaction is lost, stolen, or has not been delivered.

To address the issue of tampering and ensure the reliable delivery of messages, a common approach is to employ a concept known as Byzantine Fault Tolerance. This concept is based on the Byzantine general problem, which illustrates an allegorical scenario where to prevent the disastrous failure of a battle, all commanders of various battalions must come to a unanimous agreement on a single general's order.

This mathematical dilemma has been studied since the 80s, and the solutions proposed serve as frameworks for designing protocols and algorithms to achieve consensus and overcome potential malicious behavior or faulty communication in distributed systems.

The allegory of the Byzantine general problem involves a fictional general commanding multiple battalions in an invasion of a fortress. The general communicates with battalion leaders using simple messages: **Attack with all forces** or **retreat to a safe position**. Messengers simultaneously deliver these orders to all leaders.

There are two desired outcomes, as follows:

- All battalions attack
- All battalions retreat

Any other combination of movements can lead to disastrous consequences, as some battalions may attempt to invade while others retreat to non-aggressive positions.

In the context of messengers delivering orders, several possibilities arise due to accidents or enemy interference, as follows:

- The message is delivered within an acceptable time frame and remains authentic (desired outcome).
- The message is delayed but remains authentic.
- The message is lost accidentally without being exposed to the enemy.
- The messenger is captured, and the message is exposed to the enemy.
- The messenger is captured, and a fake message is delivered within an acceptable time frame.
- Two messages are rearranged but still arrive within an acceptable time frame.

To prevent tampering and ensure a successful battle outcome, it is crucial for the same information (general order) to be faithfully communicated to all positions (battalions) to avoid process failure (lost battle).

Going back to our times, there are many systems that face this situation when it is necessary to send signed messages to different servers and databases, and fraud should be avoided.

When a distributed system, platform, or network uses the proper algorithms to enhance protection against transaction fraud, the environment is considered to be **Byzantine Fault Tolerant (BFT)**.

Consensus is crucial for distributed systems to ensure consistent and reliable information across different locations. In scenarios like a database cluster, where multiple servers store the same key with different values, the lack of consensus can have disastrous consequences for connected systems or platforms.

Discrepancies in retrieving different results for the same key from different servers can result from network tampering attacks or conflicts arising from simultaneous digital transactions by multiple actors, commonly known as the double spending problem in the cryptocurrency world.

Regardless of the cause of transaction or information conflicts, an algorithm is needed to address such situations. When conflicts are detected, the consensus algorithm determines which transactions are deemed valid and which ones are rejected.

This resolution process is known as consensus. It ensures that distributed systems can effectively resolve conflicts and maintain a consistent state across all participating nodes.

To have a better understanding of the concept of consensus, let us do an exercise. Imagine a situation where eight people need to decide if they are going to the left or right. To make this decision, they will simultaneously raise boards showing each one's intention, as shown in *Figure 2.7*:

***Figure 2.7**: Consensus is about knowing the final decision of a group*

The final decision depends on the pre-defined consensus, after all. If it was agreed that the majority would define the result, then they would go for the right. On the other hand, if it was agreed that a vote of one person in blue counts three times the vote of one in black, then they would go for the left. It is possible to think of consensus in different ways, depending on which process you would like to apply.

In the real world, the consensus of a blockchain can take many forms depending on the blockchain itself. The first and most used one is the PoW algorithm, applied in Bitcoin and initially on Ethereum. After years of using PoW, Ethereum has moved to another algorithm called PoS. Fabric, on the other hand, uses a whole new way to achieve consensus, and as a permission blockchain, it has a different purpose since participants in the network are known.

PoW is a consensus algorithm used in blockchain networks to validate transactions and achieve agreement on the state of the ledger. In PoW, participants, known as miners, compete to solve complex mathematical puzzles using computational power. The first miner to find the solution broadcasts it to the network, and other participants verify the solution. Once the solution is verified, the miner adds a new block to the blockchain and is rewarded with cryptocurrency. This process requires a significant number of computational resources, making it computationally expensive and time-consuming.

It ensures the security of the blockchain by making it difficult for malicious actors to manipulate the transaction history. Since finding a solution to the mathematical puzzle is resource-intensive, it becomes impractical for an attacker to control more than 50% of the network's computing power. In other words, the attacker is unable to generate fraudulent but valid blocks as fast as the rest of the network.

PoS is an alternative consensus algorithm that aims to address the energy consumption issues of PoW while maintaining security. In PoS, the validators, or participants, are chosen to create new blocks and validate transactions based on the number of coins they hold and are willing to stake as collateral. Rather than solving complex puzzles, validators are randomly selected to create blocks and validate transactions in proportion to their stake. This means that the more coins a validator holds, the higher the chance of being chosen to participate in the consensus process.

By eliminating the need for extensive computational power, PoS significantly reduces energy consumption compared to PoW. It also introduces economic incentives for validators to act honestly, as they have a stake in the system. If a validator tries to validate fraudulent transactions, their stake can be forfeited as a penalty.

Ethereum has moved from PoW to PoS in 2022. The shift to PoS was driven by several factors. Firstly, PoS offers increased scalability, allowing for a higher number of transactions to be processed per second compared to PoW. This is achieved by dividing the network into smaller shards, each capable of processing its own transactions. Secondly, PoS reduces the energy consumption of the Ethereum network. Finally, PoS enables greater decentralization by allowing more participants to become validators without the need for expensive mining equipment.

In many contexts, consensus takes the form of single functions that guarantee the order of transactions in a block among many nodes. In Hyperledger Fabric, however, this guarantee takes the form of three steps known as endorsing, ordering, and validation. This consensus mechanism requires a predetermined set of nodes, known as a consortium, to agree on the order and validity of transactions. The three steps can be summarized as follows: a client sends a transaction proposal to the endorsing peers, which simulate and endorse the transaction; the endorsed transaction is then sent to the ordering service, which orders the transactions into blocks; and finally, the ordering service sends the blocks to the validating peers, which validate the transactions and commit them to the ledger. This is popularly known as the transaction flow, and we will devote the totality of *Chapter 5, Transaction Flow* to it.

Adding new blocks for data integrity

Even with the processes described above, the registers of the DLT may still be tampered, basically substituting ledger entries. In the example for *Alice, Bob, Charlie,* and *Vinnie,* someone should simply remove a signed transaction and replace it with another signed transaction.

Refer to *Figure 2.8*:

Ledger

ID	transaction	signature
0	Alice sends 20 dollars to Bob	b58ad3...
1	Bob sends 30 dollars to Charlie	f5ea32...
2	Alice sends 40 dollars to Vinnie	6feb23...
3	Vinnie sends 13 dollars to Bob	ea3b23...
4	Bob sends 40 dollars to Vinnie	6feea3...

Ledger

ID	transaction	signature
0	Alice sends 20 dollars to Bob	b58ad3...
1	Bob sends 30 dollars to Charlie	f5ea32...
2	Alice sends 40 dollars to Vinnie	6feb23...
3	Bob sends 60 dollars to Vinnie	ae3fb5...
4	Bob sends 40 dollars to Vinnie	6feea3...

***Figure 2.8**: Bob tampers a block to fool Vinnie into thinking he has sent money*

An effective way to prevent fraud is by capturing a fingerprint of a collection of transactions, known as a block. This fingerprint can be used to determine if any part of the registered data has been altered.

In the digital realm, this fingerprint is created using mathematical cryptographic functions known as hash functions or simply hashes, such as the SHA256 mentioned earlier. The analogy of a fingerprint is often used to illustrate the uniqueness of this digital identification artifact, similar to how it is highly improbable to find two non-twin individuals with identical fingerprints.

Hash functions are considered one-way encryption because it is practically impossible to retrieve the original data from the hash value alone. In other words, the hash function acts as an encryption method, with the original data serving as the key.

The process involves hashing the data using a specific algorithm, as follows:

```
hashMethod(data) => hash
```

To verify the integrity of the data, the hash is checked against a verification hash, as follows:

```
hashVerify(data, verificationHash) => hashMethod(data) == verificationHash
```

Leveraging this method to secure and organize transactions in a distributed system is more efficient. Instead of individually hashing each transaction, they can be grouped together, and the collective hash can be calculated. Additionally, each group can include the hash of the previous set to compute the subsequent digital fingerprint, creating a chain of transaction hashes.

The approach assures that if any data within the set of transactions is modified, the resulting fingerprint (hash) will be different, indicating tampering or fraud.

The amalgamation of these mechanisms guarantees reliability and trust in transactions conducted within a distributed system. This collective process laid the groundwork for what we now recognize as blockchain technology.

It is worth noting that the definition of blockchain may vary among authors. In the previous chapter, we discussed how blockchain emerged following the creation of the Bitcoin network. Consequently, different bibliographic sources may present diverse definitions of blockchain. Some authors argue that Bitcoin is the only true blockchain, while others contend that a pure blockchain has yet to be realized.

In this book, we will not rigidly defend a specific definition of blockchain. Instead, we will focus on exploring the incredible possibilities offered by blockchain technologies using the Hyperledger Fabric framework.

Pillars of blockchain technology

All of the elements we have talked about so far are built on top of structural elements that concretely make blockchain. Transactions, blocks, and nodes appear in any blockchain, but their role may vary depending on the protocol. Let us summarize what we have seen so far in these pillars.

Transactions and state

In the Ethereum whitepaper, *Vitalik Buterin* referred to Bitcoin as a state transition system. To understand this concept better, let us break it down. In our previous example, where friends planned future payments, we started with a clean slate or an empty state. This means there was no existing information registered. Our initial state is empty.

The following equation defines the initial state S_0:

$$S_0 = null$$

When the first payment information was registered, such as *Alice* sending 20 dollars to *Bob*, the state changed. Now we have knowledge that *Alice* owes *Bob* 20 dollars, and *Bob* has a balance of 20 dollars.

This updated state can be represented as follows:

$$S_1 = \{Alice: - 20, Bob + 20\}$$

This transition in the state occurred through the application of a transition function, which is essentially a transaction initiated by a participant in the network. Mathematically, we can represent it as follows:

$$S_1 = apply(S_0, T)$$

Here, T represents the transition function (transaction) that is applied to the initial state S_0 to generate the updated state S_1.

In this example, we assume there is a real-world exchange of money between friends. In decentralized systems like the Bitcoin blockchain, the state represents the total amount of spendable coins associated with each participant. For example, *Alice* can only spend $20 (or 20 BTC) if the blockchain's state reflects that.

Typically, the state is not explicitly stored anywhere. It is an abstraction that needs to be generated and verified by executing every transaction since the beginning of the blockchain. However, in systems like Hyperledger Fabric, each node maintains a world state, deviating from this general approach. This will be further explained in *Chapter 4, Fabric Concepts and Components*.

When a transaction is applied to a state and results in an invalid state or cannot be applied at all, the transaction may return an error. For instance, if *Alice* has 5 BTC and tries to transfer 7 BTC to *Bob*, it should throw an error because the current state does not allow the transaction to be applied. The blockchain determines the participants' balances and identifies errors by maintaining a transparent and immutable ledger of all transactions and account balances.

This is where wallets come into play. A wallet is an abstraction that simplifies blockchain usage for humans. Just like a physical wallet holds cash, a blockchain wallet abstractly holds digital assets such as cryptocurrencies or NFTs. More accurately, a wallet is a key pair consisting of a public key and a secret key.

When we say that *Alice* owns a certain amount of BTC, we mean that the public key associated with the secret key used by *Alice* to sign her transactions has been involved in transactions in the past, resulting in a current balance of X BTC.

Blocks

Blockchain blocks are the fundamental units of data in a blockchain network. They contain a collection of transactions that have been validated and grouped together. The process of assembling blocks involves steps associated with the consensus of the protocol. For instance, in the Bitcoin blockchain, transactions are gathered from the network and verified by nodes called miners. These miners compete to solve the PoW cryptographic puzzle. Once a miner successfully solves the puzzle, they create a new block containing the validated transactions.

To ensure the integrity and immutability of the blockchain, each block is connected to the previous block through a hash function. The hash function takes the data of the previous block, including its hash, and produces a unique fixed-length string of characters. This hash is included in the new block, effectively linking it to the previous block. Chaining these blocks together with hashes, any modification to a previous block would result in a change to its hash, which would subsequently break the chain. This property makes it extremely difficult to tamper with the blockchain since it would require modifying every subsequent block.

The frequency at which blocks are formed depends on the blockchain protocol. In most public blockchains like Bitcoin, new blocks are typically added approximately every 10 minutes. However, this can vary depending on factors such as network congestion, difficulty adjustments, or the specific consensus algorithm used. Some blockchains, such as Ethereum, have shorter block times, aiming for an average of around 15 seconds. On the other hand, Hyperledger Fabric has customizable block formation rules to accommodate their specific use cases and requirements. The block time is an essential parameter as it affects the transaction throughput, confirmation times, and overall network scalability.

Nodes

One of the main features of blockchain is decentralization. It is decentralization that is responsible for a big part of why blockchain is such an innovative technology, and it is decentralization that makes it possible to not have a centralized authority. This characteristic has everything to do with the nodes of the network. The information is decentralized to the nodes in the first place.

In public blockchains, anyone with a computer with enough storage can be a node. The node will traditionally have the full copy of the ledger locally and will receive broadcasts of new blocks created by the validators of the network. Nodes will also execute each transaction to validate if transactions are valid or not.

Nodes will have different types and responsibilities in a blockchain, and each blockchain will have its own types of nodes.

In Bitcoin, there are primarily three types of nodes: full nodes, mining nodes, and lightweight nodes. Full nodes maintain a complete copy of the Bitcoin blockchain and validate all transactions and blocks. Mining nodes, also known as miners, are responsible for creating new blocks by solving complex mathematical problems through the process of mining. Lightweight nodes rely on trusted full nodes to validate transactions and do not store the entire blockchain locally.

In Ethereum, the node types include full nodes, mining nodes, light nodes, and archive nodes. Full nodes in Ethereum maintain a complete copy of the blockchain and execute all transactions and smart contracts. Mining nodes, like Bitcoin, participate in the mining process to create new blocks. Light nodes only download block headers. Archive nodes store the entire historical data of the blockchain, including all past states and transactions, providing comprehensive access to historical information.

In Hyperledger Fabric, the node types differ from public blockchains. In fabric, there are peer nodes and ordering nodes. Peer nodes maintain a copy of the ledger and execute chain code (smart contracts) transactions. Ordering nodes are responsible for ordering transactions into blocks and distributing them to the peers.

Exploring smart contracts

In *Chapter 1, History of the Blockchain,* we have talked about smart contracts as pieces of code that are run when something is to be registered in a blockchain. They are the central part of building different applications in the blockchain.

Smart contracts are built based on the scenario they will be applied to, but all of them have common characteristics, as follows:

- **They are deterministic**: For a set of inputs and a current state, the output will always be the same.
- **They are transparent**: In public blockchains such as Ethereum, the smart contracts are stored on-chain and accessible by all participants. For Hyperledger Fabric, organizations must approve the source code before deployment.
- **They ensure data integrity on-chain**: Every piece of information for the application has to go through a transaction defined on a smart contract. This defines the state transition function we have talked about. That means that no invalid data, according to the contract rules, will make it into the ledger.
- **They are programmable**: It is nothing more than a collection of code executed once a transaction is called. Ethereum uses mainly solidity for its contracts, whereas fabric can use Go, Java, and JavaScript.

Let us clarify the concept using an example, as follows:

Suppose we want to track the ownership history of cars over the years. To achieve this, we can create a smart contract that registers cars and assigns them owners. The ownership can be transferred through the smart contract whenever a car is sold or given away.

Our contract would have two main pieces of information, as follows:

- **Car**: With information about the model, year, car plate, and current owner
- **Owner**: With the name of the person and associate with a wallet pertaining to them

To interact with the information and register transactions, the smart contract should provide the following functionalities:

- **Create a new car**: This function allows the registration of a new car into the system.
- **Create a new owner**: This function facilitates the addition of a new owner to the system.
- **Transfer car ownership**: This function enables the transfer of ownership from one owner to another.

Let us imagine that we have deployed this smart contract on a blockchain and can now utilize its functions to make the transactions. To illustrate the process, we will start by registering a new owner with the following details:

- **Name**: John Smith
- **Public key**: f012ab

Then, we register a new car for this owner, as follows:

- **Model**: Tesla Model Y
- **Year**: 2020
- **Car plate**: XPTO 1111
- **Current owner**: f012ab

All of this initial information would be recorded in blocks on the blockchain. Within the smart contract, each property can have its validation function to ensure data integrity. For example, the year field can be validated to only accept numerical values like 2020 rather than non-numeric values like two thousand and twenty. This validation helps maintain the accuracy and validity of the information stored on the blockchain ledger.

Finally, the third transaction involves transferring car ownership. This transaction takes inputs such as the car and the new owner, and it is signed by the current owner. This process creates a new transaction that is added to a subsequent block on the blockchain, allowing us to track the complete history of the car and all its previous owners.

Conclusion

In this chapter, we began delving into the technical concepts of blockchain. Our main objective was to gain a comprehensive understanding of how a blockchain system works. We started by building a foundation from scratch, gradually incorporating additional functionalities into a basic ledger. One of the key aspects we focused on was achieving consensus within a distributed system, and we explored the various methods employed by blockchain technology to accomplish this. Another crucial topic we covered was the significance of blocks in maintaining data integrity within a blockchain. We examined the contents of each block, specifically the inclusion of transactions, which play a vital role in shaping the state of a blockchain network. Lastly, we delved into the concept of smart contracts, which serve as the intelligence behind a blockchain system.

In the next chapter, we will dive deep into Hyperledger Fabric itself and begin to understand how these concepts translate into the most popular permissioned blockchain.

CHAPTER 3
Introduction to Hyperledger Fabric

Introduction

In this chapter, we will discuss the technical concepts that make blockchain technology incredibly valuable. Here, we will unravel the foundations of blockchain and explore how it differs from traditional databases. By the end, you will have a solid grasp of the fundamental elements underpinning blockchain's power.

Hyperledger Fabric stands as one of the most prominent permissioned blockchain frameworks available today. In this chapter, we will delve into the origins of this framework and its remarkable evolution over the years. Starting as an IBM project, it has emerged as one of the leading solutions for enterprise blockchain worldwide.

Our discussion will encompass the optimal use cases for this technology and the value it brings to resolving business challenges. We will explore the exceptional characteristics of security, permissions, privacy, and flexibility that make it a compelling choice for numerous scenarios.

As we venture into the technical aspects, we will acquaint ourselves with the architecture model implemented by Fabric. Understanding this model is vital as we step into the realm of Fabric, delving into concepts such as organizations, peers, and orderers.

In contrast to other private distributed ledger technologies like R3's Corda, Hyperledger Fabric is an open-source framework. This enables the contribution and utilization of the codebase. We will examine the significance of this not only for Fabric but also for other projects under the umbrella of the Hyperledger Foundation.

Lastly, we will provide essential guidance in searching for reliable information about Fabric. Given the expansive nature of the project, this book will focus on a specific aspect, making it crucial to seek information from reputable sources during your learning journey.

Structure

The chapter covers the following topics:

- Hyperledger timeline
- Fabric architecture model
- Open-source community
- Searching for information

Objectives

By the end of this chapter, you will understand why Hyperledger Fabric stands out as the preferred choice among various blockchain technologies. Through exploration, you will develop the ability to discern the specific scenarios in which Hyperledger Fabric excels and recognize situations where alternative blockchain solutions may be more suitable.

As we delve into the initial concepts of Hyperledger Fabric, we will see how its open-source community is an important asset in your learning. You will discover how this thriving community fosters collaboration, innovation, and continuous improvement. Additionally, we will unveil strategies and techniques to leverage the resources and knowledge available within the Fabric ecosystem. You will also understand the architecture model of Hyperledger Fabric.

By mastering the concepts presented in this chapter, you will not only possess the necessary knowledge to justify the implementation of Hyperledger Fabric over other blockchain types but also wield the ability to identify the ideal circumstances for its application. As you immerse yourself in the architecture and engage with the community, you will acquire a powerful set of skills to harness the full potential of Hyperledger Fabric, propelling you toward success in your blockchain endeavors.

Hyperledger timeline

The growing popularity of Bitcoin and other cryptocurrencies worldwide has generated significant excitement surrounding blockchain technology. This technology offers a reliable and trustworthy digital ledger accessible to all, allowing users to select their preferred blockchain, connect to it, and execute transactions for various purposes.

In a very short period, many Bitcoin-like technologies blossomed, slightly changing features from one to another, especially regarding the consensus algorithm. Most of them, however, are crypto-based, or in other words, it is necessary to use the tokens created in the network to register new transactions.

This model provides fantastic possibilities when it deals with processes that fit in a public blockchain setting. However, it also has some disadvantages, as follows:

- Processes that deal with sensitive information.
- Cryptocurrency may become too expensive for fiat exchange.
- Anyone with an account can place transactions.
- Consensus has known tampering methods (for example,: 50%+1 of miners in Bitcoin).

These drawbacks can pose significant obstacles for various corporate processes, as companies and organizations cannot afford to rely on unpredictable variables. For instance, consider a scenario where companies utilize the Ethereum main network for buying and selling activities. Suddenly, within a few days, the price of Ethereum surged two or three times. Such situations are deemed unacceptable, necessitating the evolution of blockchain technology to provide the advantages of cryptocurrency networks while mitigating their inherent risks.

The new blockchain model should have the following characteristics:

- Only predefined nodes can operate in the network.
- Only certain accounts can transact with the network.
- Not cryptocurrency dependent.
- Consensus algorithms that fit consortium processes.

These characteristics are the base of the permissioned blockchain technology.

It was clear that Ethereum-like blockchains would not be enough to tackle enterprise problems since they did not have the aforementioned characteristics. In 2015, the Linux Foundation, a non-profit organization that foments technology advancements, created the Hyperledger project to develop and support the next generation of enterprise blockchain. One of those early members was IBM, which committed to contributing thousands of lines of code from its Open blockchain project. The project would soon be graduated and rebranded to Hyperledger Fabric, becoming the first widely known framework for permissioned blockchain. In 2017, the Hyperledger project announced the first production version of Hyperledger Fabric v1.0.

The Hyperledger project grew and popularity, and it became the Hyperledger Foundation before achieving a greater status as the Linux Foundation Decentralized Trust. As of this writing, more than 80 companies are foundation members and actively contribute to the projects. There are currently over 6 graduated projects, including Fabric, and over 7 incubating projects. These projects are all related to blockchain in some way. Hyperledger Besu, for instance, is an Ethereum client that can be used in a permissioned manner. Hyperledger Cacti, on the other hand, is an integration tool between different blockchains.

Fabric has become one of the most successful projects in the blockchain industry and in the open-source space, with more than 300 contributors on the main codebase and dozens of associated projects, like SDKs and official libraries. Fabric is currently on version v2.5.x, which will be the version we will explore throughout this book.

Following are the most important milestones of Fabric across the years:

- **July 2017, Release v1.0.0**: The first production release of Fabric. It was the start of a remarkable success story, but many improvements would be made in the coming years.
- **March 2018, Release v1.1.x**: Included TLS communication between all components, support for chaincodes written in Node.js, and allowed peers to manage CouchDB indexes.
- **January 2019, Release v1.4.x**: The first LTS version of Fabric. Included many new features, but most notably, it added support for RAFT as the preferred protocol for the ordering service.
- **January 2020, Release v2.0.x**: Introduced a new chaincode lifecycle that allowed for decentralized governance. It also added the possibility of external chaincode builders.
- **July 2020, Release v2.2.x**: The next LTS version. Fixed many issues of the v2.0 release. Added utility functions to make the update of expired certificates possible.
- **November 2020, Release v2.3.x**: Allowed ordering services without a system channel, which dramatically simplifies the network's management.
- **November 2021, Release v2.4.x**: Introduced the Fabric Gateway service in peers that allowed for a simpler SDK implementation. Also added the unjoin channel operation for peers.
- **March 2023, Release v2.5.x**: The current LTS version of Fabric. It added native support for AMD and ARM architectures, which allows for different possibilities for deployment.
- **Future, Release v3.0.x:** This version is set to implement a new ordering service protocol with **Byzantine Fault Tolerance** (**BFT**).

Using Hyperledger Fabric

Before deciding to use the Hyperledger Fabric framework for a blockchain project, it is crucial to go through a series of checks to ensure the appropriateness and suitability of these open-source artifacts.

To assist the project manager in making an informed decision, following is a concise questionnaire to consider:

Question 1: Is the process reliant on structured information?

If the registered data can be precisely and systematically organized, it becomes feasible to define digital assets that can be created and modified in accordance with the process workflow.

Hyperledger Fabric offers a comprehensive framework for managing structured assets, offering various options for defining and upgrading assets when required.

Question 2: Is the process transaction-oriented?

If the process follows a structured workflow with defined transactions at each step, Hyperledger Fabric can utilize chaincodes to associate each step with a specific method.

As we will delve into later, in a Fabric network, data registration or updates cannot occur without the execution of chaincode methods. These methods validate data and ensure the consistency and security of the process.

Question 3: Are the profiles of the actors involved in the process known?

If the process workflow spans different entities or organizations, it is crucial to identify them. When these entities, such as companies, regulators, NGOs, etc., have well-defined structures with multiple users or employees within their hierarchy, it indicates a permissioned model. The Hyperledger Fabric framework provides a comprehensive **Private Key Infrastructure** (**PKI**) that enables the creation of a certification authority for each organization. This allows for the issuance of digital cryptographic certificates, which are used to identify each element within the blockchain network.

Question 4: Is the historical information of the process significant?

In traditional client-server systems, it is common to encounter requests for data history. This means that a digital asset undergoes multiple modifications and updates throughout its lifecycle, and retrieving previous states may be necessary for various purposes, particularly auditing.

The more crucial these historical snapshots are, the more suitable a Hyperledger Fabric schema becomes for developing such a system. Later, we will demonstrate how easily the Fabric SDK allows access to the complete data history.

Question 5: Does the process follow a hierarchical workflow?

In a distributed system, it is essential to determine how to handle transaction inconsistencies. If multiple transactions conflict with each other simultaneously, a predefined method must be implemented to resolve the dispute.

In the realm of blockchain, this dispute resolution algorithm is known as consensus. Hyperledger Fabric provides a hierarchical and adaptable consensus mechanism, often directly applied to the smart contract, as we will elaborate on later in this book.

Example

Let us apply the previous questions to a practical example: a supply chain food trust process to ensure that the product consumed by the end consumer is gluten-free.

Question 1: Is the process reliant on structured information?

Yes, the main digital information is the product itself, and this product has certain characteristics that are structured as follows:

Key	Type
Product lot ID	Number
Product type	Enum (None, Organic, Diet, Gluten Free)
Product name	String (255 char max)
Quantity	Number
Date of expiration	Date

***Table 3.1**: Key and types of product details*

Question 2: Is the process transaction-oriented?

Yes, as the product moves from the manufacturer to the store, various steps will be taken to transfer data throughout the process, as follows:

- Product lot creation
- Product lot transport
- Product lot division
- Product lot receival
- Product lot consumed

Question 3: Are the profiles of the actors involved in the process known?

Yes, the product supply chain actors are known and the only ones allowed to transact.

- Farm
- Manufacturer
- Transporter
- Distributor
- Reseller

Question 4: Is the historical information of the process significant?

Absolutely, when it comes to food safety, any mishandling within the product supply chain can lead to health issues. The ability to quickly retrieve historical information increases the chances of identifying flaws or mistakes.

Question 5: Does the process follow a hierarchical workflow?

Yes, particularly when determining the properties of a product.

If an entity, such as the consumer, wants to ensure that a product is gluten-free, the manufacturer must have hierarchical dominance over the others. The manufacturer plays a critical role in guaranteeing all the product's properties before packaging it.

In conclusion, considering the factors discussed in this example, it becomes evident that Hyperledger Fabric ticks all the boxes and is an excellent choice for implementation. Its transaction-oriented approach, the significance of historical information in ensuring food safety, and the hierarchical workflow required to determine product properties align with the capabilities and features provided by Hyperledger Fabric. Therefore, it proves to be a suitable framework for implementing the supply chain food trust process described in this scenario.

Fabric architecture model

One of the main characteristics of Hyperledger Fabric is its modular approach to network architecture, with many individual components that can be assembled in numerous combinations to result in a blockchain network tailored to the business needs of the organizations that are a part of it.

Let us think of a business situation where several partners want a blockchain to share information. If we spend some time exercising such scenarios, we might conclude that these business partners will need to be represented in some way inside the network. Initially, we might be tempted to think that a single node for each organization would suffice. However, we will see that Fabric provides a much more robust approach to representing participants in a network.

On a high level, a Fabric network is indeed very simple. It is composed of participants who know how to reach each other through a network, each one maintaining a ledger that is shared through communication over the network.

Refer to *Figure 3.1*:

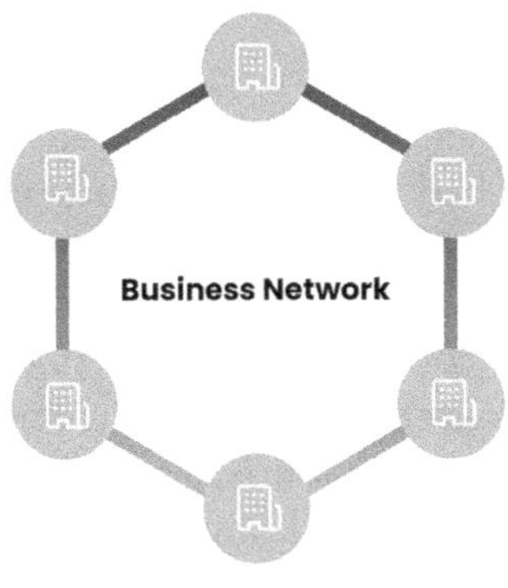

***Figure 3.1**: A high-level representation of a Fabric network*

The participants of a Fabric network are called **organizations**, which makes sense since we are dealing with a business setting. We can assume that the organization is a collection of components that will make it possible to write to and read from the shared ledger. In a Fabric network, the organizations that are part of it must be aware of the existence of every other organization and how to reach it for communication. This is achieved by a communication layer called **channel**, which will define a configuration for how to communicate and deal with the network's administration. The channel can be thought of as a group chat, where only the members of the chat are allowed to read and write messages. The administrator (or administrators) of the group chat may add new members if they want to. Similarly, in a channel configuration, organizations will be known as members of the channel, and policies describe how the administration of this channel will be done.

So far, we have defined the participants, how they will communicate, and who gets to decide who joins the network. There's one piece missing: what they will share. This is where we start to differentiate how our networks behave from case to case. By now, it has become clear that blockchain functionality is only as useful as the rules for transacting make it. These rules are programmed in the smart contract, which is known as **chaincode** in Fabric, and that is how we will refer to it from now on.

Refer to *Figure 3.2*:

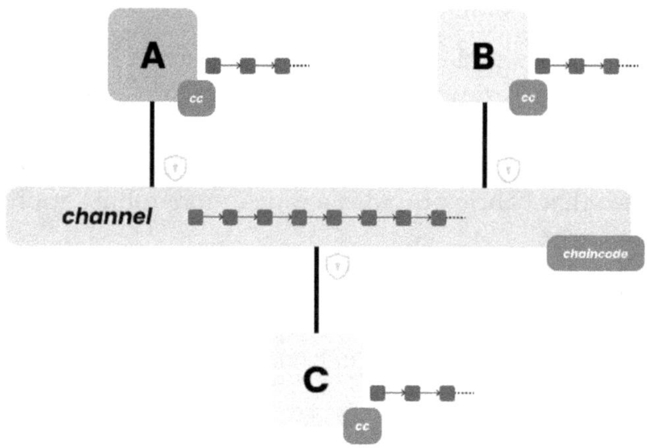

***Figure 3.2**: Illustration of a Fabric network with organizations using a chaincode to transact on a channel*

All the layers above are stitched together by the use of digital certificates when organizations communicate and when they create new signed transactions. The digital certificate's purpose is to identify the organization inside a particular channel, and that is mainly how the permissioned component of Hyperledger Fabric is achieved. In simple terms, if an organization's public certificate is in the channel's configuration, then it is part of the channel. That way, other organizations can verify communication signed by other participants and block it if it is not from a known source.

Refer to *Figure 3.3*:

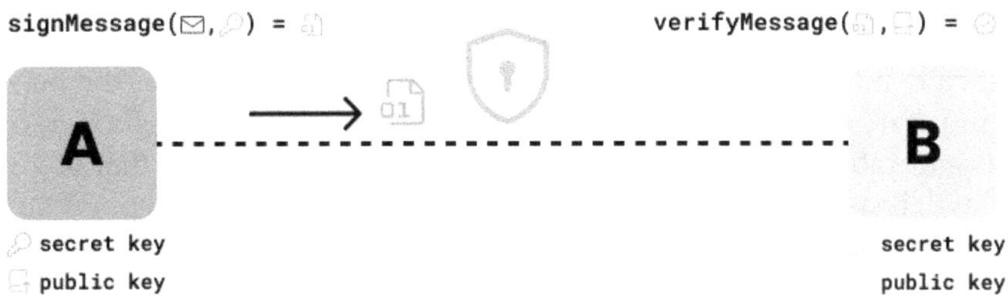

Figure 3.3: *Organization A signs a message with its secret key*

Digital certificates are provided by a **certificate authority** (**CA**), much like websites that have SSL certificates issued by a trusted authority, to ensure that users are not accessing a tampered version of the website. In Fabric, organizations have X.509 certificates issued by a CA trusted by the channel configuration to identify their components. Generally, each network organization would have its self-signed CA, usually provided by Fabric itself, called Fabric CA. That will ensure that different organizations' identities are managed in logically separate environments. Even though Fabric provides a ready-to-go CA, it is not required, and organizations can use the CA that suits them.

Organizations still need a runtime environment that will do the actual communication with other organizations in a channel. The component central to this in Fabric is the peer. Peers are the nodes that will store the ledger, hear for new blocks and update it, communicate directly with other peers, host a chaincode definition, and execute transactions defined by it. They are the concrete element that an organization will have as a means of interaction with the channel. A peer can be part of many channels and, consequently, an organization. Peers have their identities issued by the CA of their organization so that they can communicate and sign transactions.

Refer to *Figure 3.4*:

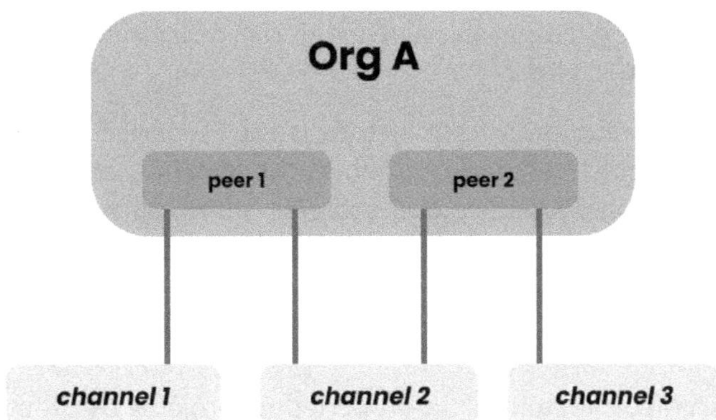

Figure 3.4: *Organization A's peers can be part of many channels*

Additional to peer nodes, a channel must include ordering nodes or orderers. Orderers are elements responsible for the consensus of block formation in Hyperledger Fabric, which is done by hearing transactions issued by the organizations and ordering them deterministically into a block, and then broadcasting it to the peers of the network. They are united in what is called the ordering service of the channel. Even though orderers are part of an organization, they serve a greater purpose in the channel, that of guaranteeing that a block will be well formed and then distributing that to peers to append to their copy of the ledger. Additionally, orderers are the gatekeepers of the channel configuration, and they will enforce access rules and administration rights to the channel. Just like peers, orderers can serve multiple channels, albeit the ordering service is exclusive to each channel. We will explore in *Chapter 4, Fabric Concepts and Components*, in more detail how these elements interact.

Refer to *Figure 3.5*:

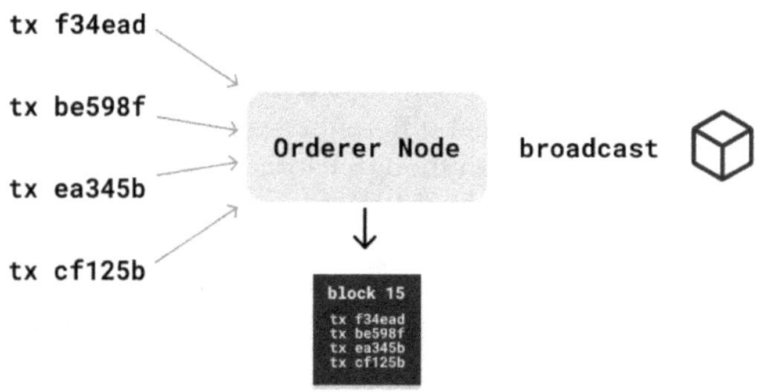

***Figure 3.5**: The orderer hears transactions, assembles a block, and broadcasts it to the network*

Open-source community

The open-source principle has revolutionized software development, leading to the creation of highly successful software products that are collaborative efforts benefiting society at zero cost. This paradigm has also given rise to entirely new business categories that were previously non-existent.

One notable organization embracing this ethos is the Hyperledger Foundation. It serves as a dynamic and interactive platform where developers, researchers, and industry experts collaborate to build open-source artifacts specifically designed for blockchain development.

The Hyperledger projects adhere to several fundamental goals and principles that underpin their success, as follows:

- **Trust**: Trust is a cornerstone of the Hyperledger projects. By promoting transparency and accountability, the community strives to create a trustworthy environment where users can confidently engage with the technology.

- **Transparency**: Openness and transparency are key tenets of the Hyperledger projects. The source code, design decisions, and governance structures are openly available for scrutiny, ensuring that the community has a clear understanding of the inner workings and can contribute to their improvement.
- **Security**: Security is of paramount importance in blockchain technology. The Hyperledger projects prioritize robust security measures to safeguard the integrity of the systems and protect against unauthorized access, fraud, and other potential threats.
- **Efficiency**: The Hyperledger projects aim to optimize the efficiency of blockchain solutions. Through continuous innovation and collaboration, the community strives to develop streamlined and performant frameworks, tools, and protocols that can support a wide range of use cases.

Crucially, all Hyperledger projects are made possible by the dedicated efforts of the open-source community. Their contributions and support are instrumental in creating and maintaining these significant projects that bring immense value to the world. Without the collaborative spirit and expertise of the community, the development and availability of these essential tools would be impossible.

Refer to *Figure 3.6*:

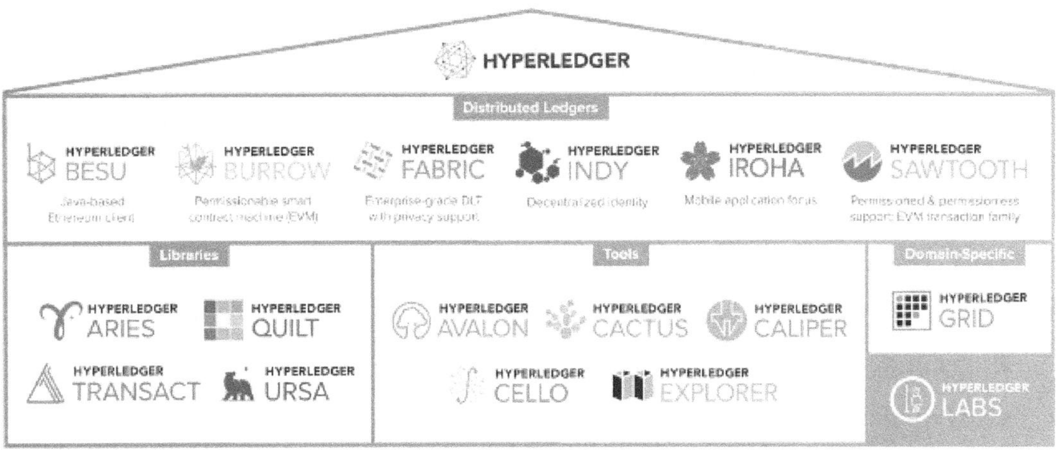

***Figure 3.6**: The Hyperledger greenhouse changes as projects evolve*

These projects have several principles that make them so special, as follows:

- **Collaboration**: The Hyperledger community emphasizes open collaboration and encourages contributors from various backgrounds, including technology companies, startups, academic institutions, and more. This diverse ecosystem facilitates the sharing of ideas and expertise to create robust and inclusive blockchain solutions.

- **Multiple frameworks**: Hyperledger hosts various blockchain frameworks and tools, each fitting specific use cases and requirements.
- **Transparency and governance**: The community operates with a transparent governance model that involves special interest groups (climate action, financial market, healthcare, etc.), regional chapters (India, Japan, Brazil, etc.), and a governing board. Decisions related to project updates, releases, and roadmap planning are made through open discussions and consensus.
- **Regular meetings and events**: The community hosts regular meetings, webinars, and conferences where members and stakeholders can discuss the latest developments, share knowledge, and explore collaboration opportunities.
- **Resourceful documentation**: Hyperledger maintains comprehensive documentation for each of its projects, including technical guides, tutorials, and reference materials. This facilitates the onboarding of new contributors and developers to the projects.
- **Focus on real-world applications**: The community is committed to driving practical implementations of blockchain technology. This includes pilots and proofs of concept in various industries such as supply chain, healthcare, finance, and more.

Searching for information

During your journey to learn Fabric, you may encounter challenges or have questions that are not covered in this book. Fabric is an evolving technology, and it undergoes continuous development by a vibrant community, resulting in a changing landscape. To empower readers to explore and learn independently, we will offer general recommendations for additional resources that can assist you along the way.

The main information sources for Hyperledger Fabric may be found at following:

- Read the docs website
- Hyperledger Wiki
- Discord
- GitHub
- Mailing list
- Issues

The main way to get information related to Fabric is the official documentation. The documentation, as of the writing of this book, can be accessed on the website:

https://hyperledger-fabric.readthedocs.io/

Dozens of contributors maintain this documentation and is where the essential information about Fabric will be found. You will find tutorials, command reference guides, installation guides, and many more in this documentation.

Note: The official documentation is versioned, and you can navigate to older versions. Make sure you check the version before exploring to make sure you have the correct information.

Refer to *Figure 3.7*:

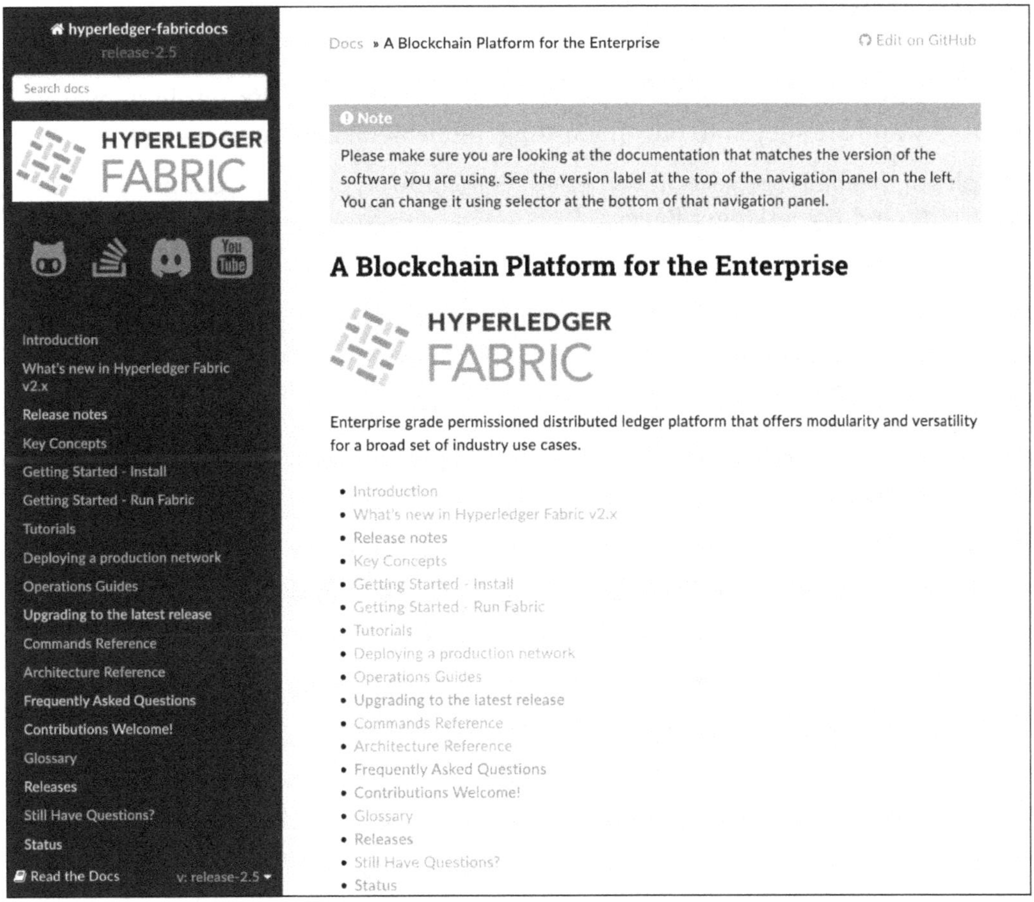

***Figure 3.7**: Hyperledger Fabric's official documentation homepage*

Hyperledger Foundation keeps the latest news on a Wiki page that can be found at the following:

- **https://wiki.hyperledger.org/**

The Hyperledger Wiki has information about all Hyperledger projects and is divided into the sections: Graduated, Incubated, and Labs.

Graduated

These projects have undergone rigorous review, testing, and development. Some characteristics of graduated projects include maturity, production readiness, community support, documentation, and resources.

Examples of graduated projects in Hyperledger include Hyperledger Besu, Hyperledger Sawtooth, Hyperledger Indy, and, of course, Hyperledger Fabric.

Incubated

These projects are in the early stages of development and are actively being worked on to reach a more mature state. These projects are typically open to contributions from the community and are subject to ongoing testing, refinement, and development.

Examples of incubated projects in Hyperledger include Hyperledger Caliper, Hyperledger AnonCreds, and Hyperledger Bevel.

Labs

Hyperledger Labs is a space within the Hyperledger community where experimental and early-stage projects reside. These projects are typically exploratory and may not have a well-defined roadmap or governance structure. Labs projects serve as a sandbox for developers to collaborate on innovative ideas and proof-of-concepts related to blockchain technology.

Refer to *Figure 3.8*:

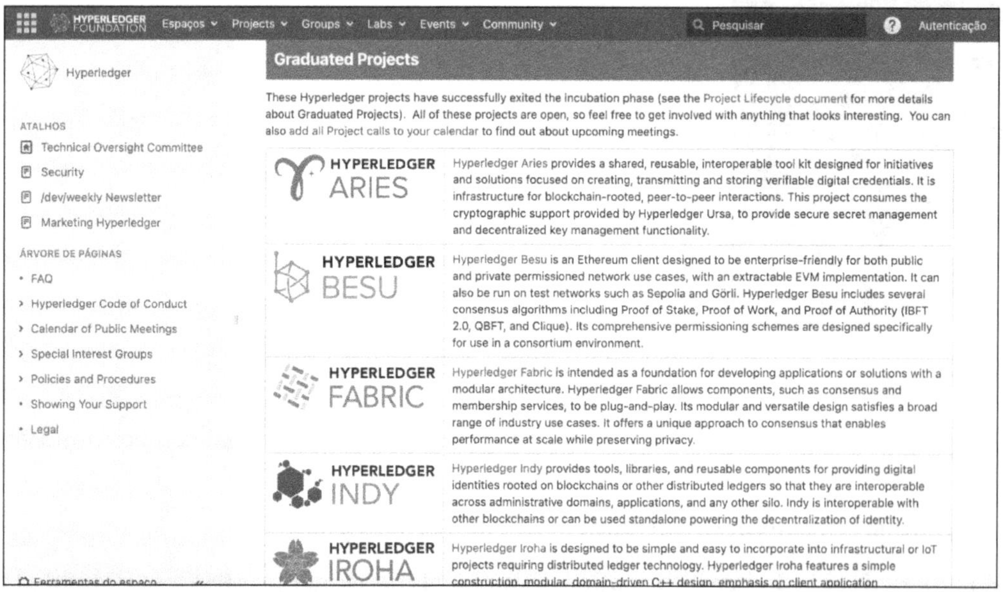

***Figure 3.8**: Hyperledger official Wiki page*

Other than the projects, the Wiki page has specific spaces for the community, like regional chapters, academic information, or scheduled events. Hyperledger Foundation fosters the development of open-source blockchain, and the code may be found on the GitHub page:

- **https://github.com/hyperledger**

There are multiple repositories utilized to store the source code for both Hyperledger Fabric itself and its associated projects, including SDKs. The Fabric core repository can be found at:

- **https://github.com/hyperledger/fabric**

The primary repository, however, recommended for application developers seeking to learn and access tutorials are:

- **https://github.com/hyperledger/fabric-samples**

The Fabric Samples repository contains chaincode examples for different purposes, from creating a test network and deploying a basic chaincode to chaincodes for tokenization like ERC-20 or ERC-721. This book will use some of these repository artifacts.

Regardless of their level of expertise, it is perfectly normal for chaincode developers to have questions or uncertainties when faced with technical challenges. Fortunately, there are numerous community platforms available for developers to engage with each other and discuss various aspects of blockchain development.

The Hyperledger Foundation provides an open space for real-time chat and collaboration on the Discord platform. Hyperledger's Discord server has dedicated channels for its projects and regional chapters. The Discord server may be accessed at the following:

- **https://discord.gg/hyperledger**

Refer to *Figure 3.9*:

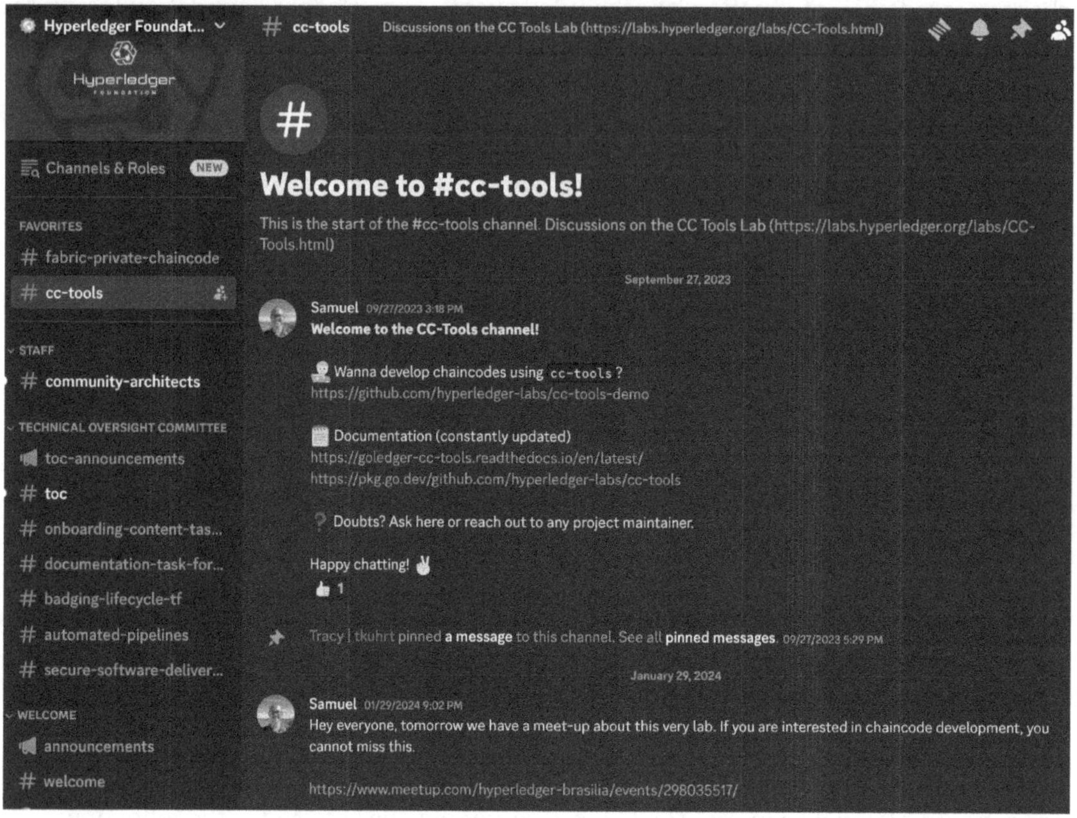

***Figure 3.9**: Hyperledger's Discord server*

The authors of this book highly recommend a subscription to the Hyperledger Fabric mailing list. Although it has the same purpose as the Discord server, the mailing list provides a forum-like experience where a thread with questions and answers on a topic can be seen uninterrupted. Its structure makes it easier to get reliable answers from the maintainers of Fabric themselves.

The complete mailing list can be found on the Wiki page:

- **https://wiki.hyperledger.org/display/CA/Mailing+List+Mapping**

Sometimes, users have questions or problems that are either bugs or unimplemented features they would like to see. On the issues section of the Hyperledger Fabric repository, planning, project management, issue tracking, and tasks can be found. It is common to find some discussions regarding bugs and new features, so it is always useful to keep an eye there. If the reader at some point wants to contribute to the project, exploring GitHub issues is a great place to start.

The issues page for Hyperledger Fabric:

- **https://github.com/hyperledger/fabric/issues**

Refer to *Figure 3.10*:

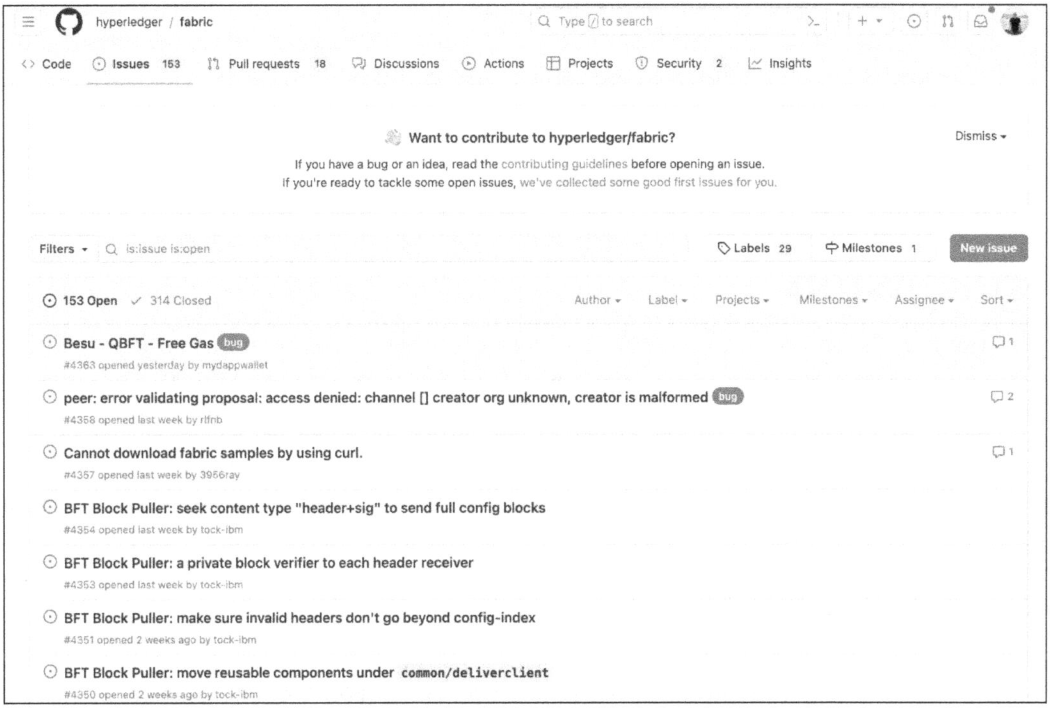

***Figure 3.10**: Hyperledger Fabric issues page*

This book will, naturally, explore Hyperledger Fabric, but also it will explore a tried and tested open-source toolset called Hyperledger Labs CC-Tools, which is a library for chaincode development. CC-Tools was accepted as a Hyperledger Labs project in September 2023 but has been used in production environments since 2019. The codebase was donated by GoLedger, a general member of the Hyperledger Foundation. The authors of this book are partners at GoLedger.

Throughout this book, we will get to know how to use this library for developing chaincode extremely fast.

The main repositories can be found at the following:

- **https://github.com/hyperledger-labs/cc-tools**
- **https://github.com/hyperledger-labs/cc-tools-demo**

The documentation for the library can be found at the following:

- **https://goledger-cc-tools.readthedocs.io/en/latest/**

Tutorials and how-to guides, which provide the package information of the library, can be found at:

- **https://pkg.go.dev/github.com/hyperledger-labs/cc-tools**

As an open-source project, CC-Tools has a growing community around it, and Hyperledger provides a space for discussion around chaincode development, which can be found under the Hyperledger Discord server. There you will have direct access to developers that use CC-Tools and to the maintainers of the project, including both authors.

Finally, both authors and the maintainer team regularly post instructional videos on YouTube on blockchain development, with many tutorials utilizing CC-Tools on Hyperledger Meetups.

Conclusion

Hyperledger Fabric is a powerful and versatile blockchain framework with great capabilities to create permissioned networks for several purposes. Auditing, integration, tracing, or tokenizing are some of the processes that may be benefited by this technology.

In this chapter, you gained insights into the distinctive advantages of Hyperledger Fabric and its suitability for specific scenarios. Furthermore, you were introduced to strategies for utilizing Fabric's resources and knowledge. The architecture model of Hyperledger Fabric was also explained, enabling you to make informed implementation decisions.

We explored the open-source community's role in fostering collaboration, innovation, and improvement. The open-source approach brings a strong and united community that may help developers all around the world throughout their journey of building blockchain platforms for registering digital transactions with efficiency, transparency, and trust in their processes.

In the next chapter, we will explore Fabric components and how they relate to one another to create a blockchain network.

Join our book's Discord space

Join the book's Discord Workspace for Latest updates, Offers, Tech happenings around the world, New Release and Sessions with the Authors:

https://discord.bpbonline.com

CHAPTER 4
Fabric Concepts and Components

Introduction

We are now ready to dive into Hyperledger Fabric and learn about all of the moving pieces and their purpose for the network. As we have seen, the Hyperledger Fabric framework provides a rich environment to work with, there are many components that allow for the creation of different permissioned blockchain networks, from the simplest to the most complex architectures.

When starting out with Hyperledger Fabric, it is common to have some difficulties in the clear understanding of all the components available and what they do. This chapter aims to explain clearly what each component is and how they interact with each other. With proper understanding, Fabric becomes one the most powerful tools available for blockchain, and that is because of its flexibility when constructing applications.

In the previous chapter, we explained the Hyperledger Fabric architecture model, showing how organizations relate to each other through nodes and channels. This chapter will build on top of that and detail each one of Fabric components. Although this book is focused on application development, represented by smart contracts or chaincodes, it is important to understand the role of each component.

In Hyperledger Fabric, one of the most important abstractions is the organization, it is where most components will have their place. An organization needs certain components to be fully functional in a Fabric network, the first one being a collection of digital certificates that will identify it in the network. These certificates are generally provided by a **certificate authority** (**CA**), an entity responsible for issuing identities for resources, in a directory structure known as the **membership service provider** (**MSP**), which allows for easy referencing of those identities. Next, organizations will need nodes that will concretely interact in the network context: peers and orderers, two node types available in Hyperledger Fabric.

Organizations are members of channels, structures of communication between parties, where they share information in the ledger. During this chapter, we will explore how these channels are created and managed by its members.

On top of a channel, organizations are able to instantiate chaincodes, where the application logic of the network is defined. This chapter will introduce chaincodes in more detail and is foundational for the next chapters.

Finally, we will explain in an introductory manner how we can assemble components ourselves to interact with the blockchain. Some Fabric tools like the Fabric Software Development Kit and Fabric Gateway allow for programmatic interaction with the ledger, allowing us to develop APIs. Those tools are code packages that can be utilized as an interaction interface with the blockchain network.

Structure

The chapter covers the following topics:

- Scalability as premise
- Organizations
- Channel and administration
- Chaincode
- Client services
- Business network

Objectives

By the end of this chapter, readers will gain a deeper understanding about Fabric components, how they can be assembled and the main reasons for why Fabric has the structure that it has.

While you, in reading this book, might not have the objective of learning about Fabric components and administration of networks, by the end of this chapter you will have a solid base from which to start if ever you might need to manage a running network. You will gain understanding of digital certificates, which are artifacts that identify Hyperledger Fabric resources.

By the end of this chapter, you will be able to identify channel policy requirements, including endorsement policies, access permissions, and governance rules that determine how transactions are validated and managed in the applications you will develop in later chapters. You will also have a foundation of chaincodes and client services for interacting with the chaincode that will allow for a smooth transition to the hands-on approach of the rest of this book.

Some of the component descriptions in Hyperledger Fabric rely on each other, so it can be confusing to understand them all at once. For example, to understand the concept of a channel, which is a private communication layer enabling specific data exchanges between network participants, you need to understand the concept of an organization, which is an entity in Hyperledger Fabric that represents a collection of members, policies, and nodes working together within the network, because organizations are composed of nodes, and nodes are also part of channels. If you are a beginner, do not worry. It is normal to feel confused at first. Just read the component descriptions more than once and try to piece together the relationships between them. Coding and testing in Hyperledger Fabric will also help you to understand the technology better.

Scalability as premise

The Hyperledger Fabric framework offers remarkable advantages in terms of flexibility and scalability for developing permissioned blockchains. With its various components, it opens up a multitude of possibilities for blockchain architecture, that is, how to structure all the resources together.

In this chapter, we will explore the essential roles played by these components, as their strategic combination defines the technical features of a permissioned blockchain network. A **strategic combination** refers to the purposeful alignment of these components, such as number of participants, governance rules, and business logic to achieve the desired network functionality, scalability, and security.

While beginners of Hyperledger Fabric might initially find the numerous components overwhelming, it is highly recommended to read and revisit these definitions to enhance understanding. Once grasped, this architectural schema, provided by the flexibility of having pluggable components, opens up a wealth of possibilities for blockchain development, solidifying Hyperledger Fabric's position as a leading development framework worldwide.

Scalability, that is, the ease of adapting the network structure and capacity is not just an added feature in Hyperledger Fabric; it is a fundamental premise that underpins the framework's design. This principle of scalability is ingrained in every aspect of the system, ensuring that it can handle a growing volume of transactions and participants without compromising performance. This is particularly critical for enterprise-level blockchain networks, where corporations and governments have the highest of standards when it comes to security, availability and maintainability.

The use of multiple components with different roles enables networks that suit many business cases. Moreover, the framework includes a feature called private channels, which are secure, isolated communication paths within the network. These channels allow specific groups of participants to share data exclusively among themselves, ensuring that sensitive information is not visible to unauthorized members. This selective visibility is crucial in business settings where different organizations may collaborate while maintaining confidentiality over certain transactions.

As the network grows with more participants and an increasing number of transactions, private channels help maintain efficiency by reducing unnecessary data exposure. This means that only relevant parties process specific transactions, which helps preserve both network performance (by reducing congestion) and security (by minimizing the risk of unauthorized access). As a result, the system can scale effectively, accommodating new members and higher transaction volumes without compromising speed or data privacy.

Refer to *Figure 4.1:*

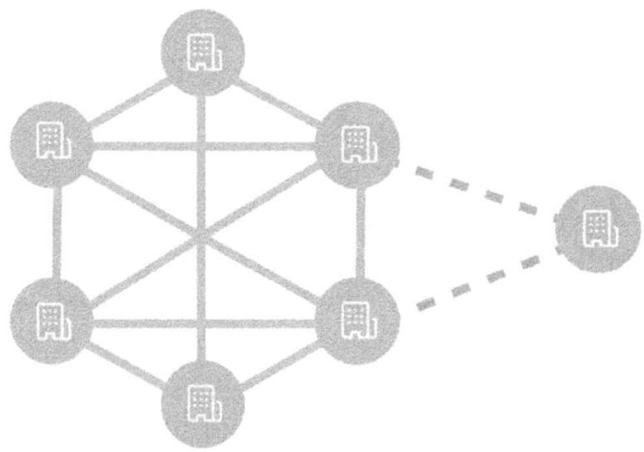

***Figure 4.1**: Hyperledger Fabric allows new organizations to join a running network*

Scalability as a premise in Hyperledger Fabric goes beyond the technical aspects; it also promotes adaptability to diverse business requirements, which can include regulatory compliance, industry-specific data privacy rules, transaction throughput needs, and governance models. Organizations can design their networks to suit their specific needs, such as a healthcare company maintaining privacy over their customers data. Those needs might involve a few trusted participants, such as a regulatory agency, or span across numerous collaborating entities, such as hospitals that need patient information. This flexibility allows enterprises to start with smaller, more focused networks and then gradually expand and interconnect with other networks as their business demands grow. Ultimately, the scalability principle empowers Hyperledger Fabric to serve as a robust and versatile foundation for building enterprise-grade, permissioned blockchain solutions that can evolve and thrive in a dynamic and ever-changing business landscape.

Let us start taking a look at how these pieces come together to give life to an organization.

Organizations

Hopefully, it has become clear that enterprise blockchain revolves around organizations, in its most formal sense. **An organization is a group that has a common objective, it can be a company, a government agency or even departments inside a big corporation**. That abstraction serves as a good starting point for understanding an organization inside a Hyperledger Fabric network.

In Fabric, the organization generally will be the logical component of the physical entity, so to speak. The Fabric organization is an abstraction to unite the nodes pertaining to the same entity. These organizations are materialized in the form of a MSP, which is a component in Hyperledger Fabric responsible for managing identities and access control within the network. An MSP defines how members are authenticated and authorized, ensuring that only verified participants can interact with the blockchain.

Each organization in the network has its own MSP, which establishes its identity and governance rules. The MSP relies on digital certificates, which are issued by a CA to validate the authenticity of network participants. These certificates are used to sign transactions, proving that they come from legitimate sources and maintaining the integrity of the system.

As with any blockchain network, Hyperledger Fabric relies on a distributed infrastructure consisting of interconnected nodes responsible for creating and validating transactions and blocks. Within the Hyperledger Fabric framework, two types of nodes exist: **peers** and **orderers**. **Peers** handle transaction endorsement and maintain the state of the ledger, while **orderers** manage the consensus and block creation process. MSPs are associated with these types of nodes in the network, namely **peers** and **orderers**.

The abbreviation of organization as org is widely used for the Fabric technical documentation and this book will also use the term org to reference to the organization definition.

In the following subsections, we will the main concepts related to the organization and how they are intertwined.

Certificate authority

As a blockchain platform, Hyperledger is strongly dependent on cryptographic signing of transactions that are registered on the network. Asynchronous encryption algorithms are used in order to provide the necessary trust and make the transactions reliable enough for the technology to work as desired.

When compared to other technologies like Ethereum, for example, that uses cryptographic key pairs at their signing functions, Hyperledger Fabric uses X.509 digital certificates that bring several advantages for a permissioned model.

Ethereum, as a public blockchain, follows a decentralized trust model where users generate their own asymmetric cryptographic key pairs without requiring permission from a central authority. These key pairs function as follows:

- **Public key**: Functions as an account address on the network.
- **Private key**: Used to sign transactions, providing proof of ownership and authorization.

This model enables pseudonymous transactions, meaning that a user's identity is not inherently tied to their key pair. While this ensures privacy, it also raises challenges related to security, accountability, and compliance. A lost or compromised private key results in irreversible consequences, as there is no authority to revoke or reassign it.

Hyperledger Fabric, designed for permissioned enterprise environments, takes a different approach by integrating X.509 digital certificates issued by a CA. Instead of relying on self-generated key pairs, each participant is explicitly registered with verifiable credentials, enabling a structured identity model.

The main functions and responsibilities of the Hyperledger Fabric CA model, as follows:

- **Identity registration**: It involves registering identities of participants in the blockchain network. It verifies and validates the identity of entities such as clients, users, admins, peers and orderers, and associates them with unique digital certificates.
- **Certificate issuance**: Once an entity's identity is verified, the CA issues X.509 certificates to those entities. These certificates contain the public key associated with the entity's identity and are used for cryptographic operations within the network. The CA digitally signs each issued X.509 certificate using its private key, ensuring authenticity and integrity. This process embeds a cryptographic signature over the certificate's public key, identity details, and validity period, which can be verified using the CA's public key to confirm its legitimacy.
- **Certificate revocation**: in case an entity's privileges need to be revoked or if a certificate is compromised, the CA can revoke the certificate. Certificate revocation generates a **Certificate Revocation List** (**CRL**) that can be informed in the network so that the participants will not trust it.
- **Certificate renewal**: The CA can also handle the renewal of certificates. Renewal involves generating a new certificate with an updated expiration date while maintaining the same identity and associated cryptographic keys.

Key characteristics of X.509 certificates in Fabric are as follows:

- **Issued by a CA**: Ensures participants are authenticated before gaining access to the network.
- **Tied to a real-world identity**: Unlike Ethereum's pseudonymous model, each certificate contains organization and role-based identity information.

- **Used for both authentication and transaction signing:** Enhances security by ensuring only verified entities can sign and submit transactions.
- **Revocable and manageable**: Certificates can be revoked or renewed without disrupting the network, allowing for better security control.

This identity-driven approach strengthens trust, compliance, and governance, making Hyperledger Fabric well-suited for regulated industries such as finance, healthcare, and supply chain management.

Refer to the following table:

Feature	Ethereum (key-pairs)	Hyperledger Fabric (X.509)
Identity Management	Pseudonymous, no real-world identity	Tied to organizations or individuals
Authentication	Based on private key ownership	Verified through a CA
Access Control	Open participation, no restrictions	Permissioned, role-based access
Security Risks	Irrevocable, private key loss is permanent	Revocable and manageable
Regulatory Compliance	Limited due to anonymity	Supports compliance with governance models

Table 4.1: *Comparison between key pairs and X.509 certificates*

The X.509 certificate model follows a hierarchical structure. This means that trust for a certain certificate in ensured by the issuer in the trust chain.

Refer to the following figure:

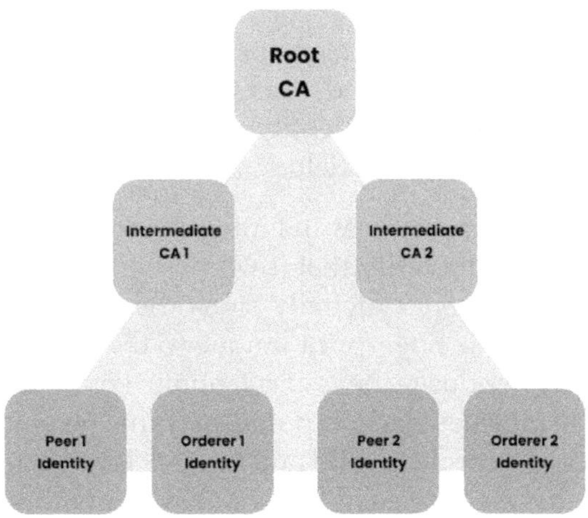

Figure 4.2: *Hierarchical characteristic of the X.509 certificate model*

The X.509 model is structures on the **Public Key Infrastructure** (**PKI**) concept. It consists of several key components, as follows:

- **Subject**: The Subject field in an X.509 certificate represents the entity whose identity is being certified. This entity can be an individual, organization, or system component (such as a server or a blockchain node). The subject is the primary identifier in the certificate and is used to validate the authenticity of the certificate holder.
- **Distinguished Name (DN)**: The DN is a structured format used to uniquely identify the subject within a certificate. It consists of multiple attributes that describe the entity, including the following:
  - **Common Name (CN)**: The primary identifier, often the entity's name or domain name.
  - **Organization (O)**: The name of the company or organization to which the entity belongs.
  - **Organizational Unit (OU)**: A subdivision within the organization, such as a department.
  - **Country (C)**: The country code (e.g., "US" for the United States).
  - **State/Province (ST)**: The region or state where the organization is located.
  - **Locality (L)**: The specific city or town.
- **Issuer**: the issuer is the entity that issues the certificate and attests to the identity of the subject by checking the issuer's digital signature on the certificate using the public key of the issuing CA to ensure it was legitimately signed and has not been tampered with. The issuer is also identified by a DN and is usually a trusted **Certification Authority** (**CA**) responsible for verifying the subject's identity.
- **Public key**: The X.509 certificate contains the subject's public key, which is used for encryption, digital signatures, and other cryptographic operations. The public key is associated with the subject's identity and is typically included in a certificate's subject's public key information field.
- **Signature**: The signature ensures the integrity and authenticity of the certificate by allowing recipients to verify that it was issued by a trusted authority and has not been altered. The issuer digitally signs the certificate using its private key, creating a cryptographic fingerprint unique to the certificate's contents. To verify authenticity, a recipient uses the issuer's public key to decrypt the signature and check whether it matches the computed hash of the certificate's contents. If the values match, the certificate is valid and trusted; if not, it may have been tampered with or issued by an untrusted source. This signature is computed over the certificate's data, including the following:

- **The subject's public key**: The key that others will use to encrypt data or verify signatures from the certificate holder.
- **DN of the subject**: Identifies the entity being certified.
- **Issuer information**: Identifies the entity that issued the certificate.
- **Validity period**: Defines the certificate's start and expiration dates.
- **Certificate serial number:** A unique identifier assigned by the issuer.

- **Validity period**: X.509 certificates have a defined validity period during which they are considered valid. This period includes a start date and an expiration date, after which the certificate is no longer considered trustworthy, in order to mitigate security risks from outdated cryptography, prevent unauthorized use, account for changes in the certificate holder's status, and ensure compliance with industry regulations requiring periodic renewal.
- **Extensions**: X.509 certificates can include various extensions to provide additional information or functionality. These extensions can define key usage constraints, specify the certificate's purpose, indicate certificate revocation status, and include other attributes as needed, as follows:
    - **Key usage constraints**: Defines allowed cryptographic operations like signing, encryption, or certificate signing.
    - **Extended key usage (EKU)**: Specifies the certificate's purpose, such as server authentication or code signing.
    - **Certificate revocation status**: Indicates if a certificate is revoked via a CRL or OCSP.
    - **Subject alternative name (SAN)**: Associates multiple identities (for example, domains, IPs) with a single certificate.
    - **Basic constraints**: Defines whether the certificate is a CA and if it can issue other certificates.

X.509 certificates are used for secure transactions and communication in a Hyperledger Fabric network. The certificates allow the parties to verify each other's identities, encrypt communication, and prevent tampering or interception of data.

In Hyperledger Fabric, the nodes are identified by a X.509 certificate, namely the peer and the orderer. During the setup of these nodes, it is necessary to provide the proper certificates so that they know who they are and how to present them for the network. These proper certificates are known as the MSP. Technically speaking, these certificates can be issued by any means: OpenSSL command-line, cryptogen command-line (a Fabric tool for development use), a self-signed CA or a trusted CA.

Refer to the following details for each certificate issuing tool:

- **OpenSSL command-line**: A widely used open-source tool for generating, signing, and managing X.509 certificates. It allows users to create self-signed certificates, issue certificates from a private CA, or generate **Certificate Signing Requests** (**CSRs**) for trusted CAs. Found in Linux, macOS, and Windows via package managers like apt, brew, or choco.
- **Cryptogen command-line (Hyperledger Fabric Tool):** A development-focused tool in Hyperledger Fabric used to quickly generate X.509 certificates and keys for Fabric networks. Unlike OpenSSL, it is designed for testing and local development, not for production environments. It is included in the Fabric binaries and can be found on the Hyperledger Fabric GitHub repository.
- **Self-signed CA:** CA that generates its own root certificate without being verified by a higher authority. Self-signed certificates are useful for internal applications, testing, or private networks, but they are not trusted by browsers or external entities. These can be created using OpenSSL or Fabric's Fabric-CA.
- **Trusted CA:** A certificate issued by a recognized third-party CA, such as DigiCert, Let's Encrypt, or GlobalSign. These certificates are widely trusted by operating systems, browsers, and external systems, making them essential for production deployments, public-facing applications, and compliance requirements.

From the perspective of the nodes, it does not matter where the certificates come from as long as they are valid.

The following is the X.509 digital certificate example:

```
Certificate:
    Data:
        Version: 3 (0x2)
        Serial Number:
            93:03:b6:58:f3:a4:92:c3:3c:cc:6a:ed:a4:34:89:51
    Signature Algorithm: ecdsa-with-SHA256
        Issuer: C=US, ST=California, L=San Francisco, O=org.example.com,
CN=tlsca.org.example.com
        Validity
            Not Before: Jun 22 15:47:00 2023 GMT
            Not After : Jun 19 15:47:00 2033 GMT
        Subject: C=US, ST=California, L=San Francisco, O=org.example.com,
CN=tlsca.org.example.com
        Subject Public Key Info:
            Public Key Algorithm: id-ecPublicKey
                Public-Key: (256 bit)
                pub:
                    04:d1:b6:a7:c6:19:c8:fc:38:22:5e:c7:ba:a7:1e:
```

```
                    76:48:a6:b8:35:f1:98:9c:1f:b8:d0:ed:9f:c6:ec:
                    0e:54:12:89:ca:67:fc:cd:21:c7:06:c4:ee:d9:6e:
                    af:6f:27:83:cb:b2:be:83:ed:3e:cc:33:07:16:3d:
                    db:74:3b:37:46
                ASN1 OID: prime256v1
                NIST CURVE: P-256
        X509v3 extensions:
            X509v3 Key Usage: critical
                Digital Signature, Key Encipherment, Certificate Sign, CRL
Sign
            X509v3 Extended Key Usage:
                TLS Web Client Authentication, TLS Web Server
Authentication
            X509v3 Basic Constraints: critical
                CA:TRUE
            X509v3 Subject Key Identifier:
                93:25:CF:24:82:46:BB:A9:59:47:76:4D:20:6C:AF:D6:2C:37
:CF:75:0E:6B:54:B2:6E:67:3A:2C:6E:4B:FE:F5
    Signature Algorithm: ecdsa-with-SHA256
         30:45:02:20:46:68:98:b3:9f:e3:2d:fd:1c:56:90:bf:fe:87:
         2b:32:02:c9:b4:ba:41:9e:fc:05:ae:ce:b6:19:4d:73:99:39:
         02:21:00:d3:c1:9f:64:ab:87:2d:e6:85:21:0f:93:01:2d:38:
         cf:45:f2:08:18:85:bb:2b:fe:2f:76:1f:23:21:44:de:2c
```

In more practical terms, however, the most common and recommended way to issue certificates is with the use of a CA. As most people do not have the access to trusted CAs (or do not want to pay for issuing certificates), Fabric provides an implementation of a self-signed CA called Fabric CA. The Fabric CA is able to provide all the needed functionality regarding certification that a Fabric project might need. The CA is responsible for managing and issuing certificates to each Hyperledger Fabric component, serving two key functions, as follows:

- **Securing communication**: The CA provides TLS certificates, ensuring that communications between Fabric nodes are encrypted and authenticated, preventing unauthorized access.
- **Signing transactions**: The CA issues identity certificates, which allow participants to prove their identity and sign transactions, enforcing access control through the MSP mechanism.

Although this book will not dive deeper into the operational details of the Hyperledger Fabric CA, there will be many examples and exercises in order to provide a better understanding of it in the next chapters.

Membership service provider

Hyperledger Fabric is based on the PKI model, a security framework that manages digital identities and cryptographic keys to enable secure communication and authentication. PKI ensures that participants in a network can verify each other's identities and exchange information securely.

Fabric relies on four essential PKI elements, as follows:

- **Digital certificates**: X.509 certificates serve as electronic credentials that authenticate network participants. These certificates bind an entity's identity to its public key and are issued by a CA.
- **Public and private keys**: A key pair is generated for each entity in the network. The public key is shared openly and is used to verify signatures, while the private key is kept secret and is used to sign transactions and prove ownership.
- **Certificate authorities (CAs)**: CAs are trusted entities responsible for issuing, managing, and revoking digital certificates. In Hyperledger Fabric, CAs validate the identity of network participants before issuing them a certificate.
- **Certificate revocation lists**: A CRL is a list of revoked certificates maintained by the CA. If a certificate is compromised, expired, or no longer valid, it is added to the CRL to prevent unauthorized use.

This allows for a flexible and secure identification architecture, meaning that Hyperledger Fabric can support multiple identity providers, role-based access control, and certificate-based authentication, adapting to different enterprise requirements while maintaining strict security.

PKI model provides cryptographic identities for network components, ensuring that each participant has a unique, verifiable digital identity. This is similar to how SSL/TLS certificates authenticate websites, enabling secure communication between browsers and web servers by verifying the server's legitimacy and encrypting data exchanges.

While PKI is essential to Fabric nodes, there still must be a way to make these identities known in the network. Having a node with an identity does not suffice. This is where the MSP comes in. The MSP will be used to verify that a particular identity is indeed allowed to operate in the network.

Let us imagine a practical situation to make the concepts clearer. In most countries, citizens have formal identities issued by government agencies. The identities carried by citizens have different purposes. Some are a general type of identification, others allow citizens to drive a vehicle, and some identify them when they are overseas. They are issued by agencies that have an established chain of trust, but the ones with specific purposes provide authorization in some regard to citizens. We know that it is unreasonable for a passport holder to be allowed to drive because of it, the citizen must hold a driver's license. It is also unreasonable to allow travelers to enter a country without a passport (in most cases). Agencies and governments are the PKI of citizens' identities while how these identities are treated is the MSP, for example at a passport control.

In the context of Fabric, a CA registers, stores and manages identities for components belonging to an organization. In practical terms, digital certificates are assigned to each identity, allowing network components to use them for authentication, secure communication, and transaction signing within Hyperledger Fabric.

MSP has a confusing name because it does not actually provide anything. In essence, the implementation of the MSP is a set of certificates that will define an organization in two contexts: inwardly and outwardly. These are known as the local MSP and the channel MSP.

The local MSP is defined by certificate definition in the context of the node itself, be it a peer or an orderer. First and foremost, the MSP structure, which in practice is a directory following a particular structure, will define the organization responsible for that node and which identities are administrators of that node. That alone will define the permissioning for most of what the peer is in the context of the organization and who can operate it. The local MSP can happen in the context of clients too, and in that context, it will define the certificates related to authentication when invoking transactions. Every single node will have an MSP folder structure defined and that will uniquely identify it in the network and as a member of an organization.

Consider the following directory structure for a glimpse of what files are needed for MSP:

```
MSP
├── admincerts
│   └── admin-cert.pem          # Admin certificate(s)
├── cacerts
│   └── ca-cert.pem             # Root CA certificate
├── intermediatecerts
│   └── intermediate-cert.pem   # Intermediate CA certificate(s)
├── keystore
│   └── <private_key_file>     # Private key of the organization
├── signcerts
│   └── peer0-cert.pem          # Peer's signing certificate
└── tlscacerts
    └── tls-ca-cert.pem         # TLS Root CA certificate
```

In Hyperledger Fabric, the channel MSP defines how an organization is recognized by other participants within a given channel. It governs identity verification, access control, and transaction policies at the channel level, ensuring that only authorized entities can interact with the channel. The channel MSP determines which organizations are permitted to read, write, endorse transactions, and enforce governance policies, making it a critical component of channel security and governance.

The channel MSP differs from the local MSP, which is simply a directory of certificates stored on a node. The local MSP is used internally by an organization to verify the identities of its own members, ensuring that only authorized users within that entity can operate on its nodes. In contrast, the channel MSP consists of public certificates that are explicitly registered in the channel configuration, known as the configuration block. These certificates define the organizations recognized within a channel and establish their permissions. Since the configuration block is shared across all participants, every member of the channel can verify the authenticity of transactions based on the registered channel MSPs.

For an organization to participate in a channel, it must be explicitly defined in the channel configuration with its correct channel MSP. This ensures that only properly authorized organizations are allowed to transact within the channel and enforce policies. If an organization's MSP is not correctly registered, its nodes and users will not be recognized, preventing them from participating in the network.

The channel MSP is the foundational element of governance in a Hyperledger Fabric network. Through its configuration, organizations can establish different governance models. In a consortium model, multiple organizations collectively define and manage the channel, each with equal authority in setting policies, endorsing transactions, and approving changes to the network configuration. This decentralized approach is often used in business networks where multiple entities need shared control. On the other hand, in a regulator-based governance model, a central entity, such as a government agency or a lead organization maintains full control over the channel's governance, dictating policies and enforcing strict access controls for participants.

By configuring the channel MSP correctly, organizations can enforce trust, compliance, and operational control within their network.

The following is an example of a configuration block defining the channel MSP:

```
{
  "channel_group": {
    "groups": {
      "Application": {
        "groups": {
          "org1MSP": {...   // channel MSP for organization org1
          },
          "org2MSP": {...   // channel MSP for organization org2
          }
        },
        "mod_policy": "Admins",
        "policies": {              // policies for the channel
          "Admins": {...
          },
```

```
            "Endorsement": {...
            },
            "LifecycleEndorsement": {...
            },
            "Readers": {...
            },
            "Writers": {...
            }
          }
        }
        ...
      }
      ...
    }
    ...
}
```

The certificates defined under an MSP structure will generally have an identity type, also known as a Node **Organizational Unit (OU)**, which is a field in the X.509 certificate that categorizes identities based on their role within the network. In Hyperledger Fabric, Node OUs help distinguish between different types of participants, such as peers, orderers, administrators, and clients, enabling the MSP to enforce access control and apply specific permissions to each entity type.

There are four types of identities in the context of Hyperledger Fabric, as follows:

- **Admin**: Used to sign the transactions for channel management in the network.
- **Client**: Identify an external application and sign transaction proposals necessary for the execution of the chaincodes.
- **Peer**: Identify the Hyperledger Fabric nodes of type `peer` and sign the proposal response of a chaincode transaction.
- **Orderer**: Identify the Fabric nodes of type `orderer` and sign the block committed in the network.

These identity types are used in MSPs to define permissioning for each element type. For example, peer nodes have a responsibility of signing a transaction response, the local MSP will define which identity the peer will use to sign this response, we say that this certificate identifies the peer. The channel MSP will define that the identity authorized to sign this kind of message is of the type `peer`. That means that if some other node signs a transaction response with a type that is not a peer, that will be rejected during signature validation.

These OUs are designed to align perfectly with Hyperledger Fabric's permissioned philosophy. Each organizational component plays a distinct role in the blockchain lifecycle, endorsing the information stored in the network.

An organization in Hyperledger Fabric is a logical grouping of nodes that are owned and operated by the same entity. As previously discussed, organizations serve as a structural unit within the network, defining which participants belong to a particular entity. The MSP is directly tied to the organization because it manages the identities, certificates, and access policies for all the nodes and participants within that organization. In other words, an organization's identity within the network is established and enforced through its MSP.

Since organizations can vary in size, from small businesses to multinational corporations, the way they manage their blockchain infrastructure can also differ. In some cases, a single MSP is sufficient to represent the entire organization, ensuring that all nodes and users operate under a unified identity and governance model. However, in larger organizations with decentralized management structures, it may be necessary to define multiple MSPs. This allows different divisions, subsidiaries, or departments to maintain their own independent identity management, access controls, and governance policies while still being part of the same overarching entity within the Fabric network. Having separate MSPs for different divisions can help streamline access control, enhance security, and support complex enterprise requirements.

Examples of MSP names are as follows:

- org1-MSP
- org2-branch1-MSP
- org2-headquarter-MSP

Peers

In a Hyperledger Fabric network, peers are critical components that serve multiple roles within an organization. A peer is responsible for storing a complete copy of the ledger, which contains all the transactional data recorded on the blockchain. This role is fundamental to the concept of a distributed network, as peers ensure the ledger is replicated across the network, providing resilience and fault tolerance.

Moreover, the peer manages chaincodes so that they can be executed when a transaction is invoked. Since it possesses a copy of the ledger and chaincodes, the peer will be able to independently execute a transaction that will be later used to achieve consensus based on the response.

Not all peers in a Hyperledger Fabric network are required to have the chaincode installed, meaning some peers are only responsible for storing and updating the ledger by receiving new blocks. However, the peers that do have the chaincode installed are referred to as **endorsing peers** or **execution peers**. These peers play a critical role in the transaction process, as they are responsible for executing the chaincode, evaluating the proposed transaction, and generating a transaction proposal response.

Endorsing a transaction involves the peer validating and signing the transaction proposal using its private key and certificate. This signed response serves as proof that the transaction was evaluated and approved according to the chaincode logic. When endorsing peers sign the transaction, it signifies that the respective organization is endorsing a proposed change to the ledger state.

Starting with version 2.4 and later, Hyperledger Fabric introduced a Gateway service running on peers. This service simplifies the process of handling transaction proposals and endorsements, serving as a centralized point for clients to interact with the network efficiently.

Peers also communicate with other nodes in the network using the gossip protocol, a mechanism for securely and efficiently disseminating information, such as private data associated with transactions. This protocol ensures that private data is shared only with authorized peers while maintaining the overall integrity and privacy of the blockchain network.

Each peer has a digital X.509 certificate issued by its organization CA, and this certificate is used to define the peer as a member of a specific organization. In other words, if a peer signs a transaction, the blockchain network will recognize it based on the channel MSP configured. Consider the following decoded X.509 certificate and note the type of the node found on the **Organizational Unit** (**OU**) field.

Refer to the following code:

```
Certificate:
    Data:
        Version: 3 (0x2)
        Serial Number:
            09:ee:0a:e0:fa:ef:2d:22:e3:8e:dd:bd:79:bd:b1:e4
    Signature Algorithm: ecdsa-with-SHA256
        Issuer: C=US, ST=California, L=San Francisco, O=org.example.com,
CN=ca.org.example.com
        Validity
            Not Before: Aug  7 22:51:00 2023 GMT
            Not After : Aug  4 22:51:00 2033 GMT
        Subject: C=US, ST=California, L=San Francisco, OU=peer, CN=peer0.
org.example.com
        Subject Public Key Info:
            Public Key Algorithm: id-ecPublicKey
                Public-Key: (256 bit)
                pub:
                    04:55:98:59:90:90:2c:85:85:91:16:96:f1:2f:ae:
                    6d:c2:00:37:dc:5d:67:de:b8:cd:0e:a3:75:2b:76:
                    ca:26:3c:fa:1b:36:a7:64:89:07:37:4e:f7:73:82:
```

```
                d5:73:32:1e:00:80:85:fc:8b:8a:c5:d6:dd:7f:d7:
                e3:50:90:67:02
            ASN1 OID: prime256v1
            NIST CURVE: P-256
    X509v3 extensions:
        X509v3 Key Usage: critical
            Digital Signature
        X509v3 Basic Constraints: critical
            CA:FALSE
        X509v3 Authority Key Identifier:

keyid:7C:07:38:A1:8F:4D:02:4A:DF:70:B6:62:CA:EB:EC:FF:CF:E6:46:02
:49:AD:3A:38:5E:AF:50:3E:25:CD:BD:2B
    Signature Algorithm: ecdsa-with-SHA256
        30:45:02:21:00:da:f4:b9:0f:4e:69:47:6c:37:54:04:f2:3b:
        4a:2f:6f:87:4c:a2:16:f8:d2:42:09:f5:a2:f4:bc:e6:a9:b7:
        69:02:20:5c:3b:a8:20:dd:e0:4e:99:45:41:a2:f1:3e:74:1a:
        97:56:31:16:af:09:2d:a9:7a:ca:ed:e4:18:4b:f0:a5:f4
```

It will be seen in detail in the next chapter, that a peer signing a transaction proposal does not necessarily mean that this transaction will be accepted by the blockchain network as it will have to be validated by the Hyperledger Fabric consensus algorithm.

A peer is able to host a copy of multiple ledgers, and that will become clear in the section about channels. Multiple ledgers simply mean that the peer has joined more than one channel. Likewise, a peer can have multiple chaincodes installed, where these chaincode access a particular channel.

Consider the following illustration of a peer with multiple ledgers and chaincodes:

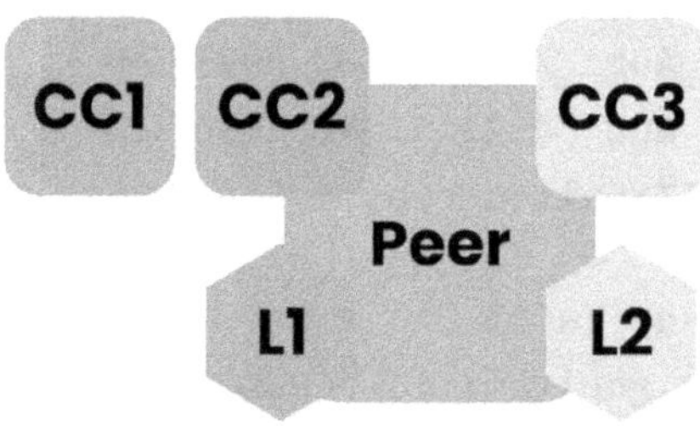

Figure 4.3: *A peer can host multiple ledgers and chaincodes*

A peer is supported by something we call a state database. The state database is responsible for maintaining the current state of the blockchain information, more commonly known as the world state. This database can be either a LevelDB or a CouchDB, both of which are non-relational databases. LevelDB provides a more basic set of functionalities, not allowing for complex queries, whereas CouchDB provides a huge set of functionalities that we can take advantage of when developing chaincodes.

Orderers

Just like peers, a Fabric network must have orderers for it to be functional. An orderer is a special type of node that has one simple but important task, to order transactions into a block and broadcast it to the network.

A Fabric channel may have many orderers and they will work together as what we call the ordering service of the channel. At the time of this writing, when Fabric is in version v2.5.x, the preferred ordering service configuration is called **Raft**. The Raft protocol provides a crash fault tolerant cluster-like service for the ordering service. This means that an orderer will be part of a channel's ordering service along with an arbitrary number of orderers, where they will elect a leader that will assemble blocks for the channel. If an orderer goes out, another election will be carried out and the system will remain operational.

Any orderer on a Fabric network will belong to a channel, just like peers. That means that they will have an identity and that a CA will issue certificates so they can be correctly identified by the local and channel MSPs.

Consider a decoded certificate of an orderer, as follows:

```
Certificate:
    Data:
        Version: 3 (0x2)
        Serial Number:
            ba:76:fa:b3:01:1a:b9:d4:19:6c:27:24:7a:98:de:77
    Signature Algorithm: ecdsa-with-SHA256
        Issuer: C=US, ST=California, L=San Francisco, O=example.com, CN=ca.
example.com
        Validity
            Not Before: Jun 22 15:47:00 2023 GMT
            Not After : Jun 19 15:47:00 2033 GMT
        Subject: C=US, ST=California, L=San Francisco, OU=orderer,
CN=orderer.example.com
        Subject Public Key Info:
            Public Key Algorithm: id-ecPublicKey
                Public-Key: (256 bit)
                pub:
                    04:8f:02:5a:37:cc:b2:43:15:6b:e0:ad:ea:31:ee:
                    1e:4f:0d:82:47:a2:0f:aa:ed:8c:28:5d:c8:5c:f6:
                    51:5f:8c:64:a4:21:93:6f:4e:d9:48:0e:c9:d9:1d:
                    57:33:04:33:34:47:cc:5f:9e:94:a3:ec:83:95:b8:
```

```
                    89:b8:cd:27:47
                ASN1 OID: prime256v1
                NIST CURVE: P-256
        X509v3 extensions:
            X509v3 Key Usage: critical
                Digital Signature
            X509v3 Basic Constraints: critical
                CA:FALSE
            X509v3 Authority Key Identifier:

keyid:7D:60:44:1B:EC:FA:02:E2:BA:ED:64:F1:C1:7E:5F:2C:14:8E:83:88:
FE:CC:5A:68:00:92:44:8F:AD:CD:63:1B
    Signature Algorithm: ecdsa-with-SHA256
         30:45:02:21:00:94:60:25:b1:7c:3b:b2:c5:fe:27:b1:13:06:
         ab:47:2b:c1:7b:4f:53:5f:0f:f5:26:6d:89:de:1f:d2:f0:14:
         f4:02:20:17:9b:81:3d:08:fc:dd:09:29:f8:05:28:6f:11:d8:
         32:f7:ad:4c:f6:17:c5:d9:60:f4:dd:a8:bb:ea:49:f8:03
```

The ordering service is also responsible for safeguarding the channel membership and configuration by maintaining and enforcing the channel's configuration policies, which are defined in the configuration block. These policies ensure that only authorized organizations, as specified by their channel MSPs, can participate in the channel. Any changes to membership or configuration must be approved according to the channel's governance rules, and the ordering service validates and applies these updates, ensuring the integrity and security of the channel's structure. When a request for joining a channel comes from a peer, the orderer is the one who enforces the access rules based on the channel MSP. If the peer is from an organization not defined by the channel configuration, that is, the channel MSP, it will be forbidden from joining it.

For example, in the finance sector, only licensed financial institutions or regulators may join, with specific roles like read-only access for oversight. In healthcare, access might be restricted to certified providers or researchers, with additional controls on sensitive patient data. For supply chain networks, rules can enforce participation for verified suppliers and manufacturers, sometimes limiting access based on geography or supply chain tiers. In government sectors, agencies may have role-based access, with certain nodes restricted to classified data. In retail networks, verified retailers or distributors may join, often with segmented access to sales data or regional information.

Orderers will also enforce rules on who can update the channel configuration. This process is governed by channel policies, which define the rules for managing and administering the channel. These policies are part of the **Channel and administration** configuration, which establishes the governance framework for the channel, including how changes are proposed, validated, and approved. It ensures that only authorized organizations or individuals can modify the channel's structure, membership, or access rules.

Channel and administration refers to the mechanism by which participating organizations collectively manage the channel. It includes setting governance rules, such as defining who can propose updates, how votes are counted, and the thresholds needed for approval.

Channel and administration

The Hyperledger Fabric channel is where the information of a Fabric network is registered. One channel always has only one ledger. A channel, however, is much more than the ledger of the blockchain. It also consists of the credentials and roles for the permissioned scheme that the Hyperledger Fabric provides, as we have seen before. Not every organization created in the Fabric model may access or modify the information in the distributed ledger. To be allowed access the channel configuration must be defined accordingly.

By now, you may have realized that the many components we are outlining here are tied to each other tightly. A channel is the structure peers rely on to share information by registering transactions in the channel's ledger. A channel is also guarded by the orderer and its ledger only exists because of the blocks assembled by it. Later we will see that the information registered in the channel's ledger is originated by the execution of a chaincode transaction by a client. All these moving parts are connected harmoniously to deliver what we call a blockchain.

The Hyperledger Fabric channel is an important structure because before a block and its transactions are registered in the ledger; the channel policies will always be verified. This is especially useful for distributed consortium processes, where only a restricted set of entities have the proper credentials to change the state of the blockchain. This is possible because of the channel configuration and how Fabric deals with the administration of a channel.

The channel configuration is essential in the understanding of the Fabric model. A channel gets created in the first place by the generation of its first block, the genesis block. The genesis block will contain the configuration of the channel at the time of creation. That means that the configuration of the channel is registered in the blockchain itself. In Fabric, the genesis block is generated by assembling a file we call **`configtx.yaml`**, where configurations for the blockchain network are defined, and running it through a tool called *configtxgen* that will return a genesis block encoded in the proto buffer format. The configuration file will detail the organizations that will be participating in the channel by informing what are the certificates to use for verifying identities, the channel MSP. It also will define the orderer nodes that will be part of the ordering service for that channel.

Following is the **`Organizations`** section of a configuration file as an example:

```
Organizations:
    - &OrdererOrg
        Name: OrdererOrg
        ID: OrdererMSP
```

```
        MSPDir: ../organizations/ordererOrganizations/example.com/msp
        Policies:
            Readers:
                Type: Signature
                Rule: "OR('OrdererMSP.member')"
            Writers:
                Type: Signature
                Rule: "OR('OrdererMSP.member')"
            Admins:
                Type: Signature
                Rule: "OR('OrdererMSP.admin')"
        OrdererEndpoints:
            - orderer.example.com:7050
    - &Org1
        Name: Org1MSP
        ID: Org1MSP
        MSPDir: ../organizations/peerOrganizations/org1.example.com/msp
        Policies:
            Readers:
                Type: Signature
              Rule: "OR('Org1MSP.admin', 'Org1MSP.peer', 'Org1MSP.client')"
            Writers:
                Type: Signature
                Rule: "OR('Org1MSP.admin', 'Org1MSP.client')"
            Admins:
                Type: Signature
                Rule: "OR('Org1MSP.admin')"
            Endorsement:
                Type: Signature
                Rule: "OR('Org1MSP.peer')"
```

In the example above, there are several boolean expressions like **`OR('Org1MSP.admin', 'Org1MSP.client')`**. These expressions are called **policies**.

Policies are responsible for the management of the Hyperledger Fabric blockchain network configuration. Typically located within the channel configuration, these policies play a crucial role. The main objective of this document is to elucidate the process of defining and how they interact with the channel configuration. Nevertheless, it is important to note that policies might also find application in other contexts, like chaincodes, by the definition of endorsement policies, thus broadening their significance beyond the confines of channel configuration.

Once we have the genesis block for the channel that will be created, an administrative operation must be issued by an administrator connected to the ordering service in order to join the orderer node to the channel with that genesis block. Only when the first orderer joins the channel can we safely say that it exists, but in truth there is no practical difference between creating the channel and joining it. The nodes will create the channel locally and start connecting with the other members.

This configuration model also allows for updates. When a new organization needs to be added to a channel, a new configuration block is appended to the blockchain with the updated configuration. This book will not focus on administrative functionalities provided by configuration blocks, but instead our focus will be on applications and what they register in channels.

Besides configuration blocks, most of the blocks in a channel will be blocks containing actual data for an application. The information inside these application blocks are the transactions that modify the state of the information in the network, and they are necessarily registered through chaincodes. Ultimately, when a transaction registers something in the ledger it will be a key and a value.

Consider *Table 4.2* with examples of what could be registered as key and value:

Key	Value
name2	Marcos
lot247	{"id": 13, "quantity": 567.3}
result9	true

***Table 4.2**: Key and value examples*

The key and value model are well known and used in many situations, like JSONs, documents in non-relational databases, Go maps, hashtables and others. In Fabric, keys and values have another dimension to it, the history. Every time a transaction is made, it is included in a new block that is appended to the chain. It means that every transaction that deals with a particular key will generate more recent versions of it.

Let us see an example.

Imagine a Fabric network with a channel where we use a simple chaincode to register anything we want for key and value. It means that any of the following transactions would be possible:

- Transaction 1: **`{ "key1": "value1"}`**
- Transaction 2: **`{ "GoLedger": "cc-tools"}`**
- Transaction 3: **`{ "John": 35 }`**

So, let us do the following sequence of transactions with a ten second interval:

- `{ "0001": "my first registration"}`
- `{ "0001": "my updated registration"}`
- `{ "0002": "my old registration"}`
- `{ "0001": "my old registration"}`
- `{ "0002": "my new registration"}`

When querying the value of our keys 0001 and 0002 we will get the following results, since the transaction will be in more recent blocks:

- Query for 0001: "my old registration"
- Query for 0002: "my new registration"

However, when checking the history for each key, old blocks will have an influence and we will be able to see every possible version of the key, as follows:

- History for 0001
  - "my first registration"
  - "my updated registration"
  - "my old registration"
- History for 0002
  - my old registration
  - my new registration

Registering a simple value might be useful but it is certainly limited. That is why when working on chaincodes we usually define more complex structures that we can register as values in JSON format, a widely used data format that represents information as key-value pairs within a structured, human-readable format. These complex structures are usually referred to as assets.

Consider another example.

When exploring the Hyperledger Fabric documentation, it is usual to come across chaincode examples that live under the Fabric Samples repository, found in **https://github.com/hyperledger/fabric-samples**. Of the many examples there the **asset-transfer-basic** shows a declaration of the format of an asset to be registered, as follows:

```
type Asset struct {
	AppraisedValue int    `json:"AppraisedValue"`
	Color          string `json:"Color"`
	ID             string `json:"ID"`
	Owner          string `json:"Owner"`
	Size           int    `json:"Size"`
}
```

Defining a structure for the assets provides pre-visibility for what is registered in the blockchain, thus allowing for validation of properties. In this manner, our registration will look something like the following:

```
"ASSET01": {
    "AppraisedValue": 100,
    "Color": "Blue",
    "ID": "ASSET01",
    "Owner": "Samuel",
    "Size": 5
}
```

Later, we will see better ways to define the format and property validation for assets by using the open-source library CC-Tools.

It is usual for a Hyperledger Fabric developer to begin the architecture of a new blockchain network with the data mapping of the assets that will be used. We can think of assets as a document in a non-relational database, because that actually constitutes an asset. That is why a peer is supported by a non-relational database, as we have seen earlier.

Chaincode

For any blockchain technology, the main function of a smart contract is to ensure trust in an automated system. In other words, the smart contract guarantees that the process, represented by a computer program able to execute a set of transactions, was not tampered with after its deployment, no matter the environment in which it is run. In Hyperledger Fabric, the smart contract concept is referred to as **chaincode**.

Chaincode is a program written in languages such as Go, Java, or Node.js, that implements business logic and defines the rules for interacting with assets on the blockchain. It runs in a secure, isolated environment and is executed by endorsing peers. Chaincode handles all transaction requests, validates them against the defined rules, and ensures that updates to the ledger comply with the predefined business logic.

The authors of this book find the name chaincode much more appropriate than smart contract, because no matter the blockchain technology the developer is using, a smart contract is not always a contract or even smart.

In *Chapter 2, Blockchain Concepts*, we have introduced smart contracts and explored some of its characteristics: they are deterministic, they are transparent, they ensure data integrity, and they are programmable. In this section we will detail those characteristics in the context of Fabric.

A chaincode is a program developed with methods that will execute the transactions that will be stored inside the blockchain distributed ledger. It is essentially the business rules and logic necessary to make registrations on-chain. A chaincode can be developed in one of three programming languages: Go, Node.js and Java. During the course of this book, we will work exclusively with Go, a fast, efficient, and secure language ideal for Hyperledger

Fabric chaincode. Its simplicity and strong community make it well-suited for blockchain development. Also, there are tools written in Go that will greatly support our journey once we start developing.

A chaincode definition is associated with a channel, that is, a specific chaincode execution will generate a new transaction for a specific channel. Traditionally, a chaincode source code is installed inside some of the peers of the network. If an org's user wants to create a new transaction, they will use an application client to send transaction proposals to the chaincode inside a peer, providing the necessary arguments for a chaincode method to be executed, such as an asset ID when querying an asset or a combination of owner ID and asset value when updating ownership. When using the chaincode-as-a-service model, the chaincode is maintained externally as we will explore later.

The chaincode must be deterministic, as will become clear in the next chapter. As a code that is executed in many different environments (think multiple orgs with multiple peers), the result of this distributed execution must be the same for everyone. If not, you would get inconsistent results among organizations. Executing chaincode methods is the only way to change the state of the ledger and this provides the core of the trust of the Hyperledger Fabric technology and other blockchains.

Chaincode definitions must be known to the organization, as they need to install the source code on their peers and approve the actual implementation before it is ever committed to the channel. This ensures transparency on what is being executed when a chaincode is invoked.

Most importantly, chaincodes are programmable. This opens up a whole field of development that will be explored in detail in this book.

Assets and transactions in Fabric

Hyperledger Fabric is designed to work in flexible ways, but it shines especially with structured data, that is, the information that will be shared among the organizations of the business network may be defined in structures. This is usually referred to as an asset or asset type. Assets are the concrete information that we register on the ledger.

An asset value can be registered as any primary type, however, most developers use a JSON representation to save asset information inside the blockchain network, like we have seen in a previous example.

Consider again the asset definition from the **asset-transfer-basic** chaincode in Fabric samples, as follows:

```
// Asset describes basic details of what makes up a simple asset
type Asset struct {
	AppraisedValue int    `json:"AppraisedValue"`
	Color          string `json:"Color"`
	ID             string `json:"ID"`
```

```
        Owner           string `json:"Owner"`
        Size            int    `json:"Size"`
}
```

The chaincode will operate on keys and values that will live inside an application block, as we have seen. To register an asset, then, it is necessary to attach it to a key, which is its uniquely defined identifier. This key will be used reading, writing, modifying or deleting the value of an asset in a particular channel.

In Hyperledger Fabric, the key is a string, but Fabric supports out-of-the-box ways to create a composite key, which combine multiple attributes for better querying and indexing. For example, a composite key like *Car~VIN~OwnerID* logically groups data, making it easier to retrieve related assets. A **shim** interface acts as a middleware layer that simplifies communication to the network. It is used when developing chaincodes and provides all needed functions to read a write to a particular key. Remember, however, that when using blockchain technology, every data that is assigned to the asset key is registered in the distributed ledger, generating a history that can be retrieved later.

Operating on ledger data is done by what we call transactions, that are usually tied to methods or functions defined in the source code. Transactions will provide the logic layer for something to be registered, altered, read or deleted from the ledger. In Hyperledger Fabric, transactions can be of two types: invoke and query. For now, it suffices to know that query transactions do not generate new blocks and are usually executed for reading data, invoke transactions on the other hand generate new blocks, and are usually executed for writing data.

Let us expand on the history example provided in the *Channel* section. The example in the table shows one asset that is modified twice, having three different states, as follows:

State	0	1	2
Timestamp	1691349245	1691349245	1691349245
Key	Asset1	Asset1	Asset1
ID	1	1	1
Color	Blue	Blue	Green
Size	10	12	9
Owner	Marcos	Marcos	Samuel
Appraised value	200	200	300

***Table 4.3**: Asset 1 in three different states*

In this example, state number 2 is the latest recorded state, making it the World State, which represents the most recent values of all keys in the ledger. This data is stored directly in the peer's state database, which can be either LevelDB, a key-value store optimized for fast lookups, or CouchDB, a JSON document database that supports rich queries based on asset attributes.

An asset can have its properties validated not only by their type but by any business logic necessary, achieving as complex a logic as possible. Let us imagine an asset defined by a group of properties and one of these properties is called **QuantityLot** and will register a number for accounting information. Let us also imagine that this number can never be lower than zero. Consider the following:

```
type MyLot struct {
	QuantityLot int `json:"QuantityLot"`
}
```

In order to ensure that **QuantityLot** will always be valid, all chaincode methods will be designed to validate this property to be greater than zero, meaning that it will be impossible to find any negative numbers for **QuantityLot** registered inside the blockchain.

Consider the following:

- {"Lot 01": 100} is valid
- {"Lot 01": -1} is invalid and will not be registered

A chaincode has access to the ledger data and world state database of the peer when executed. When an execution is invoked, the chaincode must receive the required arguments to execute the transaction and after this execution it will return a set of write and read operations that will be signed by the peer certificate that executed the call.

This is but a brief introduction of chaincodes. The main goal for this book is to teach development of chaincodes, especially to professionals that plan on applying such knowledge to production-grade Fabric networks. Most of the chapters that follow are focused on the details of chaincode development.

Private data collections

As the usage of blockchain technologies spreads around the world, concerns have arisen regarding different approaches, with privacy capabilities being one of the most discussed topics.

As discussed previously, the distributed ledger concept is encapsulated in the Hyperledger Fabric channel. Any information registered in the channel is shared among the different organizations and their peers and orderers.

To provide privacy among organizations, the main process is to create different channels. In other words, if some information should be accessed by some organization but not by others, simply create the channels that will access them accordingly.

However, in some cases it is necessary to provide privacy within one channel. This is where **private data collections** (**PDCs**) are used. PDC is a privacy group inside a channel.

Example

Imagine a channel with the following organizations:

- Distributor
- Farmer
- Wholesaler
- Retailer
- Shipper

Hyperledger Fabric allows the creation of separate PDCs to protect sensitive data from unauthorized access. This means that organizations can share some information with a subset of other organizations, while keeping other information private.

The following figure shows a PDC configuration:

***Figure 4.4**: PDC configuration example*

The information attached to a PDC is not registered in the channel like other data. Only the hash of the asset data is stored in the channel, while the asset data itself is stored in the world state database (LevelDB or CouchDB) of each peer of the PDC organizations.

This means that a chaincode executing in a peer of an organization that is part of a PDC will be able to access all information of the asset. However, if a chaincode is running on a peer that is not part of the PDC, it will not be able to make any operations on the asset.

Hyperledger Fabric provides several tools for the PDC functionality, such as special chaincode SDK functions and specific policies to guarantee the privacy of the data.

Private data is a powerful functionality that will be explored in more detail in the following chapters, with some development examples.

Endorsement policy

Hyperledger Fabric networks have a really clever feature when it comes to the consensus of a chaincode result. This feature is called endorsement policy and it is an essential part of the famous transaction flow we have been talking about. An endorsement policy in Hyperledger Fabric defines the set of rules that specify which and how many endorsing peers must approve a transaction before it can be considered valid and committed to the ledger.

Chaincodes are executed in a distributed manner, meaning that different peers from different organizations will execute a source code in an independent way. The endorsement policy will define which combination of organizations must execute and endorse a transaction for it to be considered valid. Endorsing a transaction means that a peer that receives an invoke request for a chaincode will execute it and sign the transaction proposal.

An endorsement policy is defined during the chaincode lifecycle, and therefore must be agreed by the organizations in the approval step of the process. This policy can be any combination of **ANDs** and **ORs** with the organizations, as well as an Out–Of format. These formats work in the following way:

- **AND condition**: All specified organizations must endorse the transaction.
- **OR condition**: At least one of the specified organizations must endorse the transaction.
- **Combination of AND and OR**: Logical nesting allows more complex conditions.
- **Out-Of condition**: This rule specifies that a minimum number of endorsements are required from a larger set of organizations.

Let us see some examples, as follows:

- **`AND(Org1, Org2)`**: It will be required that every transaction is endorsed by both **`Org1`** and **`Org2`**.
- **`AND(Org1, OR(Org2, Org3))`**: **`Org1`** endorsement is mandatory, but **`Org2`** and **`Org3`** are not as long as one of them endorses the transaction.
- **`OutOf(2, Org1, Org2, Org3)`**: At least 2 of the 3 organizations must endorse the transaction.

These are known as **chaincode-level endorsements**, and they are the most general way of defining the endorsement of transactions. When using PDCs, however, a chaincode-level endorsement might not be satisfied because of access limitations, that is why each PDC has its **collection-level endorsement** configuration that overrides the chaincode-level endorsement.

In the same manner, there is one other way to define endorsement that overrides the previous types. The **key-level endorsement** defines an endorsement policy for a particular key. This endorsement is defined within a chaincode and is part of the standard read-write set of a transaction, meaning that a key-level endorsement is defined by transacting in the chaincode.

Client services

When interacting with a Fabric network and its nodes, what is taught by most tutorials is the **command-line interface** (**CLI**) tools. CLI tools include binaries like **configtxgen**, **peer**, **osnadmin**, **configtxlator** and others that will allow for complete interaction with the network.

We find, however, that in most cases, and certainly in production, it is desirable to develop a programmatic way for interacting with nodes and the network. That is where client services come in. Developing client services allows both users and operators to have an easier and more predictable way for interaction, through the building of APIs that expose functionality of the blockchain, be it administrative or transactional.

We are going to explore two tools for interacting with a Fabric network: the Fabric SDKs and the Fabric Gateway service.

Consider the following architecture as an example of the usage of the Gateway SDK:

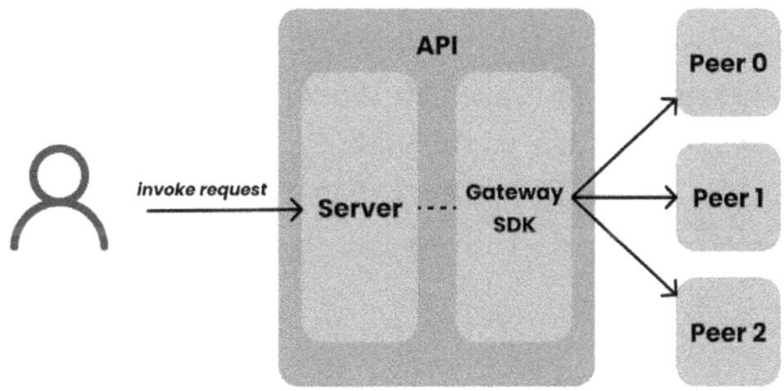

Figure 4.5*: A client application can take the form of an API for easy interaction with peers*

Fabric SDKs

As a disclaimer, the Fabric SDKs, now known as legacy SDKs, have been deprecated in favor of the Gateway service for transactional interaction and the Fabric Admin SDK for administrative interaction. At the time of this writing, the Fabric Admin SDK is still under development and it is not mature enough to be used in production, leaving us no choice but to use the legacy SDKs for managing a network.

Fabric has SDKs in four different languages: Go, Java, Node.js and Python, with the first three being the ones released officially. These SDKs can be used with v2.4.x and earlier as they do not require the new Gateway capability.

The SDK allows us to manage a network with operations like create channel, join peer, update channel configuration, querying blocks and more. So instead of running a complicated command, it is possible to write a program that will have proper error handling.

Consider the following call to do the same type of operation with Fabric SDK Go. Exposing this to an API can open up many possibilities in channel management. Fabric SDK Go to send an update channel proposal:

```
res, err := client.SaveChannel(updateChannelReq, options...)
```

The client needs the correct certificates to be able to operate in the network. When dealing with administrative operations, an admin type certificate is needed. It serves as a crucial link between the client and the blockchain network. The certificate of a client that uses an SDK will usually have an OU of type **client** or **admin,** since these roles determine the level of access within the network, **client** allows the identity to submit transaction proposals, while **admin** grants permissions to manage policies, configurations, and membership within the organization.

The following is the x509 admin digital certificate, note the OU:

```
Certificate:
    Data:
        Version: 3 (0x2)
        Serial Number:
            ef:47:58:b9:1f:5b:5b:c9:4e:bb:4c:29:25:35:06:78
    Signature Algorithm: ecdsa-with-SHA256
        Issuer: C=US, ST=California, L=San Francisco, O=org.example.com,
CN=ca.org.example.com
        Validity
            Not Before: Jun 22 15:47:00 2023 GMT
            Not After : Jun 19 15:47:00 2033 GMT
        Subject: C=US, ST=California, L=San Francisco, OU=admin, CN=Admin@
org.example.com
        Subject Public Key Info:
            Public Key Algorithm: id-ecPublicKey
                Public-Key: (256 bit)
                pub:
                    04:5c:74:5e:28:47:55:7a:9a:35:eb:57:77:5a:8f:
                    35:91:3e:e7:c6:63:ad:e0:28:3d:01:2b:67:d8:3a:
                    62:a3:4a:35:76:01:3b:9d:9d:89:77:b0:4b:f8:c5:
                    71:00:33:45:e8:00:46:9f:af:00:1e:0c:f0:c6:e5:
                    2c:a4:f3:7c:0e
                ASN1 OID: prime256v1
                NIST CURVE: P-256
        X509v3 extensions:
            X509v3 Key Usage: critical
                Digital Signature
            X509v3 Basic Constraints: critical
```

```
                CA:FALSE
            X509v3 Authority Key Identifier:
                keyid:C8:06:5D:C0:8B:AA:12:1A:2B:2D:DC:4A:EA:
50:5F:49:5D:A9:5D:0B:F4:75:65:F6:97:2C:CB:54:2B:1C:4A:19
    Signature Algorithm: ecdsa-with-SHA256
        30:44:02:20:52:d7:28:96:3b:93:81:a4:08:3e:e6:56:a1:8c:
        aa:7a:0e:17:b4:fb:9b:34:03:1f:47:57:ba:69:16:4b:d3:01:
        02:20:6d:cc:74:ba:8f:1c:fc:d3:f1:d7:cc:0d:72:74:ba:6b:
        e7:72:14:51:5b:7e:fe:f5:80:7a:68:87:06:59:c8:e5
```

Gateway service

The Gateway service was introduced in Fabric v2.4 and is a service that runs in the peer nodes and manages transaction submission and processing. When using the legacy SDKs for transaction submission there were requirements that placed a load on the client developer, namely gathering endorsements from various peers before the submission to the ordering service. With the Gateway service (or simply Gateway) this is delegated to it allowing for a simpler development experience.

The Gateway provides several benefits, besides simple development, as follows:

- Better performance since it reduces the number of connections to nodes required.
- Management of endorsement policies required with combination between chaincode-level, collection-level and key-level endorsements.
- Submission to the ordering service is made by the Gateway itself.

The Gateway can be accessed with the new Gateway SDKs written in Go, Node.js and Java. One thing to note is that the Gateway will exclusively deal with transaction submission, and administrative operations are not available.

The Gateway plays a pivotal role in overseeing a sequence of transaction steps within the context of Hyperledger Fabric, as follows:

1. **Evaluate a transaction proposal**: In this phase, the Gateway initiates a smart contract function (chaincode) on a designated peer. The outcome of this invocation is then relayed back to the client. Primarily employed for querying the present ledger state without altering its content, the Gateway typically selects a peer within its own organization. This selection is guided by a preference for the peer possessing the highest ledger block height. In the event that no suitable peer exists within the Gateway's organization, a peer from a different organization is chosen.
2. **Endorse a transaction proposal**: During this step, the Gateway collects a sufficient number of endorsement responses, a requisite for meeting the prescribed combined signature policies. Subsequently, a transaction envelope, which is

a packaged structure containing the transaction proposal, endorsements, and relevant metadata, is provided to the client, facilitating the signing process.

3. **Submit a transaction**: This phase involves the transmission of a signed transaction envelope to the ordering service. The purpose is to effectuate the ledger's commitment to the transaction.

4. **Wait for commit status events**: By undertaking this action, the client enters a waiting period to ascertain the successful commitment of the transaction to the ledger. The accompanying commit status code signifies the validation or invalidation outcome.

5. **Receive chaincode events**: Through this mechanism, client applications gain the capability to respond to events emitted by a smart contract function. These events become pertinent following the commitment of a transaction to the ledger.

To streamline the transaction submission process, the Fabric Gateway client APIs amalgamate the Endorse, Submit, and CommitStatus actions into a unified, blocking `SubmitTransaction` function available in the Gateway SDK. This simplifies transaction submission to a single line of code.

The Gateway SDK will use the same type of **client** certificate as the legacy SDKs and will use a connection configuration file for communicating with peers.

Business network

All the components we have discussed in this chapter have individual roles, but they all support one thing: a functional and distributed business network. When a group of organizations decide that an automated and secure process governed by a Fabric blockchain network is the best way to work, these components are the ones they will use.

A business network in Hyperledger Fabric is simple and will include the following:

- A group of organizations
- Each organization will be identified by a CA and an MSP
- Each organization will have one or more peers
- At least one organization with an orderer node
- Each peer will be inside one or more channels
- Orderers will be part of the ordering service of each channel
- Each channel will have one or more chaincodes

The business network represents the desire of a group of organizations to agree upon a set of rules that will manage a process. Blockchain experts have the mission of architecting the best features of blockchain business networks, bringing together the concepts and components of the technology to achieve the goal for a trustful and reliable environment.

The Fabric business network may be simple, as follows:

- 2 organizations, 2 CAs
- 1 peer per org
- 1 orderer (of any organization)
- 1 channel for both orgs
- 1 chaincode

When developing a new chaincode, it is usual to create a simple business network for the first validation steps, but Hyperledger Fabric was designed to be extremely flexible to architecture more complex designs, especially when dealing with multiple channels like the example, as shown in *Figure 4.6*:

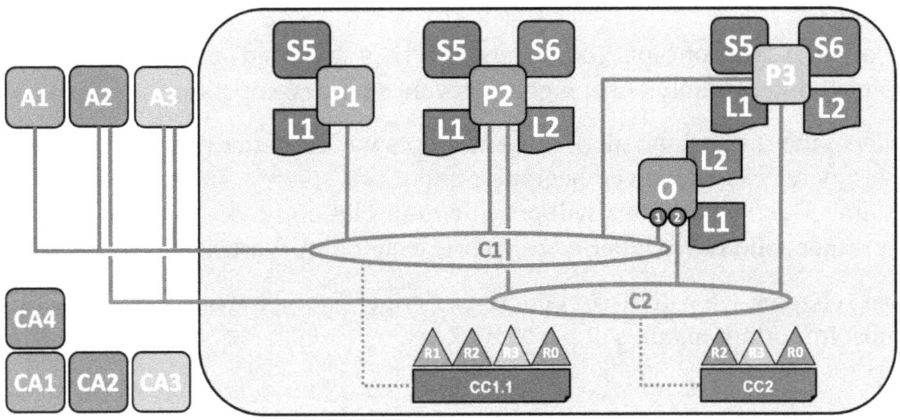

***Figure 4.6**: Multiple channels business network*

*(**Source**: The official Hyperledger Fabric read the docs page)*

This figure details the following artifacts:

- 4 organizations: R0, R1, R2 and R3
- 4 certifications authorities: CA1, CA2, CA3, CA4
- 3 peers (org1 to org3): P1, P2, P3
- 1 orderer (org4): O
- 2 channels: C1, C2 with their ledgers L1 and L2
- 2 chaincodes: CC1, CC2 with their local instances S5, S6
- 3 application clients: A1, A2, A3

Good blockchain business networks result in useful platforms and systems that are much useful to consortiums and regulators that want to provide shared governance around distributed processes.

Conclusion

In this chapter, we learned that Hyperledger Fabric is a powerful framework for architecting, developing and deploying permissioned networks and provides many possibilities for companies, consortiums or regulators so that they have the benefits of blockchain technology. This flexibility, however, comes with a degree of complexity due to the high number of components used to make the Fabric model work.

Developers tend to focus on items that are related mainly with chaincode programming, so it is usual for them to dive deeper into some components more than others. For example, after a Fabric network has been set up and deployed, the use of Hyperledger Fabric CA is usually very low, and this component is often turned off for safety after identity registration and certificate enrollment. Since its developers might not go deeper into CA comprehension.

On the other hand, concepts like assets or PDCs are used extensively for chaincode development and certainly are of bigger relevance for developers.

Developers who understand all of these concepts will be better prepared to create sound blockchain networks. However, beginners should not worry about understanding all of them at first. The next chapters will provide examples and cases that will help beginners to better understand how Hyperledger Fabric technology works.

In the next chapter, we will discuss the Hyperledger Fabric transaction flow, which is one of the most important features of the technology.

Chapter 5 Transaction Flow

Introduction

Blockchain technology became famous after the introduction of the Bitcoin paper, and over the following years, the technology was featured in many articles, technical or otherwise. Some have labeled blockchain as the **trust machine** that could bring reliability to digital registration using the distributed architecture.

Before blockchain technology and even our digital world, human society employed its methods to attain reliability, particularly when engaging in processes and transactions involving multiple parties, such as signing papers with the aid of a public notary. Signing, copying, and comparing information has been a prevalent practice for physical, fostering reliability.

As we have seen in previous chapters, the consensus of a blockchain is somewhat similar. The information to be registered in a block is agreed by the parties with some algorithm. If the necessity of checking if a block has been tampered with, all that is needed is a comparison of chains between nodes, not to mention the cryptographic manner blocks are connected.

Hyperledger Fabric has its way of ensuring data integrity in the ledger. The core of the technology lies in the transaction flow, which imparts reliability to digital data stored in the network. This process relies on the fundamental principles of trust: signing, copying, and comparing data.

The introduction of the **execute-order-validate** model for Hyperledger Fabric truly sets it apart from other blockchain projects. This model allows for increased scalability and flexibility compared to traditional **order-execute** blockchain frameworks. Unlike the order-execute model, where transactions are ordered before execution, the **execute-order-validate** model executes transactions first, then orders them, and finally validates them. This approach allows Hyperledger Fabric to handle non-deterministic transactions more effectively. It also enables parallel transaction processing, reducing bottlenecks and enhancing overall system throughput. As a result, Hyperledger Fabric can support a wider range of applications and use cases, making it a more versatile and powerful platform for building distributed ledger solutions.

To fully understand Hyperledger Fabric, the steps of the transaction flow are essential. This process is possibly the most important one to understand the technology holistically. Most of the components we have seen in *Chapter 6, Deploying Your First Chaincode,* are a part of the flow, including client applications, peers, chaincodes, orderers, channels, and many more. This process ensures data integrity in Hyperledger Fabric, which is one of the main reasons to use a blockchain.

This chapter will detail each one of the Hyperledger Fabric transaction flow steps.

Structure

The chapter covers the following topics:

- The five steps
- Step 1: Client proposal to peers
- Step 2: Peer endorsement
- Step 3: Signed proposal response
- Step 4: Transaction sent to orderer
- Step 5: Transaction is validated and committed
- Importance of the transaction flow
- Transaction flow with private data

Objectives

By the end of this chapter, readers will know the steps of the transaction flow in Hyperledger Fabric, from creating a transaction proposal to committing a block containing the transaction. By the end of the chapter, you will gain a comprehensive understanding of how Hyperledger Fabric networks provide digital trust through a distributed process. You will also have a clear view of how the components discussed in the previous chapter interact during a transaction's life cycle in normal network operations.

Hyperledger Fabric's architecture, based on the execute-order-validate model, offers significant advantages in terms of scalability, flexibility, and performance. This chapter aims to elucidate these benefits by detailing each step of the transaction flow. First, you will learn how clients initiate transactions by creating proposals that are submitted to endorsing peers for execution. This step is crucial for ensuring that transactions are simulated correctly, and endorsements are collected as per the specified policy. Next, you will understand how endorsing peers execute the transaction proposals and generate endorsements. This phase allows for parallel execution, enabling Hyperledger Fabric to handle higher transaction throughput compared to traditional order-execute models.

Additionally, you will explore how the ordering service collects endorsed transactions and orders them into blocks. Finally, you will delve into the validation phase where peers check the endorsements and ensure there are no conflicts before committing transactions to the ledger. This step ensures the integrity and consistency of the blockchain.

By the end of this chapter, you will understand how Hyperledger Fabric achieves digital trust and maintains data integrity through its innovative transaction flow. This knowledge is essential for effective chaincode programming. As a chaincode developer, you will learn that the methods you develop generate proposals to alter the world state but do not guarantee changes. Success is achieved only when orderers include the transaction in a block and peers validate and append the block to their ledger copies. In other words, true success is realized only at the end of the transaction flow.

Understanding these steps will not only enhance your technical proficiency but also enable you to leverage Hyperledger Fabric's strengths in building robust and scalable blockchain solutions. This holistic view of the transaction flow will empower you to design and implement effective chaincode, optimize network performance, and ensure the secure and reliable operation of Hyperledger Fabric networks.

The five steps

The Hyperledger Fabric transaction flow is composed of five steps that work together to achieve one goal: include a valid transaction in a block, thus making that information immutable. Naturally, this is a process that must happen not only in Fabric, but in any blockchain technology, since the desired end state is having immutable valid transactions in a block. Before we introduce the five steps used by Fabric to achieve its block registration let us understand why they exist in the first place.

Prior to Hyperledger Fabric, many blockchains supporting smart-contracts implement active replication of information, in which a consensus protocol does roughly three steps: order the transactions; propagates them to all nodes; and each node executes the transactions sequentially.

Consider a simple blockchain network with three nodes: Node A, Node B, and Node C.

Following is how the process unfolds:

1. **Transaction ordering**:
   a. Node A proposes three transactions: T1, T2, and T3.
   b. The consensus protocol orders these transactions as T1 | T2 | T3.
2. **Transaction propagation**:
   a. Node A broadcasts the ordered list [T1, T2, T3] to Node B and Node C.
   b. Nodes B and C receive and acknowledge this ordered list.
3. **Sequential execution**:
   a. Node A executes T1, updates its ledger, then executes T2, updates again, and finally executes T3.
   b. Nodes B and C do the same, executing T1, T2, and T3 in that exact order.

By following these steps, each node in the network ensures they have an identical copy of the ledger, maintaining consistency and integrity across the blockchain.

This architecture is known by the name **`order-execute`**. This requires every transaction to be deterministic, as the execution and state updates will happen separately in each node. This model can be found in basically all blockchain frameworks, from public ones like Ethereum to permissioned such as Quorum and Hyperledger Besu (which is Ethereum-based). This model poses some limitations. They often use a fixed consensus protocol. The consensus protocol also set the trust model for transaction validation, making it inflexible for different smart contract needs. Smart contracts have to be written in specific or non-standard languages (such as Solidity), which reduces adoption and increases the risk of errors. Performance is hindered by the need for all peers to execute transactions sequentially, requiring complex solutions like Ethereum's **gas** system to prevent denial-of-service attacks. Ensuring deterministic transactions is also difficult. Moreover, running every smart contract on all peers compromises confidentiality and make it impossible to restrict contract code and state to only some peers.

One curious fact is that Hyperledger Fabric's earliest versions implemented this very architecture (up to Fabric v0.6). From that experience, a new architecture model was originated.

Refer to the following figure:

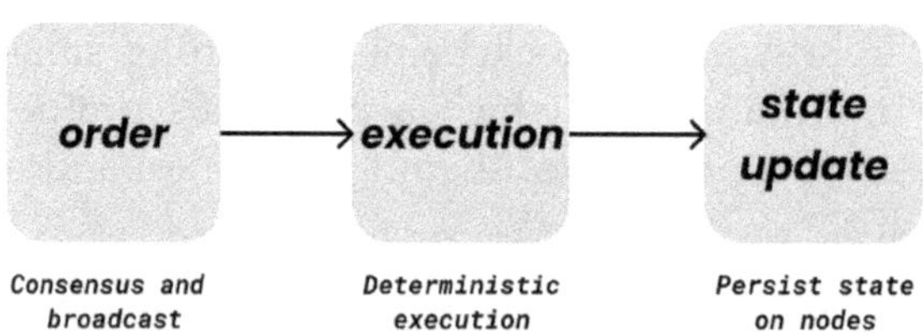

***Figure 5.1**: The order-execute model architecture*

This model is now known as the **`execute-order-validate`** architecture. It is composed of three main stages, as follows:

1. Executing the transaction and verifying if it is correct, endorsing it.
2. Ordering that transaction execution (transaction semantics do not matter here).
3. Validating the transaction.

In Fabric, there is no need for every peer to execute (or endorse) a transaction, that's done by a subset of peers. This enables a feature in chaincode lifecycle definition called **endorsement policy**, which determines which peers or how many will need to execute and endorse that executon. This will be detailed in later chapters.

Refer to the following figure:

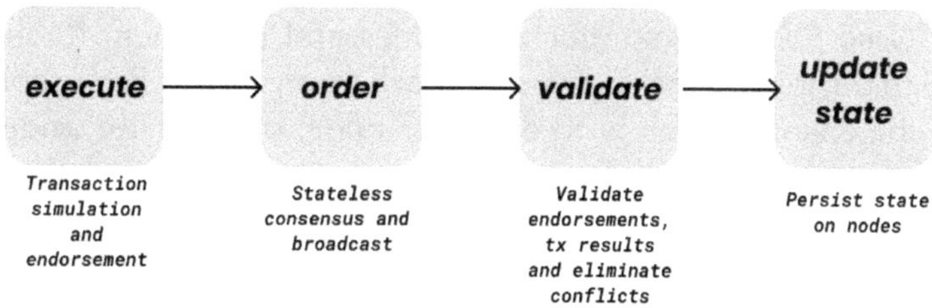

***Figure 5.2**: The execute-order-validate model architecture*

In this book, we will outline five steps which are part of the original three stages outlined above. These steps are more in accordance with the Hyperledger Fabric documentation and they provide a more practical and concrete understanding of the actual lifecycle of the transaction.

A transaction will undergo five main steps until it is committed to a block, deemed valid as a registry for the whole network.

These steps can be described shortly, as follows:

1. Client proposes a transaction to peers
2. Peers endorse the transaction proposal
3. Signed transaction responses are collected
4. Orderer receives the transaction proposal
5. Block is committed with the transaction

For a successful commit in the channel, the application client that communicates with the peers participates actively in the process, as it will have to monitor the transaction status to confirm the result of the operation.

This means the application will do more than sending a signed message to a peer (although it is possible and needed in some scenarios). It will wait for completion and treat success or error message responses.

As already mentioned, with the release v2.4 of Hyperledger Fabric, the Fabric Gateway service run by peers was introduced to simplify transaction submission. It is responsible for most transaction flow steps that previously needed to be done by the application developer with the legacy Fabric SDKs.

Although the Fabric Gateway service may simplify development, the blockchain developer must understand every step a transaction must follow to be successfully committed. Every transaction registered inside a Hyperledger Fabric blockchain network must go through the five steps described in this chapter.

Let us set up an example of a network and see what happens to it when we want to transact on it. This example will be used throughout the rest of this chapter as we explain each step.

Imagine two companies, *Good Sneakers* and *Your Shoes*, are members of a Hyperledger Fabric channel. *Good Sneakers* manufactures shoes and sells them to *Your Shoes* so that they can re-sell them to the final consumer. Each company will be represented by one organization in the channel, each with one peer node, one orderer node, and one client application.

Note: The purpose of this example is to illustrate the transaction flow. This network structure should not be used as a base for a production network. In this book, we will not cover network architecture in depth.

Consider the following figure:

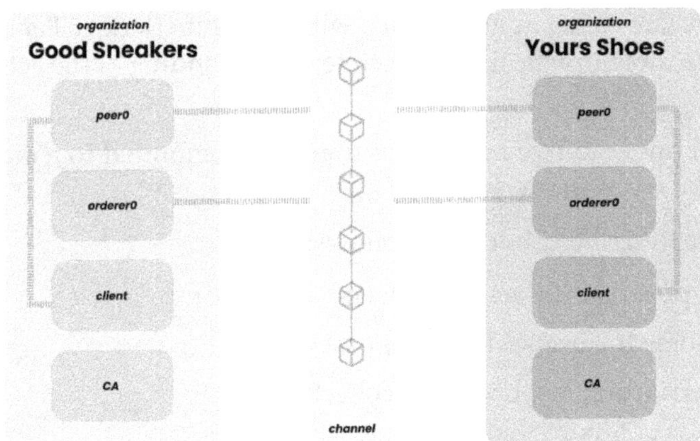

Figure 5.3: Example network

These two companies want to register the history of trades in the blockchain, so they will have a chaincode just for that. This chaincode will have one main functionality: take a lot of shoes and transfer the ownership from *Good Sneakers* to *Your Shoes* while registering a unit price. Let us call this function **`sellLot`**. To elaborate our example, we can say that both organizations need to endorse this transaction. As seen before, this is done with a chaincode-level endorsement policy.

Our asset can be detailed as shown in the following table:

Quantity in lot	number
Unit price	number
Owner	string
Lot ID	number

***Table 5.1**: Lot asset properties*

The steps outlined going forward will assume a network with the presented configuration with the chaincode described, and for simplicity, let us assume that the chaincode was initialized with the current state of lots manufactured by *Good Sneakers*; that means that some lots already exist in the network with their quantity and owned by *Good Sneakers*.

Step 1: Client proposal to peers

An organization must propose this change to change the state of an asset registered inside a Fabric channel. Hence, the process begins with a transaction proposal. *Good Sneakers* wants to sell the lot with ID 1 to *Your Shoes* for 20 dollars per pair in our example network. For that, it will use its application client to initiate the transaction, informing the chaincode method to be invoked and any arguments required, such as the unit price.

Refer to the following figure:

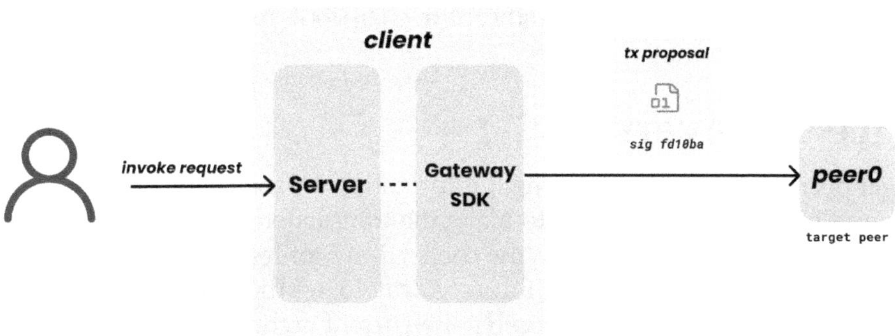

***Figure 5.4**: Good Sneakers initiating a transaction*

It is very important to remember that a transaction proposal may be successful and committed in a block or fail. In other words, initiating a transaction is not a guarantee of success, even if the chaincode method is executed successfully.

In *Chapter 3, Introduction to Hyperledger Fabric*, we detailed the component responsible for creating the transaction proposal as the **client** must have an identity registered and enrolled with the CA of its organization. The client must have the cryptographic material necessary to authenticate in the network.

The application client will use one of the available SDKs to assemble the transaction proposal object with a cryptographic signature to be sent over gRPC. The SDK will then submit the transaction proposal to a target peer. The target peer will be responsible for forwarding the proposal to other peers that must execute the transaction, as required by the endorsement policy of the chaincode.

Refer to the following figure:

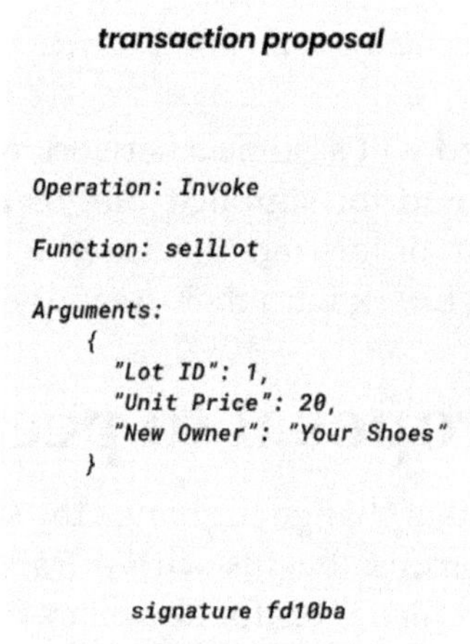

***Figure 5.5**: Illustration of an assembled transaction proposal*

In our scenario, *Good Sneakers'* client will send the proposal to its peer, which will forward it to the peer owned by *Your Shoes* since our chaincode requires both organizations to endorse the transaction.

Service discovery

The target peer must know endorsement information for the chaincode so it can forward the proposal to the necessary peers to make the transaction flow work. This information may be found statically configured in the connection profiles configuration files, but since a Fabric network may change in the future, a way to get this information dynamically is necessary. In order to dynamically receive the current architecture network information, the gateway service in peer may request this data directly from a peer using a feature known as discovery service.

The discovery service is available for peers and can retrieve the current network configuration, such as peers, orderers, and endorsing policy details for each channel. The gateway service running in each peer automatically uses the discovery service during the transaction flow.

Step 2: Peer endorsement

Once the peers receive the transaction proposal, they will take a sequence of actions to verify the request, as follows:

1. Verify that the transaction proposal is well-formed.
2. Check against replay attacks by checking if the transaction has already been submitted.
3. Check if the signature is valid and belongs to a known organization.
4. Check if the caller has permission to make the proposed operation on the channel.

Remember from the previous chapter that the MSP is used by the nodes to check the identity of incoming communication, including that from a client. That is how action number three is performed. The caller in question, in our example, is *Good Sneakers*' application client. This client's identity will be verified against the writer's policy of the application channel, which must be satisfied to invoke a transaction.

Each peer takes the proposal's payload, namely, the chaincode function and arguments to be invoked, and passes it to the chaincode for execution, usually referred to as simulation. The chaincode executes the function against the current world state data to produce a response composed of a read set, a write set, and the value returned by the function. The read set is composed of all of the keys and committed versions that the transaction reads during the transaction simulation, and the write set is composed of all the keys and values that the transaction writes.

In our example, the chaincode would have received a request to invoke the **sellLot** function with the lot ID and unit price as arguments. For instance, lot ID 1 and unit price of 20 dollars. This transaction will have to read the value of the key that represents lot ID 1 and alter it, adding the unit price of 20 dollars and changing the ownership of the lot to *Your Shoes*.

In this case, our read-and-write sets would look like the following illustration:

```
<TxReadWriteSet>
 <NsReadWriteSet name="shoes-chaincode">
  <read-set>
   <read key="ID1", version="1">
  </read-set>
  <write-set>
   <write key="ID1", value="{"ID":1,"Quantity":10,"Unit price":20, "Owner":
"Your Shoes"}">
  </write-set>
 </NsReadWriteSet>
<TxReadWriteSet>
```

It is important to note that the ledger is not updated at this point. The chaincode is executed, and it generates a transaction proposal response that includes the result of the execution signed by the peer that executed it. This is what it means to endorse a transaction.

Step 3: Signed proposal response

The target peer receives the endorsed and signed proposal responses from the peers that executed the chaincode and inspect it to make sure that the responses are the same. It means that the chaincode must yield the same result wherever it is executed.

Refer to the following figure:

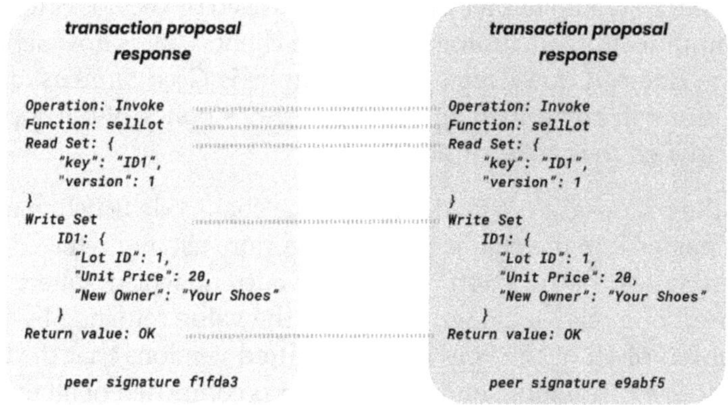

***Figure 5.6**: Proposal responses of every execution are compared*

The comparison of proposal responses is an interesting mechanic. It ensures the integrity of the data that will be registered and enforces one of the main characteristics of chaincodes. Recall from *Chapter 2, Blockchain Concepts,* that it was mentioned that smart contracts must be deterministic. In Fabric, the comparison of responses will enforce this. Imagine a chaincode that registers an asset by generating a random string as one of the properties. During the distributed execution of this chaincode, different transaction proposals would be generated, thus making the transaction invalid.

Refer to the following figure:

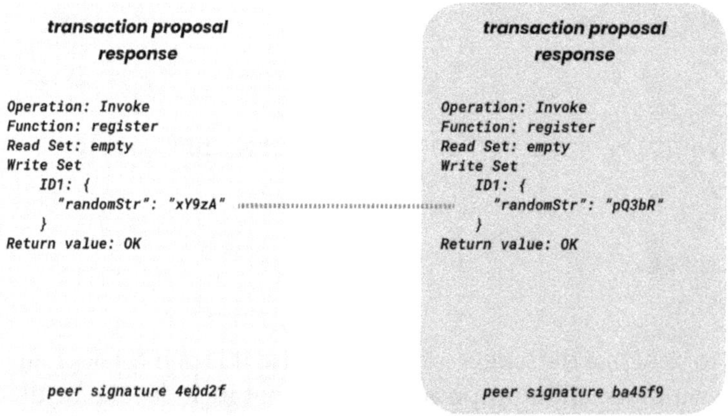

***Figure 5.7**: Proposal responses with different results yield a failure*

That using random generators in a chaincode is a bad idea might be obvious to most, but it is not uncommon for developers to run into this problem in subtler situations, such as getting the current datetime from the runtime. Peers usually run on different servers, and even if they are on the same servers, the transactions are executed at slightly different times. That means it is almost certain that the time captured during execution will not be the same. Note that this is only a problem if it affects the response of the simulation.

Step 4: Transaction sent to orderer

Once the transaction proposals are validated against the chaincode's endorsement policy, the target peer assembles a transaction message, including the proposal. This message includes the channel identification, the read asnd write sets, and the signature of every peer that endorsed the transaction.

The peer will then submit this transaction to the ordering service, which receives not only this transaction message but also every transaction message that is going through the transaction flow. The ordering service simply orders the transaction in a block to be sent back to peers. This is done deterministically.

Refer to the following figure:

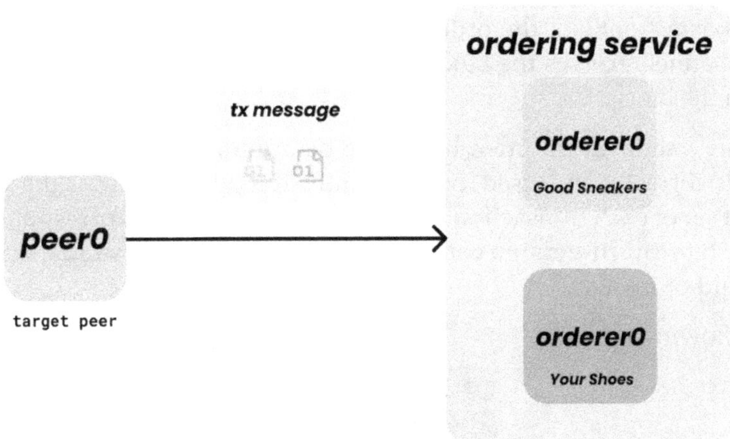

Figure 5.8: Transaction message is sent to the ordering service

Hyperledger Fabric v2.5 uses the Raft protocol as a default for the ordering service cluster. That means that when the peer submits the transaction to the ordering service, whatever the orderer receives, the message will be forwarded to the Raft leader, which will perform the ordering itself. In our example network, the target peer from Good Sneakers can send the transaction message to either orderer without affecting the functionality of the flow.

Refer to the following figure:

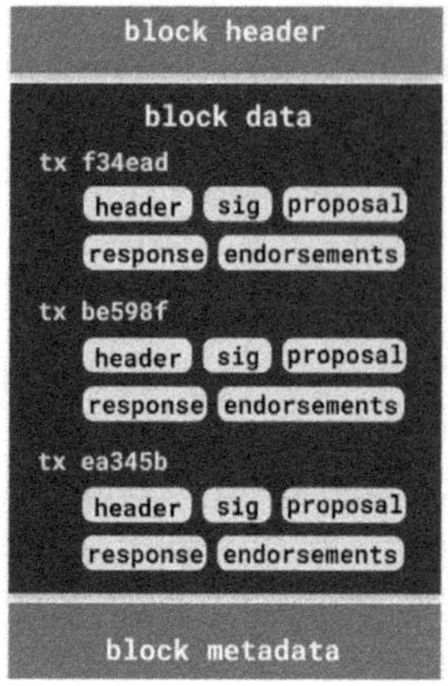

Figure 5.9: An assembled block can be represented with this structure

Step 5: Transaction is validated and committed

Once the block is assembled, the orderer sends it to the channel as a whole. Every peer joined to the channel receives the block, and each one performs its own validation of the transactions in the block.

Transactions are validated in order, hence the deterministic ordering of transactions, by checking if it is correctly endorsed. Subsequently, the peer verifies if the version of each key in the read set of each transaction matches the version of the corresponding key in the present world state (**multi-version concurrency control** (MVCC) validation). Transactions are marked valid or invalid.

Refer to the following figure:

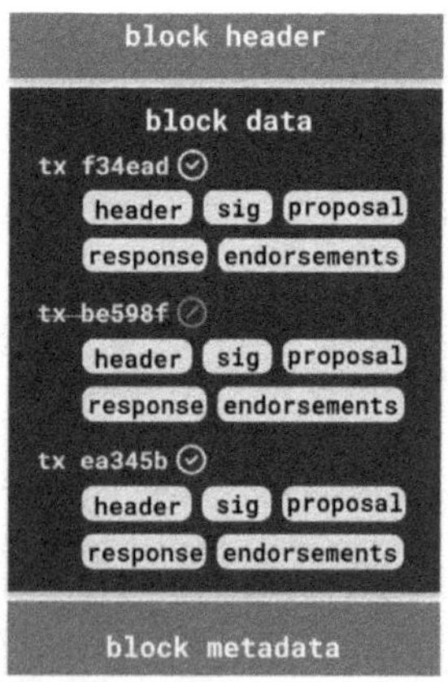

Figure 5.10: Peers validate transactions and mark them as valid or invalid

At this point, each peer will add this block to their own copy of the chain, committing the block to the channel. For every valid transaction, the write set will be committed to the world state database. Finally, a commit event is issued by the peers, which then tells the client application that the invocation was successful.

Consider the following figure representing the complete process in diagram form:

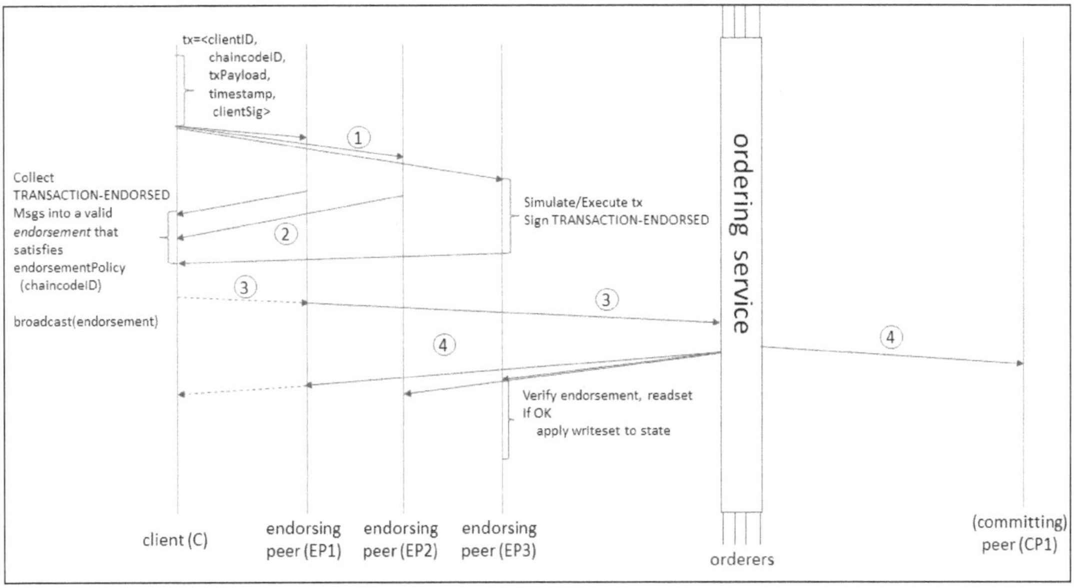

***Figure 5.11**: Diagram representing the transaction flow*

*(**Source**: Hyperledger Fabric ReadTheDocs)*

Importance of transaction flow

Even after going through all the steps outlined above, it is normal to question what the purpose of each of them in is achieving reliability. A way to answer this is to compare Hyperledger Fabric's technical approach with processes that have used notary systems historically. Let us make a simple exercise by creating of a trustful process.

When a consortium of parties shares a mutual process that impacts them collectively, it becomes imperative to establish a criterion for accepting or rejecting new transactions. This concept aligns with the endorsing policy, serving as the consensus mechanism within Hyperledger Fabric.

For any entity seeking to register or update information within this process, immediately changing it is inappropriate, as it would disrupt the consensus. Therefore, the protocol entails that a single party must propose any desired alteration to all relevant parties. In the context of Hyperledger Fabric, this mirrors the action of the client, which sends transaction proposal requests to the endorsing peers.

To verify the proper agreement on the process change, participating entities within the consensus must append their signatures of acceptance and transmit them back to the initiating party. This mirrors the role of Hyperledger Fabric's endorsing peers, which send back the signed proposal responses to the target peer.

With the original proposer now in possession of all requisite confirmations, they can proceed to record the change officially. This involves submitting all the confirmations to a designated notary entity responsible for definitive preservation. Analogously, the target peer sends the signed transaction proposals to the ordering node, which then incorporates the transaction into a block.

As emphasized earlier, the transaction flow in Hyperledger Fabric stands as an elegant mechanism for achieving reliability within digital distributed ledgers. Its elegance becomes evident when contrasted with other blockchain technologies, underscoring advantages like enhanced performance and scalability.

In contrast, Ethereum-based blockchains employ other technique and restrictions, as we've seen in the beginning of this chapter. While effective for public blockchain networks, this approach more often than not encounters performance limitations, even within private and permissioned deployments.

For a developer, a better understanding of the transaction flow will naturally lead to better production-level networks, especially because it will make them think about the distributed processing the chaincodes are involved in.

For developers, a comprehensive grasp of the transaction flow naturally translates to an improved production network, particularly as it prompts consideration of the distributed processing intrinsic to chaincode execution.

The chaincode, and by extension, the methods within it, constitute integral components of the Hyperledger Fabric transaction flow. Successful completion of this flow is essential for effecting alterations to the network's state. A common misconception among new Hyperledger Fabric developers is assuming that the successful execution of a chaincode method automatically updates the blockchain's information. The entire transaction flow must traverse each step for changes to take effect. This encapsulates the elegance of Hyperledger Fabric's technology in achieving digital trust.

Transaction flow with private data

As we have seen, private data are information that do not go openly into the blockchain. This type of data is stored locally on peers and shared only among organizations that are members of the private data collection. One might wonder if and how private data influences the transaction flow steps, specially because of parallel executions and response comparison.

The transaction flow when private data is involved is indeed slightly different in order to maintain confidentiality of the data and transactions. Let us take a look at how each step explained in this chapter differs.

In our example, two companies were sharing lot sales information, let's then assume that a third company *Sandals & Co* is now part of the network. In this setting Good Sneakers, who owns the starting set of lots will sell these lots to both Your Shoes and Sandals & Co. However, while doing that it wants to keep the data private as not to reveal sales prices to competitors. Refer to the following figure:

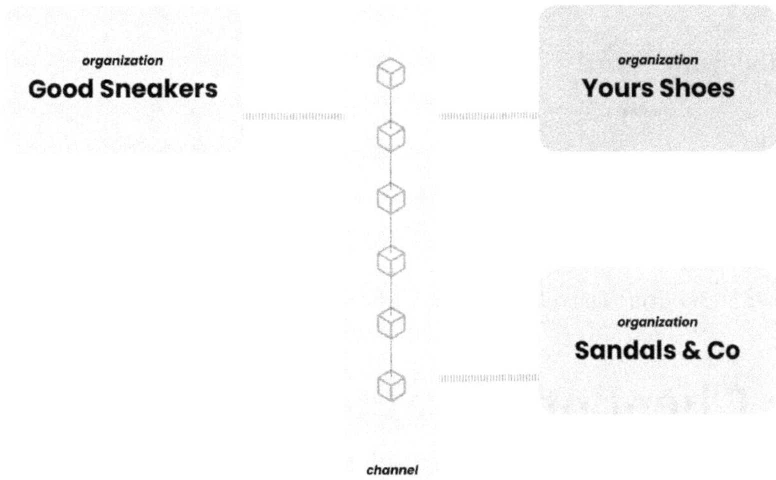

Figure 5.12: *A new organization Sandals & Co joins the network*

In this setting, our chaincode would need to change to update the asset that will still be a lot, but one property will be separated as to not reveal critical business information like sale value: unit price.

Refer to the following table with the publicly shared properties:

Quantity in lot	number
Owner	string
Lot ID	number

Table 5.2: *Lot asset properties publicly shared*

A new asset will track prices and be shared exclusively inside the private data collections. Refer to the following table with the private properties:

Unit price	number
Paid By	string
Lot ID	number

Table 5.3: *Lot asset properties for private data*

Our original transaction **sellLot** will, consequently, write two assets on the blockchain. The first one transferring ownership publicly of a lot and the second one registering the amount paid for unit for a particular lot ID, inside a collection.

Our collections configuration will, then look life this. One collection for sale information between Good Sneakers and Your Shoes and another between Good Sneakers and Sandals & Co.

Refer to the following figure:

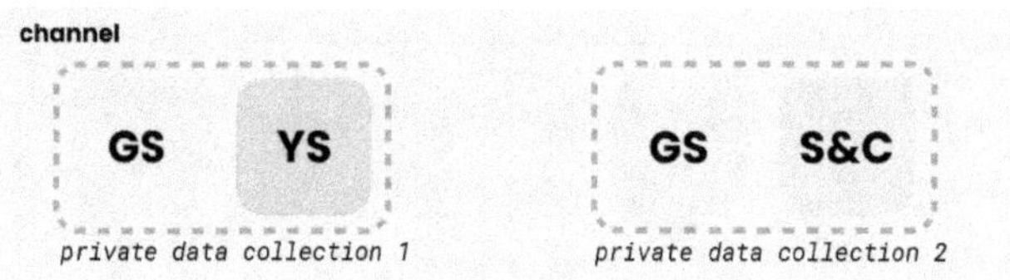

Figure 5.13: Private data collections where letters represent the initials of the organization

Step 1: Client proposal to peers

This step is generally the same. The client will submit a proposal to invoke a transaction to the target peer. One key difference is that the client will make use of the transient data argument for the information that will be kept private. This serves the purpose of hiding arguments from transaction registration when the block is formed.

In this step, the client can specify which organizations will endorse the proposal, but this can also be delegated to the target peer's gateways service just like a situation without private data.

In our example, the transaction **sellLot** would be called with new ownership information as regular arguments but with the unit price being sent as transient data.

Refer to the following figure:

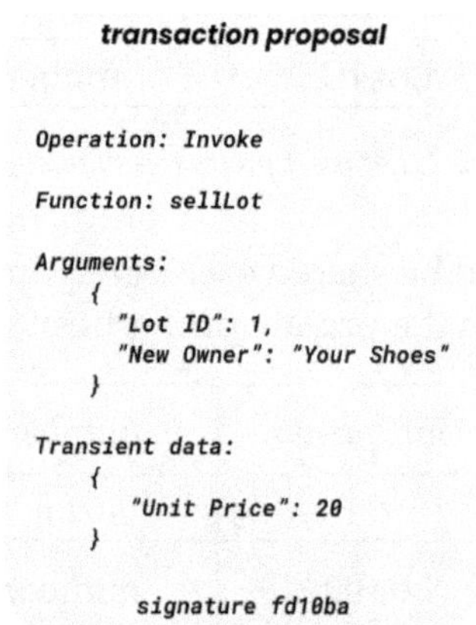

Figure 5.14: Transaction proposal with transient data representation

Step 2: Peer endorsement

The transaction is simulated and generates the result represented by the read-set and write-set. Any private data that is written during the execution of a transaction goes into a temporary storage called the **transient data store**, which is hosted locally by the peer. The write-set will contain only the hash of the data written, while the actual data will be distributed via gossip according to the collection permissions.

The `sellLot` transaction would consequently write two keys in our blockchain, the first one would be updating the owner property of the publicly available asset and the other one would be creating the asset representing the actual sale information, with the same lot ID, information of who paid and the unit price. The latter is a privately created asset inside the collection the represents the two organizations taking part in the sale. In this case, the first public asset would be in the write-set, but the second one would be only represented by the hash of the data.

Step 3: Signed proposal response

Once the proposal responses are returned to the target peer, it will check and compare them as usual. Note that, the responses will only have the hashes of the private data. That means that if executions generated the same result for the peers the endorsed that private data creation, the hash will be the same in both responses.

Refer to the following figure:

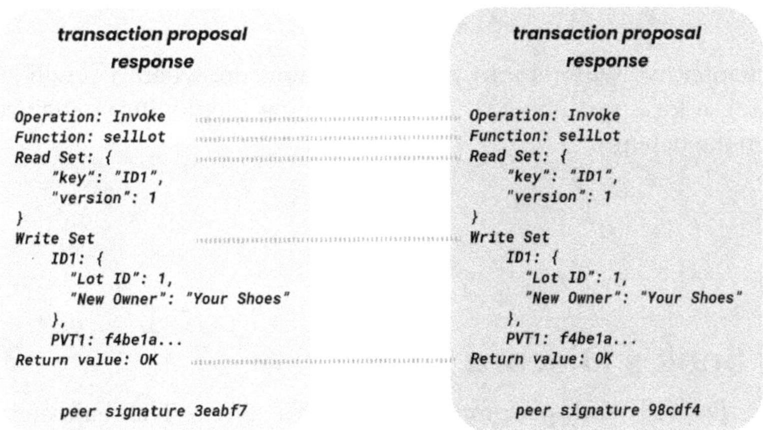

***Figure 5.15**: Comparison of responses with private data hash*

Step 4: Transaction is sent to orderer

For the ordering service, there's no difference whether there are private data hashes or not in a transactions write-set. Therefore, they are ordered as normal.

Step 5: Transaction is validated and committed

During this step, peers that have access to the private data collection will check their transient data store to fetch the private data that was saved during execution. If the data is not available, they will pull from other authorized peers in the collection.

During validation, peers will check if the data matches the hash of the data in the block. If it does the transaction and block is committed and the private data is moved to the private state database, while deleting it from the transient data store.

Conclusion

In this chapter, you have learned in detail the process Fabric uses to make ledger information consistent and trustworthy. We explained how a transaction is initiated and finalized when successful.

You have learned about how peers interact with other peers in order to ensure the chaincode is executed by the correct parties. We justified why chaincode methods must be deterministic in the context of a distributed execution environment, where it is essential for parties to get the same result from an execution.

You gained knowledge about how orderers handle block formation with the ordering of transactions and how this block is validated by every peer before it is appended to the ledger.

In the next chapter, we will get into your first chaincode, where we will go through the steps of getting a local test network up and running, deploying a chaincode to it, and transacting on the network.

Chapter 6
Deploying Your First Chaincode

Introduction

In order to gain a comprehensive understanding of Hyperledger Fabric, it is essential to blend theoretical comprehension with hands-on experience. Building upon the foundational concepts and components we have explored in earlier sections, we now transition into the practical field, where we begin deploying our first chaincode onto a Fabric network.

Chaincodes function as the logical layer of the blockchain architecture. As demonstrated in preceding chapters, the chaincode embodies the business logic that enables our application to thrive. This integration of business logic within the chaincode empowers the technology, facilitating its application across many scenarios.

Deploying a chaincode for the first time is a great opportunity to explore theoretical concepts in practice. A development environment must be set up to accommodate a local network. This can give us great insight into what is involved in deploying nodes to a network when it comes to configuration files, container parameters, and networking.

Many existing tools facilitate the local deployment of networks and chaincode, streamlining the development process. However, in this chapter, our focus will extend beyond merely using these tools. We aim to uncover and understand the underlying steps and mechanisms these tools employ during the deployment process. By doing so, we will gain deeper insights into the inner workings of Hyperledger Fabric, enabling us to troubleshoot effectively, customize deployments to specific needs, and build a solid foundation for more advanced chaincode development in subsequent chapters.

This chapter represents only the beginning of our exploration into chaincode development. We will start by examining the official examples provided by Hyperledger Fabric, available in the Fabric Samples repository. Throughout this journey, we will understand the potential of chaincode development, uncovering its details along the way.

Structure

The chapter covers the following topics:

- Development environment
- Beginning with test-network
- Asset transfer basic chaincode
- Upgrading chaincode
- World state storage in peer
- GetState
- PutState

Objectives

By the end of this chapter, readers will take a first steps in working with Hyperledger Fabric in a practical setting. You will deploy a local development network, which will serve as your sandbox environment for experimenting and understanding the core components of Fabric. This foundational experience is crucial for any future development work you undertake.

You will learn how to deploy a chaincode within this local network, providing you with hands-on experience that is essential for mastering Fabric. This chapter will guide you through each step, from setting up the environment to executing the deployment, ensuring you have a clear understanding of the process. This foundational knowledge will be indispensable as you progress in your development journey.

Additionally, you will explore the process of writing a simple chaincode using one of the main programming languages for chaincodes, Go. This exercise will cover the fundamental aspects of chaincode development, such as defining smart contract functions, managing the state, and handling transactions. You will also learn how to test your chaincode by manually interacting with the peer and orderer components of the network. This will involve using Fabric's **command-line interface** (**CLI**) tools to invoke transactions and query the ledger, providing you with a thorough understanding of how chaincode operates within the network.

This chapter will introduce you to the main operations of the chaincode lifecycle in a practical manner. You will learn how to deploy multiple chaincodes to a channel and upgrade those chaincodes, facilitating an iterative development process. Understanding these lifecycle operations is critical for managing and maintaining your blockchain applications effectively.

Furthermore, you will explore the mechanisms for registering and reading assets on the blockchain using the **`putState`** and **`getState`** functions. This will include practical examples and exercises to solidify your understanding of these essential functions. You will also learn how to query and interact with the ledger more extensively, enabling you to build more sophisticated applications that can leverage the full capabilities of the Fabric network.

By the end of this chapter, you will have a comprehensive understanding of the initial steps required to deploy and manage chaincode in a Hyperledger Fabric network. You will be equipped with the skills to continue developing more complex chaincode and to explore further capabilities of Hyperledger Fabric in subsequent chapters. This practical foundation will be critical as you move forward, ensuring you are well-prepared to tackle more advanced topics and projects.

Development environment

Before beginning to develop anything, we need to set up an environment for development. Hyperledger Fabric requires some basic tools widely available for many operating systems free of charge. In this book, we will explain how to set up an environment for Ubuntu and Mac OS systems, although many of the steps outlined here can be easily translated to other Linux distributions and Windows.

Once set up, using the environment is virtually the same for Linux and macOS, and we will only differentiate between commands where needed. This book will make exclusive use of the version cycle v2.5 for Fabric.

The prerequisites needed to run Fabric are not many, usually, Docker suffices, however for development we will need more tools, some are mentioned as follows:

- **Git:** It is necessary for cloning code repositories.
- **cURL:** It is necessary for API calls in a CLI.
- **Docker and Docker Compose:** It is necessary for deploying Fabric components.
- **Go:** It is necessary for the development of chaincodes in this book.
- **JQ:** It is necessary for some scripts that work with channel configuration.

Using Ubuntu

If Git, cURL, and JQ are not installed in your system, run the following commands in your system's terminal:

```
$ sudo apt-get install git
$ sudo apt-get install curl
$ sudo apt-get install jq
```

Now, install Docker by running the following command:

```
sudo apt-get -y install docker-compose
```

You can now run the following command to test that installation and check the version:

```
$ docker --version
Docker version 19.03.12, build 48a66213fe
$ docker-compose --version
docker-compose version 1.27.2, build 18f557f9
```

Note that the versions of Docker and Docker Compose may vary depending on the environment.

Make sure that the Docker Daemon is running, use the command as follows:

```
$ sudo systemctl start docker
```

In order to finish the Docker setup, add your user to the Docker group, so it can be used without superuser permissions, as follows:

```
$ sudo usermod -a -G docker $USER
```

In order to test if the Docker Daemon is active, use the following command:

```
$ docker ps
CONTAINER ID   IMAGE     COMMAND   CREATED   STATUS    PORTS     NAMES
```

If you still receive an error, log out and log in again.

In order to install Go, you should follow the official instructions for your system, and they can be found at **https://go.dev/doc/install**.

Using Mac

If you use Mac regularly for programming, you have probably already installed Xcode Command Line Tools, but if not, run it in your system's terminal by using the following command:

```
$ xcode-select --install
```

Xcode Command Line Tools provides a series of essential software and prerequisites for programming, including Git.

Now, we need to install Homebrew, a package manager for macOS, refer to the following command for the same:

```
$ /bin/bash -c "$(curl -fsSL https://raw.githubusercontent.com/Homebrew/
install/master/install.sh)"
```

If Git, cURL, and JQ are not installed, run the command as follows:

```
$ brew install git
$ brew install curl
$ brew install jq
```

In order to install Docker you can download Docker Desktop from the official Docker website or run the following command:

```
$ brew cask install --appdir="/Applications" docker
```

Run Docker Desktop by executing the application available in your **Applications** directory or execute the following command:

```
$ open /Applications/Docker.app
```

Check your installation by running the command as follows:

```
$ docker --version
Docker version 19.03.12, build 48a66213fe
$ docker-compose --version
docker-compose version 1.27.2, build 18f55
```

Note that the versions of Docker and Docker Compose may vary depending on the environment.

In order to install Go, you can follow the same instructions for Ubuntu or run the following Homebrew command:

```
$ brew install go@1.21
```

Using other Linux distributions

Using other Linux distributions to follow along the exercises in this book is possible and usually straightforward. It is likely that following the instructions for Ubuntu and adapting the commands for your system's package manager will suffice.

Hyperledger Fabric can be run in many systems and architectures like *CentOS, OpenSUSE, ArchLinux,* and *ARM binaries.* Fabric v2.5.x has been released, allowing developers to run Fabric natively on Apple-silicon and other ARM-based systems.

As an additional note, you can run Fabric in Windows using the Windows subsystem for **Linux version 2** (**WSL2**). This book will show commands that work on Ubuntu and Mac, so if you choose to use Windows, you might have to adapt certain commands.

Install Fabric binaries

Before we can run our local environment, we need Fabric binaries. These binaries are CLI tools that will enable the creation of certain artifacts required to deploy the network.

First, create a directory to store the binaries:

```
$ mkdir ~/fabric-installation && cd ~/fabric-installation
```

In order to install Fabric binaries, download the installation script by running the following command:

```
$ curl -sSLO https://raw.githubusercontent.com/hyperledger/fabric/main/
scripts/install-fabric.sh && chmod +x install-fabric.sh
```

This command will download the script directly from the official **hyperledger/fabric** GitHub account. Once it is downloaded, you can install the Fabric binaries by running the following command:

```
./install-fabric.sh --fabric-version 2.5.4 binary
```

This will download v2.5.4 for the binaries, thus keeping our environment consistent throughout the book.

Finally, you can add the newly created folder to your PATH environment variable in your preferred way. This will vary depending on the system's shell interface (Bash, ZSH, and others).

An example of how to do this when using Bash as follows:

```
echo 'export PATH=$PATH:~/fabric-installation/bin' >> ~/.bashrc
```

Tutorials from Fabric Samples

The Fabric Samples repository located at **https://github.com/hyperledger/fabric-samples** is possibly the first experience most developers have had with Hyperledger Fabric.

It contains many useful examples that developers can explore and tinker with different scenarios, from creating a test network to deploying an ERC-20 token chaincode. It is a good way to study Fabric and get a better understanding of technology.

Hyperledger Fabric evolves constantly with new versions being released frequently. The Fabric Samples repository is not different, so it is important to check the version that is being used by the repository and set up the environment accordingly.

In order to avoid version mismatch during this book, we will use a companion repository that will have dependency versions fixed, so that you, as the reader, can reproduce the steps in this book at any point in time. Clone the repository to get started, refer to the following command:

```
$ git clone https://github.com/goledgerdev/book-companion
$ cd book-companion
```

The companion repository will have only the files from Fabric Samples that will be used in this book, but the original repository includes several examples showing how to use different features of Hyperledger Fabric. We encourage you to take advantage of that once you are more familiar with Fabric.

Beginning with test-network

The `samples` directory in the companion repository contains artifacts to set up a simple Hyperledger Fabric network with the following characteristics:

- **Two peer organizations**: One peer node per org
- **One orderer organization**: One ordering node

It also contains a simple chaincode and a simple client application that will be explored later.

In the `test-network` directory, the script `network.sh` is used to create a complete and functional network in a local environment. Reading through the content of this script, albeit difficult for beginners, is a great way to understand details about network deployment and management. It calls many **bash** scripts that prepare certificates and configuration files to be used by the Docker containers of each Fabric component.

By running the following `network.sh` script without any flags, we can see many options that will allow developers to deploy a local network and personalize its options:

```
$ cd test-network && ./network.sh
Usage:
  network.sh <Mode> [Flags]
    Modes:
      up - Bring up Fabric orderer and peer nodes. No channel is created
      up createChannel - Bring up fabric network with one channel
      createChannel - Create and join a channel after the network is
created
      deployCC - Deploy a chaincode to a channel (defaults to asset-
transfer-basic)
      down - Bring down the network

    Flags:
    Used with network.sh up, network.sh createChannel:
    -ca - Use Certificate Authorities to generate network crypto material
    -c <channel name> - Name of channel to create (defaults to "mychannel")
    -s <dbtype> - Peer state database to deploy: goleveldb (default) or
couchdb
```

```
    -r <max retry> - CLI times out after certain number of attempts
(defaults to 5)
    -d <delay> - CLI delays for a certain number of seconds (defaults to 3)
    -verbose - Verbose mode

    Used with network.sh deployCC
    -c <channel name> - Name of channel to deploy chaincode to
    -ccn <name> - Chaincode name.
    -ccl <language> - Programming language of the chaincode to deploy: go,
java, javascript, typescript
    -ccv <version>  - Chaincode version. 1.0 (default), v2, version3.x, etc
    -ccs <sequence>  - Chaincode definition sequence. Must be an integer, 1
(default), 2, 3, etc
    -ccp <path>  - File path to the chaincode.
    -ccep <policy>  - (Optional) Chaincode endorsement policy using
signature policy syntax. The default policy requires an endorsement from
Org1 and Org2
    -cccg <collection-config>  - (Optional) File path to private data
collections configuration file
    -cci <fcn name>  - (Optional) Name of chaincode initialization
function. When a function is provided, the execution of init will be
requested and the function will be invoked.
    -h - Print this message

 Possible Mode and flag combinations
   up -ca -r -d -s -verbose
   up -r -d -s -verbose
   up createChannel -ca -c -r -d -s -verbose
   up createChannel -bft -c -r -d -s -verbose
[...]

 Examples:
   network.sh up createChannel -ca -c mychannel -s couchdb
   network.sh createChannel -c channelName
   network.sh deployCC -ccn basic -ccp ../asset-transfer-basic/chaincode-
javascript/ -ccl javascript
   network.sh deployCC -ccn mychaincode -ccp ./user/mychaincode -ccv 1 -ccl
javascript
```

By using this script, our goal is to deploy a local Fabric network with an example chaincode. Even though the script abstracts most of the process for simplicity purposes, here, we will provide more details and possibilities for this local deployment.

At any time needed, we encourage you to explore the test network tutorial from the official Fabric documentation, which can be found at **https://hyperledger-fabric.readthedocs.io / en/release-2.5/test_network.html**.

From the **`samples/test-network`** directory, we can run the following command:

```
$ ./network.sh up
```

This will generate organization certificates if they have not been generated yet and then, they will bring up the components' Docker containers.

You should see an output as follows:

```
[+] Running 4/4
 :: Container peer0.org2.example.com Started                 0.5s
 :: Container peer0.org1.example.com Started                 0.4s
 :: Container orderer.example.com    Started                 0.4s
 :: Container cli                    Running                 0.0s
```

The certificates for the organizations will be generated by a tool called **cryptogen** by default. The cryptogen tool is used for faster network deployment in development environments. It simulates a certification authority for certificate issuing. The generated certificates, however, are not recommended for production use. If you want to use certificates generated by CAs, remove the containers with the command shown below. Both options will work for the learning purpose of this book.

```
$ ./network.sh down
```

Then, call the script again with the following argument:

```
$ ./network.sh up -ca
```

The containers that are brought up are the components of a simple Hyperledger Fabric network with the following three organizations:

- org1.example.com
- org2.example.com
- orderer.example.com

The script will place the certificates in two directories, as follows:

- peerOrganizations
- ordererOrganizations

In this example network, organizations **`org1`** and **`org2`** have no ordering nodes, only peer nodes. The **`orderer`** organization, on the other hand, only has ordering nodes. Other network configurations might have organizations that have both peer and ordering nodes. Beware that this configuration is discouraged unless the **`/Channel/Orderer/BlockValidation`** channel policy is changed to limit block signing to the subset of certificates authorized for ordering.

Exploring the directory structure generated for the certificates of the organizations, we can see many elements. You can do this by using the **tree** command or exploring it on your favorite coding IDE.

Refer to the following example for a better understanding:

```
$ tree organizations/peerOrganizations/org1.example.com
organizations/peerOrganizations/org1.example.com
├── ca
│   ├── priv_sk
│   └── ca.org1.example.com-cert.pem
├── msp
│   ├── config.yaml
│   ├── cacerts
│   │   └── ca.org1.example.com-cert.pem
│   ├── admincerts
│   └── tlscacerts
│       └── tlsca.org1.example.com-cert.pem
├── peers
│   └── peer0.org1.example.com
│       ├── msp
│       │   ├── config.yaml
│       │   ├── cacerts
│       │   │   └── ca.org1.example.com-cert.pem
│       │   ├── admincerts
│       │   ├── keystore
│       │   │   └── priv_sk
│       │   ├── signcerts
│       │   │   └── peer0.org1.example.com-cert.pem
│       │   └── tlscacerts
│       │       └── tlsca.org1.example.com-cert.pem
│       └── tls
│           ├── ca.crt
│           ├── server.crt
│           └── server.key
├── tlsca
│   ├── priv_sk
│   └── tlsca.org1.example.com-cert.pem
└── users
    ├── Admin@org1.example.com
    │   ├── msp
```

```
|   |   ├── config.yaml
|   |   ├── cacerts
|   |   |   └── ca.org1.example.com-cert.pem
|   |   ├── admincerts
|   |   ├── keystore
|   |   |   └── priv_sk
|   |   ├── signcerts
|   |   |   └── Admin@org1.example.com-cert.pem
|   |   └── tlscacerts
|   |       └── tlsca.org1.example.com-cert.pem
|   └── tls
|       ├── client.key
|       ├── ca.crt
|       └── client.crt
└── User1@org1.example.com
    └── . . .
```

For a new Hyperledger Fabric developer, this directory structure might seem daunting, but for application development purposes, it is not necessary to understand it in detail. In the local environment, certain folders will be mapped to the inside of Docker containers, allowing peers and orderer to read their local **Membership Service Provider** (**MSP**) folders that identify them.

So far, we have created the organizations' cryptographic material and deployed the components as Docker containers. There are no channels or chaincodes set up, which means that there's no actual network between organizations.

You can see this by running a command to check the logs of any peer deployed. The most recent line will show that there are no active channels, refer to the following command for a better understanding:

```
$ docker logs peer0.org1.example.com
…
2023-09-16 15:51:03.285 UTC 0022 INFO ... -> No active channels passed
```

Generating a channel is a simple process, simply run the following command:

```
$ ./network.sh createChannel
…
2023-09-16 … 0001 INFO ... -> Endorser and orderer connections initialized
2023-09-16 … UTC 0002 INFO ... -> Successfully submitted channel update
Anchor peer set for org 'Org2MSP' on channel 'mychannel'
Channel 'mychannel' joined
```

This creates a new channel called **mychannel**, and to understand the configuration of the channel, we will take a quick look at the **configtx.yaml** file, under the **configtx** directory, as shown in the following code:

```
[...]
#=========================================================================
#   Profile
#   Different configuration profiles may be encoded here to be specified
#   as parameters to the configtxgen tool
#=========================================================================
Profiles:
  ChannelRaft:
    <<: *ChannelDefaults
    Orderer:
      <<: *OrdererDefaults
      OrdererType: etcdraft
      EtcdRaft:
        Consenters:
          - Host: orderer.example.com
            Port: 7050
            ClientTLSCert: ../organizations/ordererOrganizations/example.
com/orderers/orderer.example.com/tls/server.crt
            ServerTLSCert: ../organizations/ordererOrganizations/example.
com/orderers/orderer.example.com/tls/server.crt
      Organizations:
        - *OrdererOrg
      Capabilities: *OrdererCapabilities
    Application:
      <<: *ApplicationDefaults
      Organizations:
        - *Org1
        - *Org2
      Capabilities: *ApplicationCapabilities
```

The original file is longer than what is shown here, and we encourage you to look at it in its completeness. The **Profiles** section that is shown is where configurations are assembled to be used for generating the genesis block of the channel, that is, the block that starts the chain.

In this specific example, there is only the profile **ChannelRaft** which is the one used to generate the genesis block for the channel **mychannel**. Notice that there are many **yaml** references to other hidden file sections, such as **`*ChannelDefaults`**. What this shows is that the sections other than **`Profiles`** are merely descriptive, and only are applied once in a specific profile that will be used.

Also, note that certificate paths are informed. This is what makes the channel MSP generation happen during genesis creation. For that reason, we can conclude that the first step in creating any Fabric network must be certificate generation, since nodes need their local MSP, and the channel creation needs the channel MSP.

In order to get a further grasp of the configurations involved in channel creation, let us explore the **`Organizations`** section of the configuration file, as follows:

```
#=================================================================================
#   Section: Organizations
#   This section defines the different organizational identities which will
#   be referenced later in the configuration.
#=================================================================================
Organizations:
  - &OrdererOrg

    Name: OrdererOrg
    ID: OrdererMSP
    MSPDir: ../organizations/ordererOrganizations/example.com/msp

    Policies:
      Readers:
        Type: Signature
        Rule: "OR('OrdererMSP.member')"
      Writers:
        Type: Signature
        Rule: "OR('OrdererMSP.member')"
      Admins:
        Type: Signature
        Rule: "OR('OrdererMSP.admin')"
    OrdererEndpoints:
      - orderer.example.com:7050
  - &Org1
    Name: Org1MSP
    ID: Org1MSP
    MSPDir: ../organizations/peerOrganizations/org1.example.com/msp
```

```
    Policies:
      Readers:
        Type: Signature
        Rule: "OR('Org1MSP.admin', 'Org1MSP.peer', 'Org1MSP.client')"
      Writers:
        Type: Signature
        Rule: "OR('Org1MSP.admin', 'Org1MSP.client')"
      Admins:
        Type: Signature
        Rule: "OR('Org1MSP.admin')"
      Endorsement:
        Type: Signature
        Rule: "OR`('Org1MSP.peer')"
  - &Org2
[...]
```

The **Organizations** section is defined by a list of organizations with the following common properties between them. Note that **Org2** has been suppressed for clarity purposes but will have the same format as other organizations.

The following are properties of organizations in this configuration file:

- **Name**: This property specifies the name of the organization
- **ID**: This property assigns a unique identifier for the organization's MSP.
- **Policies**: This property includes the set of rules that govern various roles within the organization. Rules include roles like **admin**, **peer**, and **client** within their respective MSPs, with **member** denoting any role.
    - **Readers**: This policy specifies who can read information in the organization.
    - **Writers**: This policy defines who can write or modify information.
    - **Admins**: This policy determines who has administrative privileges.
    - **Endorsement**: This policy is specific to **Org1** and **Org2** and specifies who can endorse transactions.
- **MSPDir**: It defines the filesystem path where the MSP configuration is stored. This path is crucial for holding cryptographic materials such as certificates and keys.
- **OrdererEndpoints**: This property lists the network endpoints for the orderer organizations. Since **Org1** and **Org2** do not have orderers, this does not apply to them.

One of the most important aspects of a permissioned blockchain network is its governance, that is, which entities have the power to change it and to what extent. In Hyperledger Fabric, this is governed by policies, and we have seen that certain identity roles are configured to satisfy certain policies. The policies we have seen, however, are set on an organizational level. Let us look at policies set at the channel level, as follows:

```
#==========================================================================
#   SECTION: Application
#   This section defines the values to encode into a config transaction or
#   genesis block for application related parameters
#==========================================================================
Application: &ApplicationDefaults
  # Organizations is the list of orgs which are defined as participants on
the application side of the network
  Organizations:
  # Policies defines the set of policies at this level of the config
tree. For Application policies, their canonical path is /Channel/
Application/<PolicyName>
  Policies:
    Readers:
      Type: ImplicitMeta
      Rule: "ANY Readers"
    Writers:
      Type: ImplicitMeta
      Rule: "ANY Writers"
    Admins:
      Type: ImplicitMeta
      Rule: "MAJORITY Admins"
    LifecycleEndorsement:
      Type: ImplicitMeta
      Rule: "MAJORITY Endorsement"
    Endorsement:
      Type: ImplicitMeta
      Rule: "MAJORITY Endorsement"
  Capabilities:
    <<: *ApplicationCapabilities
```

The **`Application`** section will define configurations for the channel (or **application** channel, as Hyperledger Fabric denotes). Remember that this and other sections are referenced and potentially overwritten in the **`Profiles`** section, so always check there to get the actual configuration that will generate the channel.

The **Policies** for the application channel generally follow a different format called **ImplicitMeta** that will not reference any organization directly. It will, instead, aggregate policies defined at a lower level of the configuration hierarchy, namely the policies defined for the organizations. This allows for the creation of a high-level configuration for governance. These policies support keywords such as **ANY**, **MAJORITY**, and **ALL**.

As an example, let us evaluate the **Readers** policy. This policy requires any of the lower-level **Readers** policies to be satisfied. If at least one of the referenced **Readers** policies is met, the overall **Readers** policy is considered satisfied. The **Writers** policy is similar.

The **Admins** policy, however, is a bit different. This policy requires a majority of the lower-level **Admins** policies to be satisfied. This means that more than half of the referenced **Admins** policies must be met for the overall **Admins** policy to be satisfied.

The **Endorsement** policy, in this case, will define the default policy for endorsement in the channel. As we have seen in previous chapters, this can be overridden by other policies depending on the situation. For example, any chaincode can be committed to a channel with a different endorsement definition, and, of course, private data collection level endorsement and key-level endorsements will override this policy.

One additional policy in this configuration is the **LifecycleEndorsement**. This rule requires a majority of the **Endorsement** policies to be satisfied for lifecycle operations, that is, chaincode deployment operations. More than half of the referenced **Endorsement** policies must be met for the **LifecycleEndorsement** policy to be satisfied.

Policies govern much of the Fabric logic and configuration, so it is common to see it referenced in many places on a configtx file or in a decoded block. Modification of block configuration is always governed by the **Admin** policy, and different block levels will require different versions of this policy to be satisfied. As an example, if **Org1** wishes to change the configuration block in its section, only the **Admin** of **Org1** will be required. But if it wishes to change the application channel configuration, the majority of channel Admins will be required. We will not perform administrative operations in this book, but this explanation will be useful for the rest of the journey.

Now that we have our channel created and nodes joined, we can deploy our example chaincode. Run the following command and watch the logs:

```
$ ./network.sh deployCC -ccn basic -ccp ../asset-transfer-basic/chaincode-go -ccl go
[...]
deploying chaincode on channel 'mychannel'
executing with the following
- CHANNEL_NAME: mychannel
- CC_NAME: basic
- CC_SRC_PATH: ../asset-transfer-basic/chaincode-go
```

```
- CC_SRC_LANGUAGE: go
- CC_VERSION: 1.0
- CC_SEQUENCE: 1
- ...

[...]

+ peer lifecycle chaincode package basic.tar.gz --path
../asset-transfer-basic/chaincode-go --lang golang --label basic_1.0
+ res=0
++ peer lifecycle chaincode calculatepackageid basic.tar.gz
+ PACKAGE_ID=basic_1.0:
ee50fa374f273a42c9d5477b0a2924ff744735eff15bea7ce52bcf887af5fc01
Chaincode is packaged
```

Note that the first steps are related to packaging the chaincode source code. This generates a package with an ID that depends on the content of the source code, used to identify the deployment one it is done.

Let us continue with the logs regarding chaincode installation, as follows:

```
Installing chaincode on peer0.org1...
Using organization 1
[...]
submitInstallProposal -> Installed remotely:
response:<status:200 payload:"\nJbasic_1.0:
ee50fa374f273a42c9d5477b0a2924ff744735eff15bea7ce52bcf887af5fc01\022\
tbasic_1.0" >
2024-06-10 08:16:39.062 -03 0002 INFO [cli.lifecycle.chaincode]
submitInstallProposal -> Chaincode code package identifier:
basic_1.0:ee50fa374f273a42c9d5477b0a2924ff744735eff15bea7ce52bcf887af5fc01
Chaincode is installed on peer0.org1


Install chaincode on peer0.org2...
Using organization 2
[...]
submitInstallProposal -> Installed remotely:
response:<status:200 payload:"\nJbasic_1.0:
ee50fa374f273a42c9d5477b0a2924ff744735eff15bea7ce52bcf887af5fc01\022\
tbasic_1.0" >
2024-06-10 08:16:50.314 -03 0002 INFO [cli.lifecycle.chaincode]
submitInstallProposal -> Chaincode code package identifier:
```

```
basic_1.0:ee50fa374f273a42c9d5477b0a2924ff744735eff15bea7ce52bcf887af5fc01
Chaincode is installed on peer0.org2
```

The packaged chaincode is sent to peers and installed. Installation does not immediately make the chaincode operational but prepares the peer nodes to recognize and manage the chaincode.

Refer to the following code:

```
Using organization 1
+ peer lifecycle chaincode approveformyorg -o localhost:7050
--ordererTLSHostnameOverride orderer.example.com --tls --cafile
/goledgerdev/book-companion/samples/test-network/organizations/
ordererOrganizations/example.com/tlsca/tlsca.example.com-cert.pem
--channelID mychannel --name basic --version 1.0 --package-id
basic_1.0:ee50fa374f273a42c9d5477b0a2924ff744735eff15bea7ce52bcf887af5fc01
 --sequence 1
+ res=0
2024-06-10 08:16:52.507 -03 0001 INFO [chaincodeCmd] ClientWait -> txid
[2c1f3228ed6c21b6d46f07f873b44d808ba816edd492c4a02e6c57d0dfeff4e8]
committed with status (VALID) at localhost:7051
Chaincode definition approved on peer0.org1 on channel 'mychannel'
```

Each organization must approve the chaincode definition, including its name, version, sequence, and optional endorsement policy, to ensure all organizations consent before it becomes active on the network.

```
Using organization 1
Checking the commit readiness of the chaincode definition on peer0.org1 on
channel 'mychannel'...
[...]
{
        "approvals": {
                "Org1MSP": true,
                "Org2MSP": false
        }
}
Checking the commit readiness of the chaincode definition successful on
peer0.org1 on channel 'mychannel'


Using organization 2
Checking the commit readiness of the chaincode definition on peer0.org2 on
channel 'mychannel'...
```

```
[...]
{
        "approvals": {
                "Org1MSP": true,
                "Org2MSP": false
        }
}
Checking the commit readiness of the chaincode definition successful
on peer0.org2 on channel 'mychannel'


Using organization 2
+ peer lifecycle chaincode approveformyorg -o localhost:7050
--ordererTLSHostnameOverride orderer.example.com --tls --cafile
/goledgerdev/book-companion/samples/test-network/organizations/
ordererOrganizations/example.com/tlsca/tlsca.example.com-cert.
pem --channelID mychannel --name basic --version 1.0 --package-id
basic_1.0:ee50fa374f273a42c9d5477b0a2924ff744735eff15bea7ce52bcf887af5fc01
 --sequence 1
+ res=0
2024-06-10 08:17:00.853 -03 0001 INFO [chaincodeCmd] ClientWait -> txid
[7739d3a0814ed74d310f1796651dc3ba0ed061611da8bd42dbca4876962932ee]
committed with status (VALID) at localhost:9051
Chaincode definition approved on peer0.org2 on channel 'mychannel'
[…]
Using organization 1
Using organization 2
+ peer lifecycle chaincode commit -o localhost:7050 [...] --version 1.0
--sequence 1
+ res=0
2024-06-10 08:17:09.338 -03 0001 INFO ...
[8897813d58430d309f5852ad34a0c602606c9d9946c2858b9b951131f03e4dde]
committed with status (VALID) at localhost:9051
2024-06-10 08:17:09.342 -03 0002 INFO ...
[8897813d58430d309f5852ad34a0c602606c9d9946c2858b9b951131f03e4dde]
committed with status (VALID) at localhost:705
```

Now all that is left to do is commit the chaincode to channel. Inspect the logs that refer to this step, as follows:

```
Chaincode definition committed on channel 'mychannel'
Using organization 1
```

```
Querying chaincode definition on peer0.org1 on channel 'mychannel'...
Attempting to Query committed status on peer0.org1, Retry after 3 seconds.
+ peer lifecycle chaincode querycommitted --channelID mychannel --name
basic
+ res=0
Committed chaincode definition for chaincode 'basic' on channel 'mychannel':
Version: 1.0, Sequence: 1, Endorsement Plugin: escc, Validation Plugin:
vscc, Approvals: [Org1MSP: true, Org2MSP: true]
Query chaincode definition successful on peer0.org1 on channel 'mychannel'
Using organization 2
Querying chaincode definition on peer0.org2 on channel 'mychannel'...
Attempting to Query committed status on peer0.org2, Retry after 3 seconds.
+ peer lifecycle chaincode querycommitted --channelID mychannel --name
basic
+ res=0
Committed chaincode definition for chaincode 'basic' on channel 'mychannel':
Version: 1.0, Sequence: 1, Endorsement Plugin: escc, Validation Plugin:
vscc, Approvals: [Org1MSP: true, Org2MSP: true]
Query chaincode definition successful on peer0.org2 on channel 'mychannel'
Chaincode initialization is not required
```

Note: The logs shown above closely follow the chaincode lifecycle steps that we have just mentioned. Some logs have been suppressed for clarity purposes. These steps are required for a chaincode to be successfully committed to a channel and for peers to be able to correctly execute them. We will not cover chaincode-as-a-service deployment.

As seen, one of the first steps taken is to package the chaincode in deployable form. This will put the source code inside a compressed folder along with a metadata file for Fabric's reference. Most importantly, the packaged chaincode will get a unique ID based on its content, this will be used to make sure that the same version is being approved across every organization.

According to our channel's policies, a chaincode lifecycle must be approved (or endorsed) by the correct sub-set of organizations. Thus, each organization will approve the chaincode definition. The definition includes critical details like the chaincode name, version, sequence, and the optional endorsement policy. Approvals are the governance step mentioned previously and it is there to ensure that all organizations consent to the chaincode parameters before it becomes active on the network.

You can see on the logs that the script checks multiple times if the approvals have been made. For example, here, only **`Org1`** had approved the chaincode definition, as shown in the following code:

```
{
        "approvals": {
                "Org1MSP": true,
                "Org2MSP": false
        }
}
```

This step is referred to as checking commit readiness, which means that we are actively checking if the definition is ready to be committed to channel, that is, become active.

The commit phase is what finishes the chaincode deployment. The approved chaincode definition is committed to the channel, making the chaincode operational. With that, all peers in the channel recognize the chaincode and can execute its transactions according to the defined endorsement policies.

Now, we have a working network with a chaincode for interaction. In the following section, we will explore the chaincode's source code and the manners to interact with it.

Asset transfer basic chaincode

As we have seen in previous chapters, the chaincode is the element that brings rules to our blockchain application and it is an essential part if we want to deliver valuable solutions to the world.

In our test network, we will be using a chaincode called **asset-transfer-basic**, which is one of the most basic chaincodes. Fabric provides out of the box in its Fabric Samples repository. Although simple, exploring this chaincode is the first step to understanding what a chaincode actually does and what are the essential parts of the toolset it provides. Once we are familiar enough with it, we will understand how CC-Tools will help create more complex logic.

Under the directory **samples/asset-transfer-basic/chaincode-go**, we will find the chaincodes source code written in Go. Let us check the **assetTransfer.go** file, as shown in the following code:

```
[...]
func main() {
       assetChaincode, err := contractapi.NewChaincode(&chaincode.
SmartContract{})
       if err != nil {
              log.Panicf("Error creating asset-transfer-basic chaincode:
%v", err)
       }

       if err := assetChaincode.Start(); err != nil {
              log.Panicf("Error starting asset-transfer-basic chaincode:
```

```
%v", err)
        }
}
```

The **main** function is straightforward, it initializes a chaincode object using the *contractapi* library provided by Fabric and starts it. This is run right after the chaincode has been successfully committed in the channel, and every peer that has the chaincode installed will start their own instance of the chaincode. If you list the containers in your local environment, you can see containers starting with **dev-peer**, which means that the peers have already kickstarted their chaincode process and they are ready for execution.

Under the **chaincode** directory, we can find the implementation of the chaincode itself. The file **smartcontract.go** contains the following chaincode elements:

- **Assets:**
    - **An asset**: It is a simple example asset.
- **Transactions:**
    - **InitLedger**: It adds an initial set of assets to the ledger.
    - **CreateAsset**: It creates a new asset to the world state with the arguments.
    - **ReadAsset**: It returns the asset with the given key.
    - **UpdateAsset**: It updates an existing asset with given parameters.
    - **DeleteAsset**: It deletes an asset.
    - **AssetExists**: It returns true when an asset with a given key exists.
    - **TransferAsset**: It updates the owner field, and returns the previous owner.
    - **GetAllAssets**: It returns all assets.

The names of the transactions already provide some clarity as to what they do, however, let us verify their behavior by executing the first transactions in our network. In your terminal, make sure you are inside the **test-network** directory. Then, export the following variables so that the **peer** binary knows which organization we are representing:

```
$ export FABRIC_CFG_PATH=$PWD/../config/
export CORE_PEER_TLS_ENABLED=true
export CORE_PEER_LOCALMSPID="Org1MSP"
export CORE_PEER_TLS_ROOTCERT_FILE=${PWD}/organizations/peerOrganizations/
org1.example.com/peers/peer0.org1.example.com/tls/ca.crt
export CORE_PEER_MSPCONFIGPATH=${PWD}/organizations/peerOrganizations/org1.
example.com/users/Admin@org1.example.com/msp
export CORE_PEER_ADDRESS=localhost:7051
```

Then, to invoke a chaincode transaction using CLI tools, run the following command:

```
$ peer chaincode invoke -o localhost:7050 --ordererTLSHostnameOverride
orderer.example.com --tls --cafile "${PWD}/organizations/
ordererOrganizations/example.com/orderers/orderer.example.com/
msp/tlscacerts/tlsca.example.com-cert.pem" -C mychannel -n basic
--peerAddresses localhost:7051 --tlsRootCertFiles "${PWD}/organizations/
peerOrganizations/org1.example.com/peers/peer0.org1.example.com/tls/ca.crt"
--peerAddresses localhost:9051 --tlsRootCertFiles "${PWD}/organizations/
peerOrganizations/org2.example.com/peers/peer0.org2.example.com/tls/ca.crt"
-c '{"function":"InitLedger","Args":[]}'
```

If successful, the output for the command should be similar to the following:

```
2023-09-17 08:15:12.021 -03 0001 INFO [chaincodeCmd] chaincodeInvokeOrQuery
-> Chaincode invoke successful. result: status:200
```

The invoke command is long and can be daunting at first. Let us break it down so, that you can tinker with the command and assemble your own.

Each part of the command is explained as follows:

- **peer:** It is the binary that is being used, it provides several subcommands for many purposes.
- **chaincode:** It is the first sub-command that will interact with the chaincode in some capacity.
- **invoke:** It is the operation we want to make in the chaincode. Remember that a chaincode can be invoked or queried. Invoke submits a transaction proposal to update the state of the distributed ledger while query is used to retrieve data from the ledger (no block generation).
- **-o:** It is a flag that will receive the address of the orderer, and that will receive the transaction after the proposal is signed.
- **--ordererTLSHostnameOverride:** It is the hostname to use when validating the **Transport Layer Security** (**TLS**) connection to the orderer.
- **--tls:** It enables TLS when communicating with the orderer.
- **--cafile:** It is the path to the trusted TLS certificate for the orderer endpoint.
- **-C:** It is the name of the channel where the chaincode is located.
- **-n:** It takes the name of the chaincode.
- **--peerAddresses:** It takes the addresses of the peers we want to connect to. Note that we have two instances of this flag specifying a peer from org1 and another from org2.
- **--tlsRootCertFiles:** It takes the TLS certificates for the peers we will connect to. Each peer address informed will need this flag if TLS is enabled.
- **-c:** It is a JSON constructor message for the chaincode. This is where we determine which individual transaction will be called.

The query command is simpler since it does not require decentralized validation because it does not generate blocks. We can then use it to read the assets created by the **InitLedger** transaction.

Refer to the following command for a better understanding:

```
$ peer chaincode query -C mychannel -n basic -c '{"Args":["GetAllAssets"]}'
```

If the **InitLedger** transaction was completed successfully, you should get an output similar to the following:

```
[
  {"ID": "asset1", "color": "blue", "size": 5, "owner": "Tomoko", "appraisedValue": 300},
  {"ID": "asset2", "color": "red", "size": 5, "owner": "Brad", "appraisedValue": 400},
  {"ID": "asset3", "color": "green", "size": 10, "owner": "Jin Soo", "appraisedValue": 500},
  {"ID": "asset4", "color": "yellow", "size": 10, "owner": "Max", "appraisedValue": 600},
  {"ID": "asset5", "color": "black", "size": 15, "owner": "Adriana", "appraisedValue": 700},
  {"ID": "asset6", "color": "white", "size": 15, "owner": "Michel", "appraisedValue": 800}
]
```

You have now interacted with your chaincode successfully.

You may have noticed that interacting with the chaincode with CLI tools can be tiring since we need to assemble commands (some of them long) manually. Let us explore how to interact with it programmatically, by leveraging the Gateway SDK.

Under the directory **samples/asset-transfer-basic/application-gateway-go** you can find a Go application that uses the Fabric Gateway SDK to interact with the blockchain and transact programmatically.

The following code implements functions that will call transactions, read assets, and handle errors:

```
(...)
exampleErrorHandling(contract)
getAllAssets(contract)
createAsset(contract)
transferAssetAsync(contract)
initLedger(contract)
readAssetByID(contract)
(...)
```

The application starts by instantiating a gateway object that will be used to create the channel and chaincode objects, refer to the following code for the same:

```
// Create a Gateway connection for a specific client identity
gw, err := client.Connect(
	id,
	client.WithSign(sign),
	client.WithClientConnection(clientConnection),
	// Default timeouts for different gRPC calls
	client.WithEvaluateTimeout(5*time.Second),
	client.WithEndorseTimeout(15*time.Second),
	client.WithSubmitTimeout(5*time.Second),
	client.WithCommitStatusTimeout(1*time.Minute),
)
```

The function **`client.Connect()`** will take parameters created previously by using certificate paths defined right at the beginning of the source code, much like the **peer** CLI takes the same kind of parameters.

Let us take a look at the create asset function as an example of interaction with the chaincode:

```
// Submits a transaction synch blocking until it has been committed to the
channel ledger.
func createAsset(contract *client.Contract) {
	fmt.Printf("\n--> Submit Transaction: CreateAsset, creates new asset
with ID, Color, Size, Owner and AppraisedValue arguments \n")

	_, err := contract.SubmitTransaction("CreateAsset", assetId,
"yellow", "5", "Tom", "1300")
	if err != nil {
		panic(fmt.Errorf("failed to submit transaction: %w", err))
	}

	fmt.Println("Transaction committed successfully")
}
```

The central piece of interaction is the **`contract.SubmitTransaction()`** function which will take the chaincode function name to be called as the first parameter and arguments as the subsequent parameters. In this case, the transaction will be **`CreateAsset`** with an **`assetId`** (defined globally in the code), size, owner, appraised value, and color. Beware that these arguments are positional and must be sent in the same order as the chaincode transaction receives them.

In order to execute this code, first download dependencies with the command from the **`samples/asset-transfer-basic/application-gateway-go`** directory, as follows:

```
$ go mod vendor
```

Then, simply run the command as follows:

```
$ go run assetTransfer.go
```

Explore the output to see the results of your execution.

The Gateway SDK is essential when building Fabric applications because it will allow the solution to be integrated into many other contexts. You can leverage it to expose chaincode interaction to an API that can be used by a web application or other systems.

Upgrading chaincode

One of the essential parts of chaincode development is the iterative process of deploying a version, testing it, changing the code, and redeploying it again. Restarting the development environment is one way to develop the application, however, it will destroy your local network every time you re-run the script, and your registered asset will be gone. That is fine in some situations, but if you are working on a transaction that requires something to be on the ledger, you will need to register it every time. This is where upgrading the chaincode comes in.

Unlike blockchains like Ethereum which do not allow smart contracts to have their source code updated, Fabric not only allows it but provides a life cycle with version and sequence control for chaincodes.

In order to do this in the test network environment, we can change our command a bit from earlier. From the **test-network** directory, run the following command replacing **<version>** and **<sequence>** accordingly. Version can be any string that has not been used before and the sequence must be an integer sequential. This means that after the initial deployment, which defines sequence as one, our next value must be two, as follows:

```
$ ./network.sh deployCC -ccn basic -ccp ../asset-transfer-basic/chaincode-go
-ccl go -ccv <version> -ccs <sequence>
```

Let us create a new transaction for our basic chaincode and then upgrade it in the channel. One important functionality of a blockchain is being able to check the history of data in the ledger, for that, we can implement the following function at the end of the **smartcontract.go** file:

```
func (s *SmartContract) ReadAssetHistory(ctx contractapi.
TransactionContextInterface, id string) ([]map[string]interface{}, error) {
	resultsIterator, err := ctx.GetStub().GetHistoryForKey(id)
	if err != nil {
		return nil, err
	}
	defer resultsIterator.Close()

	assets := make([]map[string]interface{}, 0)
```

```
	for resultsIterator.HasNext() {
		queryResponse, err := resultsIterator.Next()
		if err != nil {
			return nil, err
		}

		var asset map[string]interface{}
		err = json.Unmarshal(queryResponse.Value, &asset)
		if err != nil {
			return nil, err
		}
		assets = append(assets, asset)
	}

	return assets, nil
}
```

This function will use the **GetHistoryForKey()** functionality to retrieve a list of states a particular key has already been in.

In order to ease our interactions with this new transaction, we can add a function in our application that uses the Gateway SDK to interact with it. Add the following code to the end of the file **assetTransfer.go** under the **application-gateway-go** directory:

```
// Evaluates a tx by assetID to get history.
func readAssetHistoryByID(contract *client.Contract) {
	fmt.Printf("\n--> Evaluate Transaction: ReadAssetHistory, function
returns asset history\n")

	evaluateResult, err := contract.
EvaluateTransaction("ReadAssetHistory", assetId)
	if err != nil {
		panic(fmt.Errorf("failed to evaluate transaction: %w", err))
	}
	result := formatJSON(evaluateResult)

	fmt.Printf("Result:%s\n", result)
}
```

Now, call the following function in the **main()** of the same file:

```
initLedger(contract)
	getAllAssets(contract)
	createAsset(contract)
	readAssetByID(contract)
	transferAssetAsync(contract)
```

```
exampleErrorHandling(contract)

readAssetHistoryByID(contract) // here
```

Finally, upgrade the chaincode from the **test-network** folder by running the command you learned above replacing the version and sequence accordingly. Once that is done, you can execute the command to run the application shown earlier from the **application-gateway-go** directory.

By doing this, you have successfully changed the source code of your blockchain application, upgraded it, and interacted with it.

World state storage in peer

Whenever a key is used either for registering or reading, we need to have the state of the ledger in mind. Each peer in the channel will keep the state in two different formats, the ledger itself and a non-relational database with the current version of the keys, which is called **world state**. This is especially useful because we do not need to go through all of the blocks to guarantee that we have the most recent version of the asset.

By default, the peer uses LevelDB which is stored as a file inside the peer's container. This database is non-relational, that is, it stores a key, a version, and a value, which can be in any format. Recall from *Chapter 5, Transaction Flow*, that the read set of transactions will have a version associated with each read. This version number comes from the world state and is used to validate transactions to avoid phantom items and inconsistencies.

The world state is derived from the blockchain itself. Any time a peer receives a block, it will take the transaction's write set and apply it to the world state database. This design choice means that the world state can be generated by the blockchain at any time.

Figure 6.1 shows a representation of the peer's world state, that can be generated from the blocks' write set:

Figure 6.1: *World state representation in peer*

GetState

When exploring the **asset-transfer-basic** chaincode, you may have noticed that many read transactions use the **GetState** function or some variety of it. These are the main ways developers will use to fetch data from the blockchain to be used in transactions.

The **GetState** function retrieves the value of an asset based on a provided key string. One notable feature of this function is that it does not retrieve data from the write set. This means that if a key is stored with **PutState** and subsequently accessed with **GetState** within the same transaction, the value returned will be the original value.

A read on the state of the keys can be performed to return a list of results. A function that does that is **GetStateByRange**, which takes a start key and an end key and returns an iterator that traverses the results in lexical order.

Another such function is **GetQueryResult**, which provides an important operation in chaincodes, designed for conducting rich queries on a state database. This feature is specifically tailored for state databases with rich query capabilities, such as **CouchDB**. Users provide a query string in the native syntax of the underlying state database, and in return, they receive an iterator. This iterator facilitates the traversal of all keys within the query result set. It is important to note that if the number of keys in the result set exceeds the **totalQueryLimit**, as defined in **core.yaml**, this iterator may not be able to retrieve all keys. Additionally, it is vital to understand that the query is not re-executed during the validation phase, meaning that phantom reads are not identified. This implies that other committed transactions might have added, updated, or removed keys affecting the result set, and this will not be detected during validation or commit. Consequently, applications vulnerable to this scenario should exercise caution, refraining from using **GetQueryResult** in transactions that alter the ledger, and instead, restrict its usage to read-only operations within the chaincode.

PutState

If read operations are an essential part of blockchain applications, so are write operations. This is mainly represented by **PutState**. This function is straightforward, it takes a key and a value and writes it to the blockchain.

One thing to remember is that it does not matter if the transaction is a creation or update of an asset. Ultimately, the operation made is a call to **PutState**. Differentiation between create and update operations is done by the developer. Let us check how the update function is different from the create asset function. Study the following code that creates an asset:

```
// CreateAsset issues a new asset to the world state with given details.
func (s *SmartContract) CreateAsset(ctx contractapi.
TransactionContextInterface, id string, color string, size int, owner
string, appraisedValue int) error {
```

```
	exists, err := s.AssetExists(ctx, id)
	if err != nil {
		return err
	}
	if exists {
		return fmt.Errorf("the asset %s already exists", id)
	}

	asset := Asset{
		ID:             id,
		Color:          color,
		Size:           size,
		Owner:          owner,
		AppraisedValue: appraisedValue,
	}
	assetJSON, err := json.Marshal(asset)
	if err != nil {
		return err
	}

	return ctx.GetStub().PutState(id, assetJSON)
}
```

The **CreateAsset** transaction is simple, it takes all of the asset properties as arguments. It then checks if the asset exists on the ledger, if so, an error is returned. Finally, it puts the asset with the **PutState** function.

Now, study the **UpdateAsset** transaction and try to find where they differ. Refer to the following code for a better understanding:

```
// UpdateAsset updates an existing asset in the world state with provided
parameters.
func (s *SmartContract) UpdateAsset(ctx contractapi.
TransactionContextInterface, id string, color string, size int, owner
string, appraisedValue int) error {
	exists, err := s.AssetExists(ctx, id)
	if err != nil {
		return err
	}
	if !exists {
		return fmt.Errorf("the asset %s does not exist", id)
	}

	// overwriting original asset with new asset
	asset := Asset{
		ID:             id,
```

```
            Color:          color,
            Size:           size,
            Owner:          owner,
            AppraisedValue: appraisedValue,
      }
      assetJSON, err := json.Marshal(asset)
      if err != nil {
            return err
      }

      return ctx.GetStub().PutState(id, assetJSON)
}
```

The **UpdateAsset** transaction is similar. The difference is that if the asset does not exist, an error is returned. It is not possible to update something that was not created before. Note that it also uses the **PutState** operation.

The only other operation that modifies the world state, apart from **PutState**, is **DelState**, which deletes a state. It simply takes the key and deletes it from the world state. This does not delete previous states of the key, which is impossible in a blockchain system. When checking the history of a key that has been deleted, a version history will show a property indicating that it was deleted at a point in time.

When developing chaincodes, you must keep in mind the transaction flow presented in the previous chapter. Once the chaincode returns a transaction successfully, this is only the first of many steps for the transaction to be deemed valid.

Chaincode execution is just a proposal. The chaincode execution will not affect the ledger state directly. The proposal is used by the peer to achieve transaction endorsement and then validity once it is added to a block and then validated.

Now that you know how transactions are written, let us explore another way to interact with the programmed functions by leveraging the testing environment in Go. That will allow us to run most transactions without having a blockchain running. For that, let us take a look at the **smartcontract_test.go** file, as follows:

```
// go:generate counterfeiter -o mocks/transaction.go -fake-name
TransactionContext . transactionContext
type transactionContext interface {

      contractapi.TransactionContextInterface
}

// go:generate counterfeiter -o mocks/chaincodestub.go -fake-name
ChaincodeStub . chaincodeStub
type chaincodeStub interface {
      shim.ChaincodeStubInterface
}
```

```
// go:generate counterfeiter -o mocks/statequeryiterator.go -fake-name
StateQueryIterator . stateQueryIterator
type stateQueryIterator interface {
	shim.StateQueryIteratorInterface
}

func TestInitLedger(t *testing.T) {
	chaincodeStub := &mocks.ChaincodeStub{}
	transactionContext := &mocks.TransactionContext{}
	transactionContext.GetStubReturns(chaincodeStub)

	assetTransfer := chaincode.SmartContract{}
	err := assetTransfer.InitLedger(transactionContext)
	require.NoError(t, err)

	chaincodeStub.PutStateReturns(fmt.Errorf("failed inserting key"))
	err = assetTransfer.InitLedger(transactionContext)
	require.EqualError(t, err, "failed to put to world state. failed
inserting key")
}
[...]
```

The code begins defining some interfaces that will be used as objects throughout the tests. And, by using the **go:generate** directive, it sets up mock interfaces for **chaincodeStub** and **stateQueryIterator**. This directive will run the *counterfeiter* tool which generates a mock implementation of the interface and puts it under the **mock** directory.

Right after that, we have our first test case: **TestInitLedger**. This function sets up a test for the **InitLedger** transaction of this chaincode. It uses the mocks generated to set up instances of the objects that simulate interaction with the ledger. The test first calls **InitLedger** and verifies that it completes without errors. It then simulates a failure scenario by making **PutState** return an error, and calls **InitLedger** again, this time verifying that the method returns the expected error message indicating a failure to insert a key into the world state.

Let us look at three other tests implemented in this file: **TestCreateAsset**, **TestReadAsset**, and **TestGetAllAssets** in the following code:

```
[...]
func TestCreateAsset(t *testing.T) {
	chaincodeStub := &mocks.ChaincodeStub{}
	transactionContext := &mocks.TransactionContext{}
	transactionContext.GetStubReturns(chaincodeStub)

	assetTransfer := chaincode.SmartContract{}
	err := assetTransfer.CreateAsset(transactionContext, "", "", 0, "", 0)
```

```
	require.NoError(t, err)

	chaincodeStub.GetStateReturns([]byte{}, nil)
	err = assetTransfer.CreateAsset(transactionContext, "asset1", "", 0,
"", 0)
	require.EqualError(t, err, "the asset asset1 already exists")

	chaincodeStub.GetStateReturns(nil, fmt.Errorf("unable to retrieve
asset"))
	err = assetTransfer.CreateAsset(transactionContext, "asset1", "", 0,
"", 0)
	require.EqualError(t, err, "failed to read from world state: unable
to retrieve asset")
}
```

The test initializes an instance of the **assetTransfer** smart contract and first calls the **CreateAsset** method with empty parameters, expecting it to complete without errors.

Next, it simulates a scenario where an asset already exists by having **GetState** return a non-nil value, then calls **CreateAsset** with an asset ID of **asset1** and checks that the method returns the appropriate error message indicating that the asset already exists. Finally, the test sets up **GetState** to return an error, simulating a failure to retrieve the asset from the world state, and verifies that **CreateAsset** returns the expected error message about failing to read from the world state. This test ensures that the **CreateAsset** method handles both normal and error conditions correctly.

By using the **GetStateReturns** function in the mock, it sets what the **GetState** function will return, and this allows the developer to set it, in one case, the return of an empty byte slice and in the other case, an error.

Let us now check a code for testing the **ReadAsset** function, as follows:

```
func TestReadAsset(t *testing.T) {
	chaincodeStub := &mocks.ChaincodeStub{}
	transactionContext := &mocks.TransactionContext{}
	transactionContext.GetStubReturns(chaincodeStub)

	expectedAsset := &chaincode.Asset{ID: «asset1»}
	bytes, err := json.Marshal(expectedAsset)
	require.NoError(t, err)

	chaincodeStub.GetStateReturns(bytes, nil)
	assetTransfer := chaincode.SmartContract{}
	asset, err := assetTransfer.ReadAsset(transactionContext, «»)
	require.NoError(t, err)
	require.Equal(t, expectedAsset, asset)
```

```
        chaincodeStub.GetStateReturns(nil, fmt.Errorf("unable to retrieve
asset"))
        _, err = assetTransfer.ReadAsset(transactionContext, "")
        require.EqualError(t, err, "failed to read from world state: unable
to retrieve asset")

        chaincodeStub.GetStateReturns(nil, nil)
        asset, err = assetTransfer.ReadAsset(transactionContext, "asset1")
        require.EqualError(t, err, "the asset asset1 does not exist")
        require.Nil(t, asset)
}
```

The **TestReadAsset** test starts the usual way, with a mock definition. It then defines what are the expected bytes for an **asset1** that will be read and sets up **GetStateReturns** to return that definition. The test initializes an instance of the **assetTransfer** smart contract and calls **ReadAsset**, verifying that it correctly retrieves and unmarshals the asset, matching the expected asset.

Next, the test simulates an error scenario where **GetState** fails to retrieve the asset by configuring **chaincodeStub** to return an error. It then calls **ReadAsset** again, verifying that the method returns the appropriate error message.

Ending the test, it simulates a scenario where the asset does not exist by configuring **chaincodeStub** to return nil for the asset data. When **ReadAsset** is called with the asset ID **asset1**, it verifies that the method returns the correct error message and that the asset is **nil**, as shown in the following code:

```
func TestGetAllAssets(t *testing.T) {
        asset := &chaincode.Asset{ID: «asset1»}
        bytes, err := json.Marshal(asset)
        require.NoError(t, err)

        iterator := &mocks.StateQueryIterator{}
        iterator.HasNextReturnsOnCall(0, true)
        iterator.HasNextReturnsOnCall(1, false)
        iterator.NextReturns(&queryresult.KV{Value: bytes}, nil)

        chaincodeStub := &mocks.ChaincodeStub{}
        transactionContext := &mocks.TransactionContext{}
        transactionContext.GetStubReturns(chaincodeStub)

        chaincodeStub.GetStateByRangeReturns(iterator, nil)
        assetTransfer := &chaincode.SmartContract{}
        assets, err := assetTransfer.GetAllAssets(transactionContext)
        require.NoError(t, err)
        require.Equal(t, []*chaincode.Asset{asset}, assets)

        iterator.HasNextReturns(true)
```

```
	iterator.NextReturns(nil, fmt.Errorf("failed retrieving next item"))
	assets, err = assetTransfer.GetAllAssets(transactionContext)
	require.EqualError(t, err, "failed retrieving next item")
	require.Nil(t, assets)

	chaincodeStub.GetStateByRangeReturns(nil, fmt.Errorf("failed
retrieving all assets"))
	assets, err = assetTransfer.GetAllAssets(transactionContext)
	require.EqualError(t, err, "failed retrieving all assets")
	require.Nil(t, assets)
}
```

The **TestGetAllAssets** function tests the **GetAllAssets** method of our chaincode. The test begins by creating a mock asset and serializing it into JSON. It sets up a mock **StateQueryIterator** to simulate the presence of an asset in the ledger, returning **true** on the first call to **HasNext** and false on the second, with **Next** returning the serialized asset data.

A mock **ChaincodeStub** and **TransactionContext** are also created, with the context returning the mock stub. The stub is configured to return the mock iterator when **GetStateByRange** is called. The test initializes the smart contract and verifies that **GetAllAssets** correctly retrieves the asset, matching the expected result.

The test then simulates an error during iteration by configuring the iterator to return an error on **Next**. It verifies that **GetAllAssets** returns the appropriate error message and nil assets. Finally, the test simulates a failure in retrieving the asset range by configuring the stub to return an error from **GetStateByRange**, ensuring that **GetAllAssets** correctly handles and reports this error.

If you are using a code editor with support for, Go language extensions, such as Visual Studio Code, you can execute Go tests easily by clicking the **run test** prompt on top of the function definition. However, if you have any problems running it that way, you can run the entire package with the following command:

```
$ go test github.com/goledgerdev/book-companion/samples/asset-transfer-
basic/chaincode-go/chaincode
```

Running single test functions is also straightforward. For example, in the TestInitLedger case, as follows:

```
go test -run ^TestInitLedger$ github.com/goledgerdev/book-companion/samples/
asset-transfer-basic/chaincode-go/chaincode
```

A successful output will be something like the following code:

```
=== RUN   TestInitLedger
--- PASS: TestInitLedger (0.00s)
PASS
ok      github.com/goledgerdev/book-companion/samples/asset-transfer-basic/
chaincode-go/chaincode    0.616s
```

Now, it is your turn to explore and tinker with the code that was presented. This will be invaluable for the more complex setups we will see throughout the book.

Conclusion

In this chapter, we had the opportunity to work practically with a chaincode and a development network. We also learned how to deploy a development network using helper scripts derived from the official Fabric Samples repository. Then, we successfully created a channel and deployed a chaincode to it, allowing them to interact with it using CLI tools.

We also understood the chaincode source code, how it was organized, and what a simple chaincode can do. We have also shown how you can interact with the chaincode by using the Gateway SDK to submit transactions. Then, with a chaincode upgrade and adding our custom code to it, we have seen the first glimpse of a development process.

Finally, we took some time to better understand the building blocks of ledger interaction, represented by GetState and PutState. Ultimately, that is what every single chaincode does in the ledger, despite any additional complexity applications require. And with the knowledge of those tools, we explore how we can easily test written code by leveraging mock definitions and Go testing.

In the next chapter, we will introduce the CC-Tools library, a Hyperledger Labs project, that will extend the functionality of basic chaincode development to provide many more features that allow developers to develop more complex applications.

CHAPTER 7

Introduction to CC-Tools Library

Introduction

You may have realized the power of blockchain applications and the many uses it has. Most of this power comes from the customization of the blockchain rules, which are coded in the smart contract, or chaincode, in Hyperledger Fabric.

In *Chapter 6, Deploying Your First Chaincode*, we introduced a basic chaincode that outlines the main functions and features that can be used while developing your own custom chaincodes on a Hyperledger Fabric network. This is the first chaincode experience for the majority of Fabric beginners, and moving past the basics with fewer chaincode examples can take time. Moreover, building more complex chaincodes in a reasonable time can be particularly daunting.

In this chapter, we will introduce the CC-Tools library, a Go package that aims to make the development of chaincodes easier and faster, with many built-in features that abstract certain repetitive programming patterns and allows for more complex chaincode design. This library is a Hyperledger Labs project and has full compatibility with Fabric.

Structure

The chapter covers the following topics:

- History of CC-Tools library
- Getting fast track to production mode
- CC-Tools feature details
- Comparison to chaincode asset-transfer-basic

Objectives

By the end of this chapter, you will become acquainted with the CC-Tools library's capabilities for chaincode development. Initially, you will explore its historical context, offering valuable insights into the guiding principles that inform its features. This background knowledge will lay the groundwork for addressing the challenges developers face in chaincode development and how the library adeptly resolves them.

Following this, we will present a compelling case for utilizing CC-Tools in production-level development, showcasing its potential to accelerate the delivery of applications to final customers. We will also provide a comprehensive overview of the library's feature set, ensuring you have a complete grasp of the diverse development opportunities it affords.

Furthermore, we will draw comparisons to the standard chaincode development experience, exemplified by the asset-transfer-basic chaincode. This will serve to highlight the distinct advantages of employing CC-Tools.

By the conclusion of this chapter, you will have gained a profound appreciation for the instrumental role that CC-Tools play in the Fabric development journey, particularly in the field of production-level projects.

History of CC-Tools library

The authors of this book began working with Hyperledger Fabric in 2018. Version 1.0 of Hyperledger Fabric was released in 2017 and, when we started studying it, the latest version was v1.2.

Back then, navigating Hyperledger Fabric was a test of patience due to the scarcity of documentation and a smaller community compared to what it has evolved into over the past few years. Even in the official Hyperledger Fabric Read-The-Docs were often incomplete and a source of frustration for many developers.

New developers also encountered challenges in finding fellow developers who were willing to assist them in resolving technical queries and deciphering coding intricacies encountered during the Hyperledger Fabric chaincode programming process.

During that time, people started developing chaincodes for both learning and as a service to many customers. Many features that a chaincode will have, are common to every chaincode, such as property validation. After realizing that many of the chaincodes that people developed had repetitive code snippets that had to be maintained across multiple projects.

Not only that, but as entrepreneurs, they had to train newly hired developers, since blockchain developers were rare back then. That was a hard task for the learners and the learning process usually took at least two months. When a new team member joined the technical team, they had to resort to the fabric-samples repository to experiment with

Hyperledger Fabric chaincode examples, hoping to grasp the chaincode development process.

There were not many courses or YouTube channels talking about Hyperledger Fabric earlier.

Naturally, developers could, and still can, turn to the Hyperledger Fabric open-source for assistance. However, it is a rare developer who takes pleasure in troubleshooting their projects by exploring the technology's source code.

This predicament resulted in each new programmer adopting their approach to chaincode development, potentially yielding suboptimal management outcomes, particularly in critical software engineering aspects such as accurate data mapping, code reuse, and code standardization.

The CC-Tools library was conceived for several key purposes in order to streamline development by reducing the amount of code needed, enabling intricate chaincode design, establishing standardized development practices, and simplifying the onboarding process for developers. These objectives gradually gained prominence. Initially, the library served to recycle code across various projects. As we recognized its potential, we broadened the range of scenarios it could address.

GoLedger introduced CC-Tools as an open-source project in 2020. By 2023, the project transitioned to the Hyperledger Labs initiative, transforming it into a resource for the entire Hyperledger community. The link for the official repositories is **https://github.com/hyperledger-labs/cc-tools-demo**.

The core of the library is located under `hyperledger-labs/cc-tools` and provides all the packages with functionality for various purposes. An example implementation is located under `hyperledger-labs/cc-tools-demo`.

Getting fast track to production mode

A blockchain application is only as good as the real-world problem it solves. This means that, at some point, our code will need to be in production, otherwise it is just an exercise. CC-Tools are great for creating proofs of concept efficiently, which can be used to empower research or explore new possibilities in particular markets. However, it is imperative to be able to transition to a scenario applicable to the real world.

CC-Tools will allow developers and architects to create and test business logic rapidly and to iteratively evolve their code. Including some simple alterations, such as organization permissions, this code can be transitioned to a production environment of your choice. CC-Tools do not require any special Fabric network; any Fabric network will be able to run CC-Tools.

Before CC-Tools, the GoLedger team spent on average three months to develop a new chaincode. Once CC-Tools was mature enough, a chaincode of similar complexity would only take two to three weeks.

CC-Tools feature details

CC-Tools implements many packages with functionalities that will make the life of the developer easier and at the same time allow them to develop complex chaincodes. These will include packages that deal with asset types, data types, transactions, event types, a special wrapper for additional functionality, and a testing suite.

Asset types

Similar to databases, assets are composed of properties, some of which may serve as keys for that asset. Each property is associated with a specific data type, such as string, number, boolean, and so on.

Moreover, an asset can take the form of a Hyperledger Fabric Private Data, wherein the informational content is stored in a transient database separate from the ledger, and only a select subset of organizations have access to this data, determining who can read it.

Additionally, assets can be generated dynamically during the execution of chaincode. This is facilitated through CC-Tools' Dynamic Asset Types functionality, which entails defining asset types through invoking calls to the active chaincode.

Data types

CC-Tools datatypes are essential for categorizing and defining the type of data that can be stored in an asset and used in transactions. It is crucial to validate that the entered data matches the expected datatype. The CC-Tools library provides primitive data types like string, number, integer, boolean, datetime, and **`@object`** (for JSON data). Additionally, developers can introduce custom data types. These definitions are organized in the **`chaincode/datatypes`** folder to enable tailored data handling within CC-Tools.

Transactions

CC tool transactions are methods that create a new asset or modify them in the channel. These transactions can update asset information, and this can only be done through chaincode execution in endorsing peers. The library offers pre-defined transactions like **`CreateAsset`**, **`UpdateAsset`**, **`DeleteAsset`**, **`ReadAsset`**, **`ReadAssetHistory`**, and **`Search`**. Custom transactions can be created by adding a file in the **`chaincode/txdefs`** folder.

An asset is characterized by fields including Tag (for internal reference), Label (for external application use), Description, Callers (defining which organizations can call the transaction), Args (arguments with their fields), Routine (transaction source code), and more. We will soon compare transactions built with CC-Tools with those built in **`asset-transfer-basic`**.

Event types

Hyperledger Fabric enables client applications, like the API, to receive real-time notifications called **block events,** when blocks are committed to the ledger. CC-Tools offers a convenient built-in event feature for easy registration, automatically managed by the standard chaincode API. These events in CC-Tools are available in three types, log (records event information in chaincode API logs), transaction (triggers another chaincode transaction upon event reception), and custom (executes a pre-defined custom function when the event occurs).

Stub wrapper

The **StubWrapper** enhances chaincode development by furnishing added functionalities. It manages a **`WriteSet`**, ensuring that any alterations made during chaincode execution are accurately reflected when querying the ledger state. Even if these changes have not been officially committed to the ledger, the **StubWrapper** keeps them in the **`WriteSet`**. This enables subsequent queries to incorporate the **`WriteSet`** for delivering updated data, thus maintaining the consistency and precision of information throughout the chaincode execution.

The wrapper will also provide many additional functions for putting, updating, and deleting assets while verifying the validity of data properties.

Comparison to chaincode asset-transfer-basic

Let us go back to the last chapter's chaincode: **`asset-transfer-basic`**. This chaincode implements functions to deal with the following asset structure:

```
type Asset struct {
  AppraisedValue int    `json:"AppraisedValue"`
  Color          string `json:"Color"`
  ID             string `json:"ID"`
  Owner          string `json:"Owner"`
  Size           int    `json:"Size"`
}
```

The chaincode asset-transfer-basic, for example, implements a **`CreateAsset`** function. Refer to the following code for a better understanding:

```
// CreateAsset issues a new asset to the world state with given details.
func (s *SmartContract) CreateAsset(ctx contractapi.TransactionContextIn-
terface, id string, color string, size int, owner string, appraisedValue
int) error {

    exists, err := s.AssetExists(ctx, id)
    if err != nil {
```

```
        return err
    }
    if exists {
        return fmt.Errorf("the asset %s already exists", id)
    }
    asset := Asset{
        ID: id,
        Color: color,
        Size: size,
        Owner: owner,
        AppraisedValue: appraisedValue,
    }
    assetJSON, err := json.Marshal(asset)
    if err != nil {
        return err
    }

    return ctx.GetStub().PutState(id, assetJSON)
}
```

This is a basic chaincode example that deals exclusively with a single asset type, namely **Asset**. All methods are designed to furnish information about it. For instance, if there is a need to update or delete information about an asset, the client would invoke the **UpdateAsset** or **DeleteAsset** method.

However, actual chaincodes tend to be more complex than this example. It is common to have multiple asset types defined within the source code. In such cases, Hyperledger Fabric developers will often use the same modeling strategy to implement the required functionality for the additional asset type.

Let us imagine the addition of a new asset type, refer to the following code:

```
// SecondAsset description
type SecondAsset struct {
  IDPrimary       string    `json:"IDPrimary"`
  IDSecondary     string    `json:"IDSecondary"`
  AnyValue        string    `json:"AnyValue"`
}
```

In order to use this second asset type, the developer would need to create several similar methods like a **CreateSecondAsset**, let us use the following code to understand this better:

```
// CreateSecondAsset issues a new second asset to the world state
func (s *SmartContract) CreateSecondAsset(ctx contractapi.TransactionCon-
textInterface, id1, id2,  value string) error {
```

```
    exists, err := s.AssetExists(ctx, id1 + id2)
    if err != nil {
      return err
    }

    if exists {
      return fmt.Errorf("the asset %s already exists", id)
    }

    asset := Asset{
      IDPrimary: id1,
      IDSecondary: id2,
      AnyValue: value,
    }

    assetJSON, err := json.Marshal(asset)
    if err != nil {
      return err
    }

    return ctx.GetStub().PutState(id1+id2, assetJSON)
}
```

In this scenario, the introduction of the **CreateSecondAsset** transaction mirrors the **CreateAsset** transaction, albeit with distinct parameters representing the asset properties, including variations in the primary key that identifies the asset. This necessitates the creation of transactions for updating and deleting the state of the newly added asset definition. As the complexity and number of asset types in a chaincode increase, this approach becomes less efficient. Furthermore, all these transactions must be integrated into the corresponding application, such as an API, for end-user utilization.

For companies engaged in various Hyperledger Fabric projects with separate teams, it is imperative to establish standardized coding practices. If each team adopts its approach to program a Hyperledger Fabric chaincode, inconsistencies may arise. This lack of standardization can ultimately lead to significant challenges in maintaining the codebase.

CC-Tools provide a structured approach to project organization and implementation.

Let us take a look at how similar functionalities would be implemented by using CC-Tools. The examples below are taken from the **hyperledger-labs/cc-tools-demo** repository.

Declaring the structure of an asset now includes more details. Let us look at the following code:

```
var Person = assets.AssetType{
  Tag:          "person",
  Label:        "Person",
  Description: "Personal data of someone",
```

```
  Props: []assets.AssetProp{
    {
      // Primary key
      Required: true,
      IsKey:    true,
      Tag:      "id",
      Label:    "CPF (Brazilian ID)",
      DataType: "cpf",     // Datatypes are identified at datatypes folder
      Writers:  []string{`org1MSP`},
    },
    {
      // Mandatory property
      Required: true,
      Tag:      "name",
      Label:    "Name of the person",
      DataType: "string",
      // Validate funcion
      Validate: func(name interface{}) error {
        nameStr := name.(string)
        if nameStr == "" {
          return fmt.Errorf("name must be non-empty")
        }
        return nil
      },
    },
    {
      // Optional property
      Tag:      "dateOfBirth",
      Label:    "Date of Birth",
      DataType: "datetime",
    },
    {
      // Property with default value
      Tag:          "height",
      Label:        "Person's height",
      DefaultValue: 0,
      DataType:     "number",
    },
  },
}
```

Upon closer inspection, this format, with property definitions, is much more complete. It will define tags and labels for the asset and its properties, as well as description, allowing a developer to provide documentation in the code, which can be retrieved via a get schema transaction, allowing anyone that is interacting with the blockchain to check the format of the data and any descriptions.

Similar to the simple definition of asset-transfer-basic, the CC-Tools definition provides a field for data type but many functions can be. CC-Tools provide primary types such as string, boolean, number, and datetime, and each one will be validated automatically before a put state is performed. These values can be used as keys for the asset by using the IsKey field. CC-Tools take the values marked with true and assemble a unique key that will identify the asset with a deterministic **Universally Unique Identifier** (**UUID**) that depends on the content. This relieves the user of sending an ID value like the ones received in asset-transfer-basic.

Sometimes, a primary type will require some additional simple validation, such as a string length or a number greater than zero. For this, the validate property allows the developer to implement a simple validation that will be applied to the value and return an error if it is not satisfied. In the example above, this can be seen in the name property, which validates the string to be non-empty.

In addition, it is possible to add custom-coded data types with their validation. In the example above, the **`id`** property has a type **`cpf`**, which is the official Brazilian government-issued ID number. This will refer to a custom type, coded by the developer with the validation logic for this particular type.

The validation is as follows:

```
var cpf = assets.DataType{
  AcceptedFormats: []string{"string"},
  Parse: func(data interface{}) (string, interface{}, errors.ICCError) {
    cpf, ok := data.(string)
    if !ok {
      return "", nil, errors.NewCCError("property must be a string", 400)
    }

    cpf = strings.ReplaceAll(cpf, ".", "")
    cpf = strings.ReplaceAll(cpf, "-", "")

    if len(cpf) != 11 {
      return "", nil, errors.NewCCError("CPF must have 11 digits", 400)
    }

    var vd0 int
    for i, d := range cpf {
      if i >= 9 {
        break
```

```
      }
      dnum := int(d) - '0'
      vd0 += (10 - i) * dnum
    }
    vd0 = 11 - vd0%11
    if vd0 > 9 {
      vd0 = 0
    }
    if int(cpf[9])-'0' != vd0 {
      return "", nil, errors.NewCCError("Invalid CPF", 400)
    }

    var vd1 int
    for i, d := range cpf {
      if i >= 10 {
        break
      }
      dnum := int(d) - '0'
      vd1 += (11 - i) * dnum
    }
    vd1 = 11 - vd1%11
    if vd1 > 9 {
      vd1 = 0
    }
    if int(cpf[10])-'0' != vd1 {
      return "", nil, errors.NewCCError("Invalid CPF", 400)
    }

    return cpf, cpf, nil
  },
}
```

If the validation is performed without failure, the asset will be deemed valid.

The data type functionality enables developers to reference another arbitrary asset within a property, providing a valuable capability for building more complex interactions. This brings a relational component to the assets we create and powers much more complex applications with ease of use since CC takes care of all reference validation for the developer.

Additionally, a data type can be an enumeration with pre-defined types. Consider the following example:

```
const (
  BookTypeHardcover BookType = iota
```

```
  BookTypePaperback
  BookTypeEbook
)

// CheckType checks if the given value is defined as valid BookType consts
func (b BookType) CheckType() errors.ICCError {
   [...]
}

var bookType = assets.DataType{
  AcceptedFormats: []string{"number"},
  Parse: func(data interface{}) (string, interface{}, errors.ICCError) {
    var dataVal float64
    switch v := data.(type) {
    case float64:
      dataVal = v
    case int:
      dataVal = (float64)(v)
    case BookType:
      dataVal = (float64)(v)
    case string:
      var err error
      dataVal, err = strconv.ParseFloat(v, 64)
      if err != nil {
        return "", nil, errors.WrapErrorWithStatus(err, "asset property
must be an integer, is %t", 400)
      }
    default:
      return "", nil, errors.NewCCError("asset property must be an integer,
is %t", 400)
    }

    retVal := (BookType)(dataVal)
    err := retVal.CheckType()
    return fmt.Sprint(retVal), retVal, err
  },
}
```

Sometimes, the absence of a value means that a default value must be filled, for that, we can use the **DefaultValue** option which is being used in the **Height** property.

Finally, we can add permissions intrinsic to the asset by defining its writers. For that, each property can have a field such as **Writers: []string{`org1MSP`}**, which will determine which MSPs are allowed to write to that asset. This is granular, so your chaincode logic can account for permission where one organization can only write some properties of an asset. This is useful when you have an asset creation being done by one org and another org is responsible for updating a subset of properties of the asset.

Let us take a look at the difference in developing transactions. CC-Tools provide many functions that wrap up the **`PutState`** functionality to perform validation.

These functions are as follows:

- **Put:** It checks if org is the writer, injects metadata, validates references, and puts assets in blockchains.
- **PutNew:** It checks if the asset already exists, checks if org is the writer, injects metadata, validates references, and puts the asset in the blockchain.
- **PutRecursive:** It does the same as **`Put`** while also putting sub-assets recursively on the blockchain.
- **PutNewRecursive:** It does the same as **`PutNew`** while also putting sub-assets recursively on the blockchain.
- **Update:** It is similar to the same as **`Put`**, but it allows the user to pass only the fields to be updated instead of the whole asset.
- **UpdateRecursive:** It does the same as **`PutRecursive`**, but it allows the user to pass only the fields to be updated instead of the whole asset.

We can see the following example of a simple create a transaction for an asset called **`Library`**:

```
var CreateNewLibrary = tx.Transaction{
  Tag:         "createNewLibrary",
  Label:       "Create New Library",
  Description: "Create a New Library",
  Method:      "POST",
  Callers:     []string{"$org3MSP"}, // Only org3 can call this transaction

  Args: []tx.Argument{
    {
      Tag:         "name",
      Label:       "Name",
      Description: "Name of the library",
      DataType:    "string",
      Required:    true,
    },
  },
  Routine: func(stub *sw.StubWrapper, req map[string]interface{}) ([]byte,
```

```
errors.ICCError) {
    name, _ := req["name"].(string)

    libraryMap := make(map[string]interface{})
    libraryMap["@assetType"] = "library"
    libraryMap["name"] = name

    libraryAsset, err := assets.NewAsset(libraryMap)
    if err != nil {
      return nil, errors.WrapError(err, "Failed to create a new asset")
    }

    // Save the new library on channel
    _, err = libraryAsset.PutNew(stub)
    if err != nil {
      return nil, errors.WrapError(err, "Error saving asset on blockchain")
    }

    // Marshal asset back to JSON format
    libraryJSON, nerr := json.Marshal(libraryAsset)
    if nerr != nil {
      return nil, errors.WrapError(nil, "failed to encode asset to JSON
format")
    }

    // Marshall message to be logged
    logMsg, ok := json.Marshal(fmt.Sprintf("New library name: %s", name))
    if ok != nil {
      return nil, errors.WrapError(nil, "failed to encode asset to JSON
format")
    }

    // Call event to log the message
    events.CallEvent(stub, "createLibraryLog", logMsg)

    return libraryJSON, nil
  },
}
```

There are many elements to this example, and we will see it in more detail later. Like the asset definition, a transaction will also have a definition with a tag, label, and description. The arguments are very much like the ones defined in the asset, each with its data type, primary or customized, a tag or a label. In the routine field, we define the function that will be executed when the transaction is called. In this example, we take the argument, assemble an asset, and use PutNew to put it in the blockchain before returning the JSON we put to the caller.

Like the writers of an asset, a transaction has its callers, which will limit which organizations can call a given transaction.

Conclusion

In this chapter, we have introduced the CC-Tools library and its role in chaincode development. You started by exploring the historical context of CC-Tools, which provided essential insights into the principles that shape its features. This foundation helped you comprehend the challenges developers face in chaincode development and how CC-Tools effectively addresses them.

You have also seen a compelling case for using CC-Tools in production-level development, demonstrating its potential to accelerate application delivery to end users. A comprehensive overview of the library's features was provided, ensuring you now have a complete understanding of the various development opportunities it offers.

Finally, by comparing CC-Tools to the standard chaincode development experience, such as the asset-transfer-basic chaincode, you've identified the distinct advantages of employing CC-Tools. With this knowledge, you can now fully appreciate the instrumental role CC-Tools plays in the Fabric development journey, particularly in production-level projects.

In the next chapter, we will explore in detail functionalities of CC-Tools that help developers implement assets, transactions, and custom data types.

Join our book's Discord space

Join the book's Discord Workspace for Latest updates, Offers, Tech happenings around the world, New Release and Sessions with the Authors:

https://discord.bpbonline.com

CHAPTER 8
Asset, Data Types, and Transactions

Introduction

Now that you have a solid understanding of what CC-Tools provide, this chapter explores the practical aspects of creating and managing assets, data types, and transactions using CC-Tools within the Hyperledger Fabric ecosystem. Our journey begins with a discussion into the fundamental components of assets, exploring their properties and how they can be customized to meet specific requirements. We also examine embedded data types, uncovering their role in asset creation, and learn how the asset list facilitates efficient asset management.

Custom data types, such as enumerations and objects, take center stage as we explore their usage in defining complex asset structures. Additionally, we tackle the essential CRUD transactions, covering how to create, read, update, and delete assets, along with methods for searching and reading asset history.

In addition to asset management, our exploration in this chapter extends to the critical field of transactions. Transactions form the backbone of any blockchain-based system, enabling the manipulation and exchange of assets. Furthermore, we equip you with the skills to efficiently search for specific assets using the CC-Tools library. Beyond these foundational transactional operations, we also cover the vital aspect of reading asset history, a crucial capability for auditing, compliance, and maintaining a transparent and trustworthy blockchain network.

This chapter is more than just technical details. We underscore the significance of standardization in the development process and the importance of careful data mapping. Flexibility in Hyperledger Fabric chaincode development can lead to non-homogeneous code and hinder team productivity. CC-Tools not only provides a set of chaincode functions but also establishes a standard approach to registering assets, data types, and transactions, ensuring a balanced and productive development process, regardless of project complexity.

As we progress through this chapter, you will gain the knowledge and tools needed to excel in asset management and blockchain development using CC-Tools on Hyperledger Fabric.

Structure

The chapter covers the following topics:

- Anatomy of an asset
- Advanced data types in CC-Tools library
- CRUD transactions
- Extra transactions

Objectives

By the end of this chapter, readers will gain a comprehensive understanding of the details of assets, data type, and transaction definitions along with the key components that play pivotal roles in the architectural process. From deciphering the coding scheme to navigating the directory structure, we will provide you with a wealth of insights into the initial stages of data mapping and transaction management.

This chapter is organized into three distinct parts: assets, data types, and built-in transactions, each accompanied by numerous illustrative examples designed to enhance your grasp of the subject matter. By the conclusion of this chapter, you will have the proficiency to create your very first chaincode using CC-Tools. Readers will gain an understanding of how the development of Hyperledger Fabric smart contracts becomes more accessible through the utilization of this library's capabilities. Prepare to gain knowledge about what demystifies the complexities of blockchain development and empowers you to craft efficient and robust solutions with ease.

Anatomy of an asset

In the context of Hyperledger Fabric, an asset is characterized by a key-value pair, with both components being flexible in terms of format. As demonstrated in the book's *Chapter 6, Deploying Your First Chaincode*, the structure of an asset is exemplified. The asset value is typically a Go struct, which is then marshaled into a JSON format for use, and the asset key, in this example represented as **CAR0**, is received as an input parameter. This design allows for significant versatility in how assets are defined and utilized within the Hyperledger Fabric framework, but it expects users to have a thorough understanding of the underlying data structures and the ability to effectively marshal and unmarshal these structures as needed.

The introduction of CC-Tools further refines this process. By using CC-Tools, the format of asset definitions becomes more uniform and predictable. This standardization is particularly beneficial when managing a larger number of assets, especially those of increased complexity. It simplifies the declaration process, making it easier to work with and manage these assets effectively in more demanding and diverse scenarios. This approach ultimately enhances the efficiency and scalability of asset management within the Hyperledger Fabric ecosystem.

Asset properties

Let us go back to an example introduced in *Chapter 7, Introduction to CC-Tools Library*, of an implementation provided by the repository found in GitHub, under **https://github.com/hyperledger-labs/cc-tools-demo**. When exploring the project, assets will be found under the **assettypes** folder in separate files. For example, the **person.go** file will have the following asset definition:

```
var Person = assets.AssetType{
  Tag:          "person",
  Label:        "Person",
  Description: "Personal data of someone",

  Props: []assets.AssetProp{
    {
      // Primary key
      Required: true,
      IsKey:    true,
      Tag:      "id",
      Label:    "CPF (Brazilian ID)",
      DataType: "cpf",     // Datatypes are identified at datatypes folder
      Writers:  []string{`org1MSP`},
    },
    {
      // Mandatory property
      Required: true,
      Tag:      "name",
      Label:    "Name of the person",
      DataType: "string",
```

```
      // Validate function
      Validate: func(name interface{}) error {
        nameStr := name.(string)
        if nameStr == "" {
          return fmt.Errorf("name must be non-empty")
        }
        return nil
      },
    },
    {
      // Optional property
      Tag:      "dateOfBirth",
      Label:    "Date of Birth",
      DataType: "datetime",
    },
    {
      // Property with default value
      Tag:          "height",
      Label:        "Person's height",
      DefaultValue: 0,
      DataType:     "number",
    },
  },
}
```

This definition uses a CC-Tools package imported from **github.com/hyperledger-labs/cc-tools/assets**. There, the **`AssetType`** type will be defined with many properties and functions associated with it. The main properties that must be filled are as follows:

- **Tag**: This is the name of the asset type. This property will be used to identify the asset type along with the CC-Tools methods.
- **Label**: This is a simple label for the asset type.
- **Description**: This contains a more detailed description of the asset type.

The **`Tag`** property is the most important information about the asset type, as this information will be referenced throughout the chaincode development process. It works as an identifier for the asset type.

`Label` and **`Description`** are used only as metadata about the asset, this can be important while assembling the data to be shown to the end user.

The properties of the assets are defined by setting the **`Prop`** field to a list of **`AssetProp`**, which will have the details of each asset property. This is similar in concept to the definition of columns in a database table.

Properties have the following possible configurations:

- **Tag**: This is a unique identification of the property in the scope of the asset type.
- **Label**: This is a simple label for the asset type property.
- **Description**: a more detailed description of the asset type property.
- **IsKey**: It is a flag to define if the property is part of the asset key construction.
- **Required**: It is a flag to define if the property is mandatory. If absent, the value is considered false.
- **DataType**: It is the data type of the property which can be a primary data type, a custom data type, or a reference to another asset.

These fields cover more than 80% of the customization a property needs which is mainly deciding whether the field is a key or not, is required or not and the type of data to be registered. However, CC-Tools provides us with even more customization options. The full list can be found under the struct definition for **`AssetProp`** in file **`assets/assetProp.go`**.

The additional configurations are as follows:

- **ReadOnly**: When this property is true, it will only allow the property to be written during asset creation. If the asset already exists, the property cannot be changed.
- **DefaultValue**: This allows the developer to define a value that will be filled in case the asset is created without any value. It is useful when there is a default state for an asset when created.
- **Writers**: This defines a list in a particular syntax which will define what organizations and certificate types are allowed to write on that property. Using this functionality, the developer can create an asset in which property X can only be altered by organization A and property B can only be altered by organization B.
- **Validate:** This takes a function that can perform any custom validation the user wants to whenever an asset object is created during runtime. This provides consistency amongst every registration of the asset regardless of which transaction was responsible for writing it.

Each tag defined for the asset properties will serve as a key in the JSON marshaled when putting a state and will consequently be the key to be used when accessing each value of the asset, which will be treated by CC-Tool as a **`map[string]interface{}`** with additional functionality.

For example, the **`Person`** asset shown above will be assembled in a JSON like the one illustrated as follows:

```
{
  "@assetType": "person",
  "@key": "person:6ddf6d82-6a89-5c31-90c4-168abf86f44a",
  "@lastTouchBy": "orgMSP",
  "@lastTx": "createAsset",
  "@lastUpdated": "2023-12-23T15:53:28Z",
  "dateOfBirth": "2023-11-01T03:00:00Z",
  "height": 120,
  "id": "75576998073",
  "name": "John"
}
```

In the Hyperledger Fabric framework, when defining an asset, the properties set by the developer are translated into keys and values within a JSON structure. CC-Tools, an additional tool in this environment, automatically incorporates various metadata elements into each asset. Among these, the two most crucial metadata are **`@assetType`** and **`@key`**.

The **`@assetType`** metadata is essential for encoding the specific asset definition that should be applied when interacting with the given key. It plays an important role in ensuring the correct asset type is utilized during various operations within the blockchain network.

The **`@key`** metadata, on the other hand, serves as the primary identifier of the asset within the blockchain. It is constructed based on the properties marked as **`IsKey: true`** by the developer. This metadata uniquely distinguishes each asset, allowing for precise identification and handling within the blockchain system. The format of the **`@key`** metadata follows a specific rule set, which governs its structure and representation, ensuring consistency and clarity in asset identification across the network, as follows:

```
@key = asset type tag + ":" + UUID(list of key properties)
```

The complete algorithm can be found under **`assets/generateKey.go`** into the **`hyperledger-labs/cc-tools`** repository.

Let us turn our attention to the other metadata registered with the asset; some are mentioned as follows:

- **"@lastTouchBy":** This is the MSP identifier of the client that changed the asset state most recently.
- **"@lastTx":** It is the name of the last transaction that created or changed the asset.
- **"@lastUpdated":** It is the timestamp of the transaction proposal signed by the client that changed the asset state most recently.

Built-in data types

One of the most essential pieces of information for asset definition is the type of data that will go into each property. The data type definition is used to validate the property whenever an asset object is created, thus guaranteeing that the blockchain will always have consistency according to business rules.

When developing blockchain applications, it is important to maintain consistency and coherence for the data that will be registered and changed over time. However, when using the **PutState** method, the asset format and behavior can change without notice, leading to unexpected results. For example, it is possible to save an asset with text properties, as follows:

```
asset := map[string]interface{}{"info": "this is a string"}
assetJSON, _ := json.Marshal(asset)
ctx.GetStub().PutState("asset1", assetJSON)
```

You can change the property type for a number by changing the object, as follows:

```
asset := map[string]interface{}{"info": 1000.0}
assetJSON, _ := json.Marshal(asset)
ctx.GetStub().PutState("asset1", assetJSON)
```

CC-Tools internal methods always validate the property data types. If a transaction attempts to register or modify this property with a data type that does not match, like using a number instead of a string, CC-Tools will promptly return an error. This mechanism of data type verification, although straightforward, plays a critical role in maintaining data consistency within the blockchain channel. It acts as an effective guardrail, ensuring that the data stored in the blockchain remains reliable and conforms to pre-defined structures. This validation process contributes significantly to the overall integrity and orderliness of the data managed within the Hyperledger Fabric ecosystem.

In our previous example for the **Person** asset, the property **height** has a data type number, as shown in the following code:

```
{
    // Property with default value
    Tag:          "height",
    Label:        "Person's height",
    DefaultValue: 0,
    DataType:     "number",
},
```

This makes every single method deal with the person's asset to validate whether the information is a number, otherwise, the transaction will fail.

CC-Tools provides many built-in data types, some are mentioned as follows:

- **boolean:** This is a binary property with values that can be true or false.
- **number**: This is a numeric property that represents a floating-point value.
- **string**: This is a property that represents plain text.

- **datetime**: This is a property that represents a time. Time Go type, formatted in RFC3339.
- []**boolean**: This is a property that represents an array of boolean values.
- []**number**: This is a property that represents an array of floating-point numbers.
- []**string**: This is a property that represents an array of plain text strings.
- []**datetime**: This is a property that represents an array of time values in RFC3339 format.

Also, built-in into the library is the ability to create new data types and reference other asset instances in a property.

Asset list

Each asset that we want to use inside a chaincode should be defined, according to the CC-Tools Demo project organization standard, inside the **`chaincode/assettypes`** directory in separate files, as follows:

```
chaincode/assettypes
├── book.go
├── library.go
├── person.go
└── secret.go
```

The CC-Tools library that is imported must be informed about each definition that was created by the developer. This is done in the file **`assetTypeList.go`**, found under the **`chaincode`** directory in the **`hyperledger-labs/cc-tools-demo`**. This file will provide a way to inform a list of assets known to the library which will then be used to reference each definition. Refer to the following code for a better understanding:

```
var assetTypeList = []assets.AssetType{
	assettypes.Person,
	assettypes.Book,
	assettypes.Library,
	assettypes.Secret,
}
```

When the chaincode is first started by a peer, CC-Tools will execute a startup check to ensure that the data types and asset references are consistent with what has been declared, thus preventing an inconsistent chaincode from being instantiated. For example, if a property is declared with a non-existent data type such as **double**, the CC-Tools startup check will issue an error during chaincode commit.

Advanced data types in CC-Tools library

CC-Tools defines its own primitive data types by defining a parsing function and the accepted formats of input. This characteristic allows the developer to extend the definition of data types in CC-Tools. Let us see how CC-Tools defines a string data type in the following example:

In the file **assets/dataType.go** of the **hyperledger-labs/cc-tools** repository, we can find the definition of the primitive data types that the library offers, as follows:

```
// dataTypeMap contains the "standard" primitive data types
var dataTypeMap = map[string]*DataType{
	"string": {
		AcceptedFormats: []string{"string"},
		Parse: func(data interface{}) (string, interface{}, errors.
ICCError){
			parsedData, ok := data.(string)
			if !ok {
				return parsedData, nil, errors.
NewCCError("property must be a string", 400)
			}
			return parsedData, parsedData, nil
		},
	},
	...
}
```

For an input to be considered a string, whatever the input received must be type assertable to the string type. After parsing, the function returns the value in a fixed string format and as its actual type, in this case, string. This will become clearer with the **datatime** type, as follows:

```
	"datetime": {
		AcceptedFormats: []string{"string"},
		Parse: func(data interface{}) (string, interface{}, errors.
ICCError){
			dataTime, ok := data.(time.Time)
			if !ok {
				dataVal, ok := data.(string)
				if !ok {
					return "", nil, errors.NewCCError("asset
property must be a RFC3339 string", 400)
				}
				var err error
				dataTime, err = time.Parse(time.RFC3339, dataVal)
				if err != nil {
```

```
                                return "", nil, errors.
WrapErrorWithStatus(err, "invalid asset property RFC3339 format", 400)
                        }
                }

                return dataTime.Format(time.RFC3339), dataTime, nil
        },
}
```

Note that the function accepts a string for the **datetime** data type, this is because JSON format is used when sending a request payload, and in JSON, there are no standard date or time formats. However, a string or integer representation of a date and time can be used. CC-Tools by default will accept a string representation formatted in the RFC3339 standard, such as **1985-04-12T23:20:50.52Z**. The **AcceptedFormat** field is only metadata that will inform the user of the chaincode what kind of data is expected, data type enforcement is completely done by the **Parse** function.

The **Parse** function in this example handles quite more situations than the previous string example. Let us explain step-by-step as this process might be insightful when creating custom data types.

The first verification that is done is checking whether the interface received is of type **time.Time**. This is done because the parsing function is not only called when a transaction is received but also whenever the developer creates an asset object with the **assets.NewAsset** function. In order to allow the developer to send the default type for dealing with time in Go, that is **time.Time**, the parse function will expect it to handle it accordingly. If the type of assertion fails, the parse function falls back to assuming it is receiving a string. The string is then parsed to confirm that it is indeed a datetime representation. This is then returned in string format and in its **time.Time** format. Not coincidentally, the standard JSON library in Go marshals **time.Time** into a string in RFC3339 format.

Custom data types

The developer can extend data type for a particular chaincode as much as they need to. For that, new data types can be created in the **datatypes** directory and then listed as a **CustomDataTypes** in **datatypes/datatypes.go** which is found in **hyperledger-labs/cc-tools-demo.**

The flexibility allows for simple new data types that will validate a string formatting, such as email, phone, or a national id, but it also allows for the creation of enumeration types. Let us check both examples as follows:

The Brazilian National ID, called **CPF**, is used as an example in the repository.

```
var cpf = assets.DataType{
        AcceptedFormats: []string{"string"},
        Parse: func(data interface{}) (string, interface{}, errors.ICCError)
```

```
{
        cpf, ok := data.(string)
        if !ok {
                return "", nil, errors.NewCCError("property must be a
string", 400)
        }

        cpf = strings.ReplaceAll(cpf, ".", "")
        cpf = strings.ReplaceAll(cpf, "-", "")

        if len(cpf) != 11 {
                return "", nil, errors.NewCCError("CPF must have 11
digits", 400)
        }

        var vd0 int
        for i, d := range cpf {
                if i >= 9 {
                        break
                }
                dnum := int(d) - '0'
                vd0 += (10 - i) * dnum
        }
        vd0 = 11 - vd0%11
        if vd0 > 9 {
                vd0 = 0
        }
        if int(cpf[9])-'0' != vd0 {
                return "", nil, errors.NewCCError("Invalid CPF", 400)
        }

        var vd1 int
        for i, d := range cpf {
                if i >= 10 {
                        break
                }
                dnum := int(d) - '0'
                vd1 += (11 - i) * dnum
        }
        vd1 = 11 - vd1%11
        if vd1 > 9 {
                vd1 = 0
        }
        if int(cpf[10])-'0' != vd1 {
                return "", nil, errors.NewCCError("Invalid CPF", 400)
        }

        return cpf, cpf, nil
```

```
	},
}
```

The code above parses the ID number according to the official rules for ID formation. This data type is then added to the custom data type list, so it can be used in asset declaration, which you can see in the **Person** asset shown at the beginning of the chapter.

The following structure can be found in the **datatypes.go** file:

```
// CustomDataTypes contain the user-defined primary data types
var CustomDataTypes = map[string]assets.DataType{
	"cpf":      cpf,
	"bookType": bookType,
}
```

Enum data types

Additionally, it is possible to define enumeration data types in a way that can be leveraged inside custom transactions. Let us take a look at the following example defining book type and its options: hardcover, paperback, or e-book:

```
// Example of a custom data type using enum-like structure (iota)
// This allows the use of verification by const values instead of float64,
improving readability
// Example:
//		if assetMap["bookType"].(float64) == (float64)
(BookTypeHardcover)
//			...

type BookType float64

const (
	BookTypeHardcover BookType = iota
	BookTypePaperback
	BookTypeEbook
)

// CheckType checks if the given value is defined as valid BookType consts
func (b BookType) CheckType() errors.ICCError {
	switch b {
	case BookTypeHardcover:
		return nil
	case BookTypePaperback:
		return nil
	case BookTypeEbook:
		return nil
```

```
	default:
		return errors.NewCCError("invalid type", 400)
	}

}
```

In the code above, an enumeration was defined for the custom data type that is being created. This will serve as the discreet values that the data type will be allowed to have.

In the following, we continue with the definition of the data types and its **`Parse`** function:

```
var bookType = assets.DataType{
	AcceptedFormats: []string{"number"},
	DropDownValues: map[string]interface{}{
		"Hardcover": BookTypeHardcover,
		"Paperback": BookTypePaperback,
		"Ebook":     BookTypeEbook,
	},
	Description: ``,

	Parse: func(data interface{}) (string, interface{}, errors.ICCError)
{
		var dataVal float64
		switch v := data.(type) {
		case float64:
			dataVal = v
		case int:
			dataVal = (float64)(v)
		case BookType:
			dataVal = (float64)(v)
		case string:
			var err error
			dataVal, err = strconv.ParseFloat(v, 64)
			if err != nil {
				return "", nil, errors.WrapErrorWithStatus(err,
"asset property must be an integer, is %t", 400)
			}
		default:
			return "", nil, errors.NewCCError("asset property must
be an integer, is %t", 400)
		}

		retVal := (BookType)(dataVal)
```

```
            err := retVal.CheckType()
            return fmt.Sprint(retVal), retVal, err
        },
}
```

We start defining a custom Go type **BookType** with an underlying type of **float64**, specifically designed to represent various book formats in a clear, type-safe manner. This type serves as the foundation for defining constants **BookTypeHardcover**, **BookTypePaperback**, and **BookTypeEbook**, utilizing Go's **iota** for clean, sequential numeric assignment. The elegance of this approach lies in its simplicity and clarity, allowing for easy expansion or modification in the future. The **CheckType** method attached to **BookType** plays a critical role, ensuring that any book's type is within the pre-defined range, thereby, maintaining data integrity and enforcing valid categorizations. This method leverages custom error handling for robustness, a common practice in Go for ensuring program stability and reliability. The **bookType** variable is an **assets.DataType** provides a template for parsing and validating book types. The Parse function will expect multiple types to allow for flexible use by the developer: **string**, **int**, **float64**, and **BookType**.

Object data types

In some situations, a property of a given asset can be an object in its own format. Sometimes that justifies the creation of a separate asset type that will be referenced inside another asset. Other times, it suffices to have the object defined in the asset itself and validated according to a particular format. CC-Tools allows both to be done easily by the developer. Let us explore both.

Referencing an asset is as straightforward as defining the data type of any property with the following syntax: **assetTypeTag**. Let us check with an example, the **Book** asset type found in **assettypes/book.go** inside the **chaincode** directory in **hyperledger-labs/cc-tools-demo**:

```
var Book = assets.AssetType{
        Tag:          "book",
        Label:        "Book",
        Description: "Book",
        Props: []assets.AssetProp{
                {
                        // Composite Key
                        Required: true,
                        IsKey:    true,
                        Tag:      "title",
                        Label:    "Book Title",
                        DataType: "string",
                        Writers:  []string{`org2MSP`, "orgMSP"},
```

```
            },
            {
                    // Composite Key
                    Required: true,
                    IsKey:    true,
                    Tag:      "author",
                    Label:    "Book Author",
                    DataType: "string",
                    Writers:  []string{`org2MSP`, "orgMSP"},
            },
            {
                    /// Reference to another asset
                    Tag:      "currentTenant",
                    Label:    "Current Tenant",
                    DataType: "->person",
            },
            {
                    // String list
                    Tag:      "genres",
                    Label:    "Genres",
                    DataType: "[]string",
            },
            {
                    // Date property
                    Tag:      "published",
                    Label:    "Publishment Date",
                    DataType: "datetime",
            },
            {
                    // Custom data type
                    Tag:      "bookType",
                    Label:    "Book Type",
                    DataType: "bookType",
            },
        },
}
```

The **currentTenant** property will register who is the person who currently holds a book in a library. Since, we have registrations of people under the **Person** asset, with the reference syntax we can easily point one asset to another existing asset. CC-Tools will perform any validation needed to ensure the reference format is done correctly and that the asset exists. When registered in the blockchain, CC-Tools will register references as follows:

```
{
    "@assetType": "book",
    "@key": "book:...",
    "currentTenant": {
        "@assetType": "person",
        "@key": "person:..."
    }
    ...
}
```

In the upcoming chapters, when exploring transaction calling and custom transactions, it will become clearer how to deal with the asset object in code.

When a separate asset is not an interesting decision during asset mapping, the developer can have a property and be an arbitrary object with the **@object** data type. CC-Tools will treat the object as it is, without making any validation to it, which might be ideal in some specific settings.

However, most of the time, developers will aim for a well-defined property, and a custom data type will serve well for this definition. Just like an ID or book type, we can define a data type that will be an object (for example, **map[string]interface{}**) and that will have a certain rule for parsing.

A data type that is a generic object is defined as follows

```
var customObject = assets.DataType{
       AcceptedFormats: []string{"@object"},
       Parse: func(data interface{}) (string, interface{}, errors.ICCError)
{
              // Validation of data as an object can be done here
              // The returned interface{} must be a map[string]interface{}
with @assetType == @object
              returnedProp["@assetType"] = "@object"
              return fmt.Sprint(returnedProp), returnedObject, nil
       }
}
```

The only restriction is that the returned parsed property must have a key **@assetType** set to **@object** so the CC-Tools can deal with the object properly and not be confused with whether it should be a reference or just an object.

CRUD transactions

Now that we have learned how to define the assets that will be registered by a chaincode transaction, we need a way to work with them. CC-Tools implements a set of standard transactions here referred to as CRUD transactions, which are created, read, updated, and deleted. Whatever the asset is created by a developer, this set of transactions will be available. We will also explore two other extra, but essential, transactions: search and read asset history.

Although all these transactions are implemented, exploring their implementation and explaining them will allow us to explore features of the library that are essential for custom transaction implementation.

Create asset

The create asset transaction is a transaction that will take one or more assets, regardless of their asset type, and register them as a new asset in the blockchain. Consider the following implementation, available in the **hyperledger-labs/cc-tools** repository in the path **transactions/createAsset.go**:

```
var CreateAsset = Transaction{
	Tag:         "createAsset",
	Label:       "Create Asset",
	Description: "",
	Method:      "POST",

	MetaTx: true,
	Args: ArgList{
		{
			Tag:         "asset",
			Description: "List of assets to be created.",
			DataType:    "[]@asset",
			Required:    true,
		},
	},
	Routine: func(stub *sw.StubWrapper, req map[string]interface{}) ([]
byte, errors.ICCError) {
		// This is safe to do because validation is done before
calling routine
		assetList := req["asset"].([]interface{})

		responses := []map[string]interface{}{}
		for _, assetInterface := range assetList {
			// This is safe to do because validation is done before
calling routine
			asset := assetInterface.(assets.Asset)

			// Marshal asset back to JSON format
			res, err := asset.PutNew(stub)
```

```
                if err != nil {
                        return nil, errors.WrapError(err, "failed to
write asset to ledger")
                }

                responses = append(responses, res)
            }

            resBytes, err := json.Marshal(responses)
            if err != nil {
                return nil, errors.WrapError(err, "failed to marshal
response")
            }

            return resBytes, nil
        },
}
```

The transaction definition is made by creating a variable that will be of the type **Transaction**, which is a custom type defined by CC-Tools. Much like the **AssetType** that was used to structure asset definitions, the **Transaction** type will allow us to give it a name, description, list of arguments, and a routine. The complete definition of the type can be seen in the **hyperledger-labs/cc-tools** repository in the path **transactions/transaction.go**.

For this particular transaction, the tag was defined as **createAsset** which encodes the string that will match this transaction when we call it from the **command-line interface** (**CLI**) or the **software development kit** (**SDK**).

In the **Args** field, CC-Tools expects a list of arguments, satisfied by the type **ArgList**. Each object described in this list will be an entry in the JSON sent in the request payload. In this case, our JSON will have one entry **asset** that will be composed of a list of objects representing assets. The **@asset** tag is a special datatype for transaction arguments that will validate the asset based on the **@assetType** informed.

For example, consider the following JSON as a payload:

```
{
    "asset": [
        {
            "@assetType": "person",
            "id": "75576998073",
            "name": "John Doe",
            "dateOfBirth": "2023-11-01T03:00:00Z"
```

```
        },
        {
            "@assetType": "company",
            "id": "01",
            "name": "Acme Inc."
        }
    ]
}
```

The first asset will be validated against the person asset definition and the second asset against the company asset definition.

These arguments are received in a **map[string]interface{}** in the **Routine** function. Each item in the argument list will become an entry in the map accessible by its tag. The first action of the routine is to access the **asset** entry and type assert it to a list that we can work with.

For each of the interfaces in the list, we type assert it to the correct underlying type and simply use the **PutNew** function which will put the asset in the ledger while verifying if there is a key conflict, in this case, it will return an error. The responses are appended together and then returned.

Read asset

The **readAsset** transaction is a transaction designed to retrieve the details of a specific asset from the blockchain. It queries the blockchain for an asset using its unique identifier, regardless of the asset type, and returns the current state and information of that asset. An example of this can be found in the **hyperledger-labs/cc-tools** repository under the path **transactions/readAsset.go**. This transaction is crucial for verifying asset details and ensuring transparency and accuracy in the blockchain ledger.

Following is a transaction's behavior:

```
var ReadAsset = Transaction{
      Tag:         "readAsset",
      Label:       "Read Asset",
      Description: "",
      Method:      "GET",

      MetaTx: true,
      Args: ArgList{
            {
                  Tag:         "key",
                  Description: "Key of the asset to be read.",
                  DataType:    "@key",
```

```
                Required:    true,
            },
            {
                Tag:         "resolve",
                Description: "Resolve references recursively.",
                DataType:    "boolean",
            },
        },
        ReadOnly: true,
        Routine: func(stub *sw.StubWrapper, req map[string]interface{}) ([]
byte, errors.ICCError) {
            var assetJSON []byte
            var err error

            // This is safe to do because validation is done before
calling routine
            key := req["key"].(assets.Key)

            resolve, ok := req["resolve"].(bool)

            if ok && resolve {
                var asset map[string]interface{}
                asset, err = key.GetRecursive(stub)
                if err != nil {
                    return nil, errors.WrapError(err, "failed to read
asset from blockchain")
                }

                assetJSON, err = json.Marshal(asset)
                if err != nil {
                    return nil, errors.WrapErrorWithStatus(err,
"failed to serialize asset", 500)
                }
            } else {
                assetJSON, err = key.GetBytes(stub)
                if err != nil {
                    return nil, errors.WrapError(err, "failed to get
asset state")
                }
            }

            return assetJSON, nil
        },
```

```
}
```

This transaction requires two arguments, similar to the create asset transaction. The key is received in the **@key** format which has been shown earlier in the chapter. The transaction also takes an argument that indicates if it should resolve any asset references, sending the value true will traverse the references and resolve each one recursively.

Note that once we get the key inside the routine function, an if statement verifies if the resolve is true or false. If true, we will use a special CC-Tools function called **GetRecursive** that will get the asset and any references inside it. If false, we will simply retrieve the asset bytes and return them.

Update asset

The **updateAsset** transaction is a transaction that allows for the modification of an existing asset's details on the blockchain. This transaction is used when there is a need to change or update the information associated with an asset, such as its owner, status, or other attributes while maintaining the integrity and history of the asset on the ledger. Similar to creating and reading transactions, this operation is a fundamental aspect of blockchain asset management. The implementation of this transaction is in the **hyperledger-labs/cc-tools** repository, specifically in the path **transactions/updateAsset.go**.

We can see the full implementation as follows:

```
var UpdateAsset = Transaction{
	Tag:         "updateAsset",
	Label:       "Update Asset",
	Description: "",
	Method:      "PUT",

	MetaTx: true,
	Args: ArgList{
		{
			Tag:         "update",
			Description: "Asset key and fields to be updated.",
			DataType:    "@update",
			Required:    true,
		},
	},
	Routine: func(stub *sw.StubWrapper, req map[string]interface{}) ([]byte,
errors.ICCError) {
		var err error
		request := req["update"].(map[string]interface{})
		key, _ := assets.NewKey(request)
```

```
		// Check if asset exists
		exists, err := key.ExistsInLedger(stub)
		if err != nil {
			return nil, errors.WrapError(err, "failed to check asset
existance in ledger")
		}
		if !exists {
			return nil, errors.NewCCError("asset does not exist", 404)
		}

		// Update asset
		response, err := key.Update(stub, request)
		if err != nil {
			return nil, errors.WrapError(err, "failed to update asset")
		}

		resBytes, err := json.Marshal(response)
		if err != nil {
			return nil, errors.WrapError(err, "failed to marshal
response")
		}

		return resBytes, nil
	},
}
```

CC-Tools has another metadata type, **@update**, which translates to an asset with only some of the fields filled. This allows a transaction caller to send only the fields that are supposed to be updated for a particular key without CC-Tools enforcing required properties since they might already be filled in the ledger.

The routine is straightforward and will send the fields to update as **map[string]interface{}** to the **Update** transaction.

Delete asset

The **deleteAsset** transaction is a transaction designed to remove an existing asset from the blockchain ledger. This operation is used when an asset needs to be permanently retired or is no longer relevant, ensuring that the blockchain reflects the current and accurate state of its asset registry. The **deleteAsset** transaction effectively nullifies the record of the asset, though the history of its existence and transactions remains intact in the blockchain for auditability and transparency. A specific example may be found in the **hyperledger-labs/cc-tools** repository under the path **transactions/deleteAsset.go**.

Refer to the following example for a better understanding:

```
var DeleteAsset = Transaction{
	Tag:         "deleteAsset",
	Label:       "Delete Asset",
	Method:      "DELETE",
	Description: "",

	MetaTx: true,
	Args: ArgList{
		{
			Tag:         "key",
			Description: "Key of the asset to be deleted.",
			DataType:    "@key",
			Required:    true,
		},
		{
			Tag:         "cascade",
			Description: "Delete all referrers on cascade",
			DataType:    "boolean",
		},
	},
	Routine: func(stub *sw.StubWrapper, req map[string]interface{}) ([]
byte, errors.ICCError) {
		// This is safe to do because validation is done before
calling routine
		key := req["key"].(assets.Key)
		cascade, ok := req["cascade"].(bool)
		if !ok {
			cascade = false
		}

		var err error
		var response []byte
		if cascade {
			response, err = key.DeleteCascade(stub)
			if err != nil {
				return nil, errors.WrapError(err, "failed to
delete asset recursively")
			}
		} else {
			response, err = key.Delete(stub)
			if err != nil {
```

```
                        return nil, errors.WrapError(err, "failed to
delete asset")
                    }
                }

                return response, nil
        },
}
```

This transaction receives the key to the asset that needs to be deleted and a flag to indicate whether cascade deletion should be done, that is, deleting the parent asset and all the assets referenced by it, recursively. The delete cascade is an experimental feature and may not work as intended.

The **Delete** function will check if the asset is referenced in other assets to ensure that all references remain valid. If it is, the user must update the properties that reference the asset before deleting it.

Extra transactions

CC-Tools has other transactions defined under its framework. Such transactions are very important for reading fetching blockchain's most current data and its history. Those transactions are Search and Read Asset History.

Search

The search transaction is designed to facilitate the querying and retrieval of assets from the blockchain's world state using a selector string. This transaction enables users to perform complex searches based on specific criteria, such as asset type, owner, date range, or any other relevant attribute defined within the asset's structure. The selector string acts as a query parameter that filters and identifies the desired assets from the entire ledger.

This functionality is crucial for efficient data retrieval efficiently, especially in scenarios where users need to access specific information without knowing the exact asset IDs. It enhances the usability of the blockchain by providing a flexible and powerful search mechanism.

In the **hyperledger-labs/cc-tools** repository, for example, you might find this transaction under a path like **transactions/search.go**. The search transaction significantly contributes to the blockchain's practicality, allowing for a more dynamic interaction with the ledger's data, as follows:

```
var Search = Transaction{
        Tag:          "search",
        Label:        "Search World State",
        Description:  "",
```

```
	Method:     "GET",

	MetaTx: true,
	Args: ArgList{
		{
			Tag:         "query",
			Description: "Query string according to CouchDB
specification: https://docs.couchdb.org/en/stable/api/database/find.html.",
			DataType:    "@query",
			Required:    true,
		},
		{
			Tag:         "collection",
			Description: "Name of the private collection to be
searched.",
			DataType:    "string",
		},
		{
			Tag:         "resolve",
			Description: "Resolve references recursively.",
			DataType:    "boolean",
		},
	},
	ReadOnly: true,
	Routine: func(stub *sw.StubWrapper, req map[string]interface{}) ([]
byte, errors.ICCError) {
		var err error

		query, _ := req["query"].(map[string]interface{})

		// Check if search is inside a private collection
		privateCollection, _ := req["collection"].(string)

		resolve, _ := req["resolve"].(bool)

		response, err := assets.Search(stub, query, privateCollection,
resolve)
		if err != nil {
			return nil, errors.WrapErrorWithStatus(err, "query
error", 500)
		}

		responseJSON, err := json.Marshal(response)
```

```
            if err != nil {
                  return nil, errors.WrapErrorWithStatus(err, "error
marshaling response", 500)
            }

            return responseJSON, nil
      },
}
```

For instance, when retrieving all **book** assets resolving references, the request payload JSON would be similar to the following code:

```
{
  "query": {
    "selector": {
      "@assetType": "book"
    }
  },
  "resolve": true
}
```

More information on how to assemble selectors can be found in the official CouchDB documentation, under the **Find** functionality page.

Read asset history

This is arguably one of the most important transactions in any blockchain application. Read asset history provides the ability to check all previous versions a particular key has had.

This transaction explores the blockchain's immutable ledger to retrieve the entire lifecycle of an asset with every update made to the key.

This ability to access a comprehensive history is fundamental to the value proposition of blockchain technology, emphasizing transparency, traceability, and auditability. It is especially crucial in applications requiring strict accountability and historical record-keeping, such as in supply chain management, financial services, and legal documentation.

Developers looking to understand this transaction can find the code in the **hyperledger-labs/cc-tools**, under the **transactions/readAssetHistory.go**. By providing a detailed view of an asset's history, this transaction ensures that users can fully leverage the blockchain's capabilities for maintaining an accurate and tamper-proof record of asset changes over time. We can see the full implementation that allows CC-Tools to fetch historic data for assets as follows:

```
var ReadAssetHistory = Transaction{
  Tag:          "readAssetHistory",
```

```
  Label:       "Read Asset History",
  Description: "",
  Method:      "GET",

  MetaTx: true,
  Args: ArgList{
    {
      Tag:         "key",
      Description: "Key of the asset to be read.",
      DataType:    "@key",
      Required:    true,
    },
    {
      Tag:         "timeTarget",
      Description: "Optional parameter to retrieve specific version of the
asset.",
      DataType:    "datetime",
    },
  },
  ReadOnly: true,
  Routine: func(stub *sw.StubWrapper, req map[string]interface{}) ([]byte,
errors.ICCError) {
    // This is safe to do because validation is done before calling routine
    key := req["key"].(assets.Key)
    timeTarget := req["timeTarget"]

    // Get asset's history from blockchain
    historyIterator, err := stub.GetHistoryForKey(key.Key())
    if err != nil {
      return nil, errors.WrapError(err, "failed to read asset from
blockchain")
    } ...
```

Upon this point, the transaction has fetched an iterator object that will allow us to iterate over each asset version that has been registered since the first block of the blockchain.

We continue by navigating the versions, as follows:

```
...
    if historyIterator == nil {
      return nil, errors.NewCCError("history not found", 404)
    }
    defer historyIterator.Close()
```

```
    if !historyIterator.HasNext() {
      return nil, errors.NewCCError("history not found", 404)
    }

    if timeTarget == nil {
      response := make([]map[string]interface{}, 0)
      for historyIterator.HasNext() {
        queryResponse, err := historyIterator.Next()
        if err != nil {
          return nil, errors.WrapError(err, "error iterating response")
        }

        data := make(map[string]interface{})

        if !queryResponse.IsDelete {
          err = json.Unmarshal(queryResponse.Value, &data)
          if err != nil {
            return nil, errors.WrapError(err, "failed to unmarshal
queryResponse's values")
          }
        }
        data["_txId"] = queryResponse.TxId
        data["_isDelete"] = queryResponse.IsDelete
        data["_timestamp"] = queryResponse.Timestamp.AsTime().Format(time.
RFC3339)
        response = append(response, data)
      }
      responseJSON, err := json.Marshal(response)
      if err != nil {
        return nil, errors.WrapError(err, "error marshaling response")
      }

      return responseJSON, nil
    }
...
```

Upon. The transaction utilizes the optional parameter **timeTarget** to filter asset versions from specific points in time.

You can see the implementation using **timeTarget**, as follows:

```
...
   else {
```

```
      target := timeTarget.(time.Time)

      // Check if time target is in the future
      if target.After(time.Now()) {
        return nil, errors.NewCCError("timeTarget must be in the past", 400)
      }
      closestTime := time.Time{}

      response := make(map[string]interface{})
      for historyIterator.HasNext() {
        queryResponse, err := historyIterator.Next()
        if err != nil {
          return nil, errors.WrapError(err, "error iterating response")
        }

        timestamp := queryResponse.Timestamp.AsTime()
        if timestamp.Before(target) && timestamp.After(closestTime) {
          closestTime = timestamp
          if !queryResponse.IsDelete {
            err = json.Unmarshal(queryResponse.Value, &response)
            if err != nil {
              return nil, errors.WrapError(err, "failed to unmarshal
queryResponse's values")
            }
          }
          response["_txId"] = queryResponse.TxId
          response["_isDelete"] = queryResponse.IsDelete
          response["_timestamp"] = timestamp.Format(time.RFC3339)
        }
      }

      responseJSON, err := json.Marshal(response)
      if err != nil {
        return nil, errors.WrapError(err, "error marshaling response")
      }

      return responseJSON, nil
    }
  },
}
```

Similar to the read asset transaction, we receive the key of the asset for which we want to query the history. Additionally, an optional parameter **`timeTarget`** can be sent and will retrieve the version in which the timestamp of the registry is closest.

A special function **GetHistoryForKey** is called and will return an iterator allowing the developer to resolve all versions into a return object or check the timestamp to get the version closest to the **timeTarget** parameter.

This function will return, for each asset version, three extra pieces of information identified by **_txId**, **_isDelete**, **_timestamp**, as follows:

- **_txId:** It is the ID of the transaction that changed or created the asset on that particular version.
- **_isDelete:** Indicates whether the specific version represents a change the deletes the asset.
- **_timestamp:** It is the date and time the transaction took place.

Conclusion

In this chapter, we explained the main concepts implemented by the library CC-Tools in depth. You have learned how to define assets in CC-Tools and what are the possibilities when choosing data types, validation functions, and more. You have also learned what data types exist in CC-Tools and the variations allowed, such as lists and references along with the fact that data types can be extended to support whatever use case you are developing. Additionally, we provided an in-depth explanation of the primary transactions facilitated by CC-Tools. While these are intrinsic to the library, understanding them is crucial as it lays the groundwork for the creation of custom transactions, a topic we will further explore in the subsequent sections of this book. This chapter has set a strong foundation, preparing you to explore the advanced functionalities and possibilities that CC-Tools offers.

In the next chapter, we will explore how these concepts come together to create reliable custom data workflows in smart contracts, ensuring seamless execution and robust chaincode development using CC-Tools.

Join our book's Discord space

Join the book's Discord Workspace for Latest updates, Offers, Tech happenings around the world, New Release and Sessions with the Authors:

https://discord.bpbonline.com

CHAPTER 9
Custom Transactions

Introduction

This chapter explores the significant benefits of the creation of precise data workflows in smart contracts, ensuring their consistent execution regardless of external circumstances. These workflows are built on several foundational concepts previously discussed, including assets, data types, validation processes, and rules governing data registration on the blockchain ledger. CC-Tools, a robust framework, facilitate the construction of these components, essential for good chaincode development.

A key aspect of blockchain use cases is its need for customization, which is necessary for addressing the specific requirements of various blockchain applications. This chapter will provide an in-depth exploration of custom transaction development using the capabilities of CC-Tools. It builds on the knowledge acquired in *Chapter 8, Asset, Data Types, and Transactions*, focusing on the built-in functions of CC-Tools.

We will specifically examine how custom transactions empower developers to tailor blockchain applications to meet diverse needs. This includes but is not limited to, the implementation of tokens adhering to the ERC-20 standard and the creation of unique assets like carbon credits, which must comply with specific regulations. The potential applications of these transactions are extensive, offering considerable flexibility in blockchain development.

Custom CC-Tools transactions can take advantage of many resources native to the library, such as argument definition for transactions, access control for transaction callers, specific functions for writing and reading into the blockchain, and built-in type validation.

Finally, this chapter will present transactions as any series of operations that deterministically interact with the blockchain ledger, either by writing to or reading from it. This broader understanding of transactions opens new possibilities for innovation and customization in blockchain technology and examples will guide us in that understanding.

Structure

The chapter covers the following topics:

- Importance of custom transactions
- Anatomy of transaction
- Arguments
- Write functions
- Read functions
- Transaction testing

Objectives

By the end of this chapter, readers will gain an understanding of how to use CC-Tools for creating transactions suitable for various blockchain applications. These sections will examine the importance of custom transactions and the anatomy of a transaction, detailing how CC-Tools organizes transaction definitions. We will uncover the essential elements shared by the routines they encompass, providing the knowledge to handle and define arguments within each routine effectively, thus giving you control over how they are used.

A key focus of this chapter is on exploring CC-Tools' functions for working with the ledger. You will understand their features and differences, whether you want to get information from the ledger, add new data to it, or perform both actions. The section on write functions, including **`Put`**, **`Update`**, and **`Delete`**, will equip you with the skills to use these functions effectively. Following this, the exploration of read functions like **`Get`**, **`Search`**, and **`History`** will ensure you are knowledgeable in retrieving and analyzing ledger data. Additionally, practical insights into using both write and read functions will be covered, helping you integrate them into your blockchain projects.

Transaction testing is another critical aspect addressed, with comprehensive guidance on both offline and online testing methods. By the end of this chapter, you will be prepared to navigate the world of blockchain using CC-Tools transactions with confidence, equipped with the skills to optimize functionality and ensure robustness in your blockchain applications.

Importance of custom transactions

Blockchain technology, be it public or permissioned, highly benefits from custom-programmed transactions. Smart contracts were a huge step for the technology and have unlocked new possibilities, allowing the blockchain registration logic to be programmed. Now, they are essential tools that enable businesses and developers to customize blockchain functionality to meet their specific needs. This level of customization is important for blockchain applications to effectively address unique requirements, including data handling, business rules, and industry-specific processes.

One of the key benefits of custom transactions is their ability to give organizations ways to implement data privacy and security measures. In a digital landscape, the ability to design transactions that conform to specific security protocols is invaluable. By doing so, businesses can protect sensitive information, bringing trust among participants in the blockchain network. In Hyperledger Fabric, we will be able to use private data collections to achieve these characteristics.

Beyond security, custom transactions play a significant role in streamlining complex business processes. They have the capability to automate tasks, thereby reducing the need for manual intervention. This automation not only leads to improved operational efficiency but also results in cost savings and faster transaction processing times.

Another critical aspect of custom transactions is their contribution to interoperability within the blockchain ecosystem. These transactions allow organizations to define clear terms of engagement within a blockchain network. This flexibility is key to enabling different stakeholders to collaborate effectively while ensuring that the integrity of each participant's data and operations is maintained.

In the field of regulatory compliance, custom transactions offer an efficient solution for businesses that operate within legal frameworks. By embedding compliance-related logic directly into blockchain applications, organizations can ensure they adhere to necessary legal requirements. This integration simplifies audit processes and helps maintain regulatory compliance, a crucial factor for many industries.

The ability to create custom transactions is a driver of innovation within the blockchain space. It allows businesses to experiment with new approaches and solutions, adapting to changing market conditions. This capability not only gives organizations a competitive edge but also opens doors to exploring novel opportunities within the blockchain ecosystem. In conclusion, custom transactions are not just a feature of blockchain technology; they are a cornerstone that enables security, efficiency, interoperability, compliance, and innovation.

Anatomy of transaction

Much like asset types, explained in detail in *Chapter 8, Asset, Data Types, and Transactions*, transactions are defined structures provided by the CC-Tools library, with many properties that allow developers to customize them while maintaining a standardized code and implementation that will prove itself very useful when implementing a client for interaction with the chaincode.

The structure of a transaction has some similarities with the asset type, such as tag, label, and description. However, some changes exist.

Let us go through all properties of the type transaction, as follows:

- **Tag**: It identifies the transaction uniquely. When calling a transaction with a CLI or SDK tool, the tag is sent as the transaction name, for example, **`createNewLibrary`**.
- **Label**: It describes shortly the tag. It can be useful when consuming the chaincode metadata, for example, Create New Library.
- **Description**: A longer description of the transaction. It can be a good way to document the transaction behavior and inform chaincode users what to expect.
- **Args**: A list of arguments, each one with its own tag, label, description, data type, and required information.
- **Method**: A metadata that can inform the user of the chaincode what type of transaction this is. It is based on HTTP methods. Note that this value does not influence how the transaction works.
- **ReadOnly**: A metadata that can inform the user of the chaincode if the transaction alters the world state or not.
- **MetaTx**: A metadata used generally by CC-Tools to inform that the transaction does not encode business rules but rather encodes an internal process of the chaincode, for example, the transaction **`getSchema`** returns the list of asset types.
- **Routine**: The implementation of the transaction itself. This is the heart of the transaction.
- **Callers**: A list of which organizations and identity types can call the transaction. This will identify the MSP of the organization, and additionally the identity role, and block the ones not listed as callers. This restriction does not protect the ledger data from being read by other organizations, for this private data should be used.

In *Chapter 8, Asset, Data Types, and Transactions*, when exploring transactions, we focused completely on the built-in transactions that CC-Tools provides, which are built using the same tools available for custom transactions. In this chapter, we propose the construction of a custom transaction while we explain each of the details that influence transaction development.

As a pre-requisite for this construction, we have asset types. Indeed, it is possible to bypass CC-Tools to access the **`PutState`** function directly and add anything to the ledger, but that defeats our purpose here. CC-Tools works by writing and reading asset instances based on defined asset types, that's what every transaction will ultimately do. Let us start then with two asset types as pre-requisites, so we can build our transaction with something to read and write in mind.

Let us define a person and its properties, as follows:

```
var Person = assets.AssetType{
      Tag:         "person",
      Label:       "Person",
      Description: "Personal data of someone",

      Props: []assets.AssetProp{
            {
                  Required: true,
                  IsKey:    true,
                  Tag:      "name",
                  Label:    "Name",
                  DataType: "string",
            },
            {
                  Tag:      "dateOfBirth",
                  Label:    "Date of Birth",
                  DataType: "datetime",
            },
      },
}
```

Let us now define a car as an asset that belongs to a person, as follows:

```
var Car = assets.AssetType{
      Tag:         "car",
      Label:       "Car",
      Description: "Car belonging to a person",

      Props: []assets.AssetProp{
            {
                  Required: true,
                  IsKey:    true,
                  Tag:      "carPlate",
                  Label:    "Car Plate",
                  DataType: "string",
            },
            {
                  Tag:      "model",
```

```
                    Label:     "Model",
                    DataType: "string",
                },
                {
                    Tag:       "owner",
                    Label:     "Owner",
                    DataType: "->person",
                },
        },
}
```

For the **person** asset, we have two properties, the **name** will identify this person uniquely as it's marked as a key, and **dateOfBirth** is optional information. The **car** asset is identified by the **carPlate** property and has two more properties, an optional **model** field and an **owner** field that represents a **person** asset that is already registered on the blockchain.

If we were to use built-in transactions to work with these two assets, we could perform two asset creations with **createAsset**. First, we would create a person and then create the car referencing the person that was just created.

In order to showcase the possibilities for a transaction, let us then start the construction of a transaction that will take both a person's information and their car and register them in the same transaction, while linking them with the asset reference.

Refer to the following code:

```
var CreatePersonCar = tx.Transaction{
        Tag:          "createPersonCar",
        Label:        "Create Person and Car",
        Description: "Create a New Person and Car linked together",
        Method:       "POST",

        Args: []tx.Argument{}

        Routine: func(stub *sw.StubWrapper, req map[string]interface{}) ([]
byte, errors.ICCError) {}
}
```

This will be the base for our transactions. In the next section, we will assemble the arguments for this transaction.

Arguments

Transaction arguments are their own type in CC-Tools and have properties that govern their behavior, much like asset types and their properties. These properties are as follows:

- **Tag**: It identifies the argument in the payload JSON.
- **Label**: It shortly describes the tag.
- **Description**: It is the longer description of the argument, if needed.
- **DataType**: The type of the argument. It can be one of the primary types, custom data types, asset references, or meta-arguments. For example, **`type`**, **`[]type`**, **`->assetType`**, **`@asset`**, **`@key`**, **`@update`**, **`@query`**, **and** **`@object`**.
    - o **type and []type**: The type keyword here, represents datatype or meta datatype supported by CC-Tools. For example, type can be a **string** or a list of strings, **`[]string`**. It can also be a list of person asset references, **`[]->person`**.
    - o **->assetType**: This will reference any asset defined in the Asset Type list.
    - o **@asset**: This will allow the argument to be any asset type defined in the assets package. Property validation is done based on the **`@assetType`** property.
    - o **@key**: This will allow the argument to be a reference to any asset defined in the assets package. The key must exist on the ledger.
    - o **@update**: This is similar to **`@asset`**, being able to receive and validate properties from any asset definition. The only difference is that required properties won't be mandatory.
    - o **@query:** This will require a CouchDB selector to be sent as property.
    - o **@object**: This can be an arbitrary object that will not be validated.
- **Required:** This indicates whether the argument is mandatory or not.
- **Private:** Whether the argument is sent as private or not. If so, CC-Tools will search for the argument in the transient request, which will be explained in detail in *Chapter 11, Using Private Data Collections*.

Now, we may attempt to assemble the **`Args`** section of our transaction definition, as follows:

```
var CreatePersonCar = tx.Transaction{
	Tag:         "createPersonCar",
	Label:       "Create Person and Car",
	Description: "Create a New Person and Car linked together",
	Method:      "POST",

	Args: []tx.Argument{
		{
			Required: true,
			Tag:      "name",
```

```
                Label:    "Person's Name",
                DataType: "string",
            },
            {
                Tag:      "dateOfBirth",
                Label:    "Date of Birth",
                DataType: "datetime",
            },
            {
                Required: true,
                Tag:      "carPlate",
                Label:    "Car Plate",
                DataType: "string",
            },
            {
                Tag:      "model",
                Label:    "Model",
                DataType: "string",
            },
    },
    Routine: func(stub *sw.StubWrapper, req map[string]interface{}) ([]
byte, errors.ICCError) {}
}
```

Highlighted in bold are the arguments defined for our transaction. Note that they mimic the properties of the assets we want to create. The person's name and car plate are both required since they are also required in the asset types and they are used as keys. We can suppress the owner argument since we are already receiving the person who will be linked as the owner. Also, receiving an owner as an asset reference to a person would mean that the person must already exist in the ledger before this transaction.

Write functions

CC-Tools provides many functions that write on the ledger. Ultimately, all of them perform a **PutState** in the ledger for a key and value. However, CC-Tools functions add many additional functionality to writing on the ledger.

Let us explore these functions so we can start creating the routine for our example transaction, as follows:

- **Put function:**
  - Put

    - PutNew
    - PutRecursive
    - PutNewRecursive
- **Update functions:**
    - Update
    - UpdateRecursive
- **Delete functions**
    - Delete
    - DeleteCascade

Most of these functions are related to the type **`asset`**, which means we need an **`asset`** object prior to using them. The function call creates an asset object from a map with asset properties, as follows:

```
assetObject, err := assets.NewAsset(assetMap)
```

Put

Four different functions can be used to put assets in the ledger. Each of them has slight differences to support different situations. The basic **`Put`** is the simpler option, this function will check if the organization that called the transaction has the proper permissions to write the asset properties. Then, it injects metadata into the asset, such as information on the timestamp, which organization changed the asset, and which transaction has changed the asset. All references made by the asset are validated to ensure that they are consistent with ledger data, and then CC-Tools puts the asset on the ledger with **`PutState`**.

There is an experimental function called **`PutRecursive`** that will take an asset with sub-assets inside it and put all of them recursively while assembling consistent references. That is, instead of registering an asset with a reference for an existing asset, all assets and sub-assets would be registered in one function. The same verifications done by the **`Put`** function are done by **`PutRecursive`**.

`PutNew` and **`PutNewRecursive`** do the same thing as their counterparts with the additional verification of the existence of the asset in the ledger. If the asset already exists with the same key, a conflict error will be returned.

One interesting fact about the **`PutState`** function provided by the official **`fabric-chaincode-go`** package is that it will only take effect once the transaction has gone through the transaction flow completely. That means that running a **`PutState`** for a key and immediately trying to retrieve it with **`GetState`** will return the committed state, which will be the previous state for the key.

CC-Tools wraps the official **PutState** to add to-be-committed assets to a local execution copy of the write set. This enables **GetState** to fetch non-committed states in the transaction while keeping consistency of the data regardless of when put and get functions are called.

Update

The **Update** function follows a similar logic to the **Put** functions. One benefit of using **Update** instead of **Put** is that the update allows the developer to send only the properties they want to update instead of the complete asset with repeated fields that will not be updated. Properties are validated according to asset type definition, as well as references. Metadata with transaction information is added and then the asset is put on the ledger. Like **PutRecursive**, **UpdateRecursive** updates the asset and all sub-assets that are sent in the update map.

Delete

Deleting an asset from the ledger is also a write operation, even though it does not use **PutState** and instead uses **DelState**. This function will delete the key from the ledger, that is, add a state for the key where it does not have a defined value and a flag indicates its deletion. Let us be reminded that data history is never lost in a ledger. Before deleting the key, CC-Tools performs a check to see if the asset is referenced by any other asset in the ledger. If so, the operation is halted, and the user is instructed to remove references before deleting them from the ledger. This is done to make sure that references are consistent across ledger data.

An experimental function can be used if the user wants to delete the asset and all that reference it, **DeleteCascade**.

Using write functions

Before using any of these functions, we must take the arguments of our transaction and assemble them into the assets that we want to put on the ledger. The function passed to **Routine** has the following signature **func(stub *sw.StubWrapper, req map[string] interface{}) ([]byte, errors.ICCError)**, and **req** is the object where the arguments sent to the transaction live. In order to access them, we can do the following:

```
name, _ := req["name"].(string)
dateOfBirth, _ := req["dateOfBirth"].(time.Time)
carPlate, _ := req["carPlate"].(string)
```

model, _ := req["model"].(string)

For each argument, we are accessing it in the **req** map using the defined **Tag**. This will return us an **interface{}** type, which can be type asserted to their respective primary type. This can take some getting used to because CC-Tools types do not always map one-to-one with Go types.

Now that we have the argument values in variables, we can assemble the assets accordingly, as follows:

```
personMap := map[string]interface{}{
	"@assetType":  "person",
	"name":        name,
	"dateOfBirth": dateOfBirth,
}

personAsset, err := assets.NewAsset(personMap)
if err != nil {
	return nil, errors.WrapError(err, "Failed to create a new asset")
}

person, err := personAsset.PutNew(stub)
if err != nil {
	return nil, errors.WrapError(err, "Error saving asset on
blockchain")
}
```

First, we assemble a map with the information regarding the person's asset. This serves as a parameter for the **NewAsset** function which returns an actual object with a generated key and many functions associated with it, one of which is the next step of the transaction, **PutNew**. **PutNew** takes **stub** as a parameter, which is the object that will interact with the read and write sets of the transaction, or in practice, the object that interacts with the ledger. **PutNew** returns a map with all the information of the person's asset. This has virtually the same information as **personMap** and **personAsset**.

Now that this asset is in the write set, let us move and do the same with the car asset, which has a reference to its owner.

Refer to the following example for a better understanding:

```
carMap := map[string]interface{}{
	"@assetType": "car",
	"plate":      carPlate,
	"model":      model,
	«owner»:      person,
}

carAsset, err := assets.NewAsset(carMap)
if err != nil {
	return nil, errors.WrapError(err, "Failed to create a new asset")
}

// Save the new library on channel
car, err := carAsset.PutNew(stub)
```

```
if err != nil {
	return nil, errors.WrapError(err, "Error saving asset on
blockchain")
}
```

Note that adding the reference is as simple as adding the returned variable of the previous **PutNew** to the **carMap** owner entry. In this case, **personMap** and **personAsset** would work as well.

Let us add some final touches and see our full transaction assembled, as follows:

```
var CreatePersonCar = tx.Transaction{
	Tag:         "createPersonCar",
	Label:       "Create Person and Car",
	Description: "Create a New Person and Car linked together",
	Method:      "POST",

	Args: []tx.Argument{
		{
			Required: true,
			Tag:      "name",
			Label:    "Person's Name",
			DataType: "string",
		},
		{
			Tag:      "dateOfBirth",
			Label:    "Date of Birth",
			DataType: "datetime",
		},
		{
			Required: true,
			Tag:      "carPlate",
			Label:    "Car Plate",
			DataType: "string",
		},
		{
			Tag:      "model",
			Label:    "Model",
			DataType: "string",
		},
	},
	Routine: func(stub *sw.StubWrapper, req map[string]interface{}) ([]
byte, errors.ICCError) {
		name, _ := req["name"].(string)
		dateOfBirth, _ := req["dateOfBirth"].(time.Time)
```

```
		carPlate, _ := req["carPlate"].(string)
		model, _ := req["model"].(string)

		personMap := map[string]interface{}{
			"@assetType":  "person",
			"name":        name,
			"dateOfBirth": dateOfBirth,
		}

		personAsset, err := assets.NewAsset(personMap)
		if err != nil {
			return nil, errors.WrapError(err, "Failed to create a
new asset")
		}

		// Save the new library on channel
		person, err := personAsset.PutNew(stub)
		if err != nil {
			return nil, errors.WrapError(err, "Error saving asset
on blockchain")
		}

		carMap := map[string]interface{}{
			«@assetType»: «car»,
			"plate":      carPlate,
			"model":      model,
			"owner":      person,
		}

		carAsset, err := assets.NewAsset(carMap)
		if err != nil {
			return nil, errors.WrapError(err, "Failed to create a
new asset")
		}

		// Save the new library on channel
		car, err := carAsset.PutNew(stub)
		if err != nil {
			return nil, errors.WrapError(err, "Error saving asset
on blockchain")
		}

		response := map[string]interface{}{
			"person": person,
			"car":    car,
		}
```

```
		responseBytes, nerr := json.Marshal(response)
		if nerr != nil {
			return nil, errors.WrapError(err, "Error marshalling
response")
		}

		return responseBytes, nil
	},
}
```

Before ending the transaction, a good practice is to assemble a response that indicates what assets have been created in the ledger. Of course, this is context-dependent and the developer is free to decide what is the return of a transaction.

This is not the only way to implement a transaction that has the same general behavior. As it is common with programming in general, the programmer is the ultimate architect and decision-maker of their implementation. CC-Tools follows these themes, providing tools to empower developers.

Another option for this transaction would be using **PutNewRecursive** with the map object of the car asset, including its sub-asset in the **owner** entry. Take time to study the differences in this implementation.

Following is a sample implementation for your reference:

```
var CreatePersonCarRecursive = tx.Transaction{
	Tag:         "createPersonCarRecursive",
	Label:       "Create Person and Car Recursive",
	Description: "Create a New Person and Car linked together using
recursive PutNewRecusive",
	Method:      "POST",

	Args: []tx.Argument{
		{
			Required: true,
			Tag:      "name",
			Label:    "Person's Name",
			DataType: "string",
		},
		{
			Tag:      "dateOfBirth",
			Label:    "Date of Birth",
			DataType: "datetime",
		},
		{
			Required: true,
```

```
                Tag:      "carPlate",
                Label:    "Car Plate",
                DataType: "string",
            },
            {
                Tag:      "model",
                Label:    "Model",
                DataType: "string",
            },
        },
        Routine: func(stub *sw.StubWrapper, req map[string]interface{}) ([]
byte, errors.ICCError) {
            name, _ := req["name"].(string)
            dateOfBirth, _ := req["dateOfBirth"].(time.Time)
            carPlate, _ := req["carPlate"].(string)
            model, _ := req["model"].(string)

            personMap := map[string]interface{}{
                "@assetType":  "person",
                "name":        name,
                "dateOfBirth": dateOfBirth,
            }

            carMap := map[string]interface{}{
                "@assetType": "car",
                "plate":      carPlate,
                "model":      model,
                "owner":      personMap,
            }

            car, err := assets.PutNewRecursive(stub, carMap)
            if err != nil {
                return nil, errors.WrapError(err, "Error saving asset
on blockchain")
            }

            responseBytes, nerr := json.Marshal(car)
            if nerr != nil {
                return nil, errors.WrapError(err, "Error marshalling
response")
            }

            return responseBytes, nil
        },
}
```

Read functions

Data that has been put on the blockchain at some point will be read. The most basic function used to read a key from the blockchain is **`GetState`**, available as one of the **`fabric-chaincode-go`** package standard functions. Additionally, with the standard Fabric functions, it is possible to get the history and query the world state database. CC-Tools wrap all that into functions that bring additional functionalities.

Following are the read functions available in CC-Tools:

- Get functions
  - Get
  - GetMap
  - GetMany
  - GetCommitted
  - GetRescursive
- Search
- History

Get

Get functions are used when the key value or all the key properties of the asset are known. **`Get`** and **`GetMap`** have essentially the same behavior, retrieving the asset from the ledger or the transaction's write set. The difference is that **`Get`** returns an asset object and **`GetMap`** returns a map object. **`GetMany`** receives a list of keys and returns a list of asset objects from the ledger or the transaction's write set. Sometimes, though, developers may want to get only the committed state of a key. That can be achieved with **`GetCommitted`**.

For assets with references to other assets, **`GetRecursive`** allows the retrieval of the assets while resolving all references recursively. This can be quite more intensive than fetching just a single asset; however, it can prove itself useful.

Search

The **`Search`** function makes use of the set of Fabric functions that get query results from the world state database. CC-Tools, particularly, is made to work with CouchDB rich queries and one of the parameters that must be sent to CouchDB is a selector that will be used for the query. **`Search`** also supports pagination and page size parameters. You can find an example of a selector as received by the **`Search`** function below. This will get every car in which a particular person is owner.

```
query := map[string]interface{}{
```

```
    "selector": map[string]interface{}{
        "@assetType": "car",
        "owner.@key": personKey,
    },
}
```

CouchDB selectors are a powerful way to query blockchain data. They allow users to specify complex criteria for selecting data based on their content. Selectors are, generally, expressed in JSON format and can include various options to refine queries. In CC-Tools, they can be expressed as maps and then marshaled to JSON plain text, which allows developers to easily parameterize the selector.

The key options include logical operators (**`$and`**, **`$or`**, **`$not`**, **`$nor`**), comparison operators (**`$eq`**, **`$ne`**, **`$gt`**, **`$gte`**, **`$lt`**, **`$lte`**), and array operators (**`$in`**, **`$nin`**, **`$all`**, **`$size`**). Additionally, selectors can utilize special operators such as **`$exists`** to check for the existence of a field and **`$type`** to verify the field type. These options enable precise and flexible querying capabilities.

Following are some examples:

- **$and**: It combines multiple conditions, all of which must be true.
- **$or**: It combines multiple conditions, sufficing one to be true.
- **$not**: It inverts any condition.
- **$nor**: It combines multiple conditions, none of which can be true.
- **$eq**: It matches data where the field is equal to the specified value. When an operator is suppressed, **`$eq`** is assumed.
- **$ne**: It matches all data where the field is not equal to the value.
- **$gt**: It matches all data where the field is greater than the value.
- **$gte**: It matches all data where the field is greater than or equal to the value.
- **$lt**: It matches all data where the field is less than the value.
- **$lte**: It matches all data where the field is less than or equal to the value.
- **$in**: It matches data where the field's value is included in a specified array of values.
- **$nin**: It matches data where the field's value is not included in a specified array of values.
- **$all**: It matches data where the field's array contains all specified values.
- **$size**: It matches data where the field's array is equal to the specified value.
- **$exists**: It matches data where a field exists, independent of value.
- **$type**: It matches data where the field matches the specified type.

You can find some examples of selectors in their final JSON form, as follows:

```
{
  "selector": {
    "$and": [
      { "type": { "$eq": "user" } },
      { "age": { "$gt": 30 } }
    ]
  }
}
================================================================================
{
  "selector": {
    "$or": [
      { "status": { "$eq": "active" } },
      { "status": { "$eq": "pending" } }
    ]
  }
}
================================================================================
{
  "selector": {
    "$nor": [
      { "status": { "$eq": "inactive" } },
      { "age": { "$lt": 18 } }
    ]
  }
}
================================================================================
{
  "selector": {
    "age": { "$gt": 30 }
  }
}
================================================================================
{
  "selector": {
    "status": { "$nin": ["inactive", "deleted"] }
 }
}
```

CouchDB selectors also support nested queries, enabling more complex filtering. For instance, to find documents where the address field contains a city that equals *New York* and a postal code greater than 10000, you can use a query structured, as follows:

```
{
  "selector": {
    "address": {
      "$and": [
        {
          "city": {
            "$eq": "New York"
          }
        },
        {
          "postal_code": {
            "$gt": 10000
          }
        }
      ]
    }
  }
}
```

In CouchDB, certain operators can significantly benefit from indexing to enhance query performance. The comparison operators such as **`$eq`**, **`$gt`**, **`$gte`**, **`$lt`**, and **`$lte`** are particularly effective when used with indexed fields. These operators are commonly used to filter documents based on specific criteria, and indexing the relevant fields allows CouchDB to quickly locate and retrieve matching documents without scanning the entire dataset. Generally, it is best to avoid using operators that will result in a full scan of the database or the indexes, such as **`$or`** and **`$in`**.

In CC-Tools, the **`Search`** function also supports receiving a bookmark and limit parameter for pagination purposes, as follows:

```
query := map[string]interface{}{
      "selector": map[string]interface{}{
            "@assetType": "book",
            "author":     authorName,
      },
      "bookmark": "",
      "limit":    10,
}

response, err := assets.Search(stub, query, "", true)
```

History

History is also a CC-Tools function that serves as a wrapper for **GetHistoryForKey** with additional functionality. It returns a list of all previous versions of the asset given a particular key.

In order to use **history**, the asset key string must be sent with a Boolean indicating if references should be resolved. Note that, references will be resolved with the current version of the referenced asset, as follows:

```
history, err := assets.History(stub, assetKey, false)
```

Using read functions

The structure for a transaction that uses read functions is the same as the one for write functions. Let us see a function that retrieves all cars owned by a particular person, as follows:

```
var GetCarsByOwner = tx.Transaction{
	Tag:         "getCarsByOwner",
	Label:       "Get Cars by the Owner",
	Description: "Return all the cars from a Owner",
	Method:      "GET",

	Args: []tx.Argument{
		{
			Tag:         "owner",
			Label:       "Owner's key",
			Description: "Reference to the owner",
			DataType:    "->person",
			Required:    true,
		},
		{
			Tag:         "limit",
			Label:       "Limit",
			Description: "Limit",
			DataType:    "number",
		},
	},
	Routine: func(stub *sw.StubWrapper, req map[string]interface{}) ([]
byte, errors.ICCError) {
		personKey, _ := req["owner"].(assets.Key)
		limit, hasLimit := req["limit"].(float64)
```

```
		if hasLimit && limit <= 0 {
			return nil, errors.NewCCError("limit must be greater
than 0", 400)
		}

		// Prepare couchdb query
		query := map[string]interface{}{
			"selector": map[string]interface{}{
				"@assetType": "car",
				"owner.@key": personKey.Key(),
			},
		}

		if hasLimit {
			query["limit"] = limit
		}

		var err error
		response, err := assets.Search(stub, query, "", true)
		if err != nil {
			return nil, errors.WrapErrorWithStatus(err, "error
searching for book's author", 500)
		}

		responseJSON, err := json.Marshal(response)
		if err != nil {
			return nil, errors.WrapErrorWithStatus(err, "error
marshaling response", 500)
		}

		return responseJSON, nil
	},
}
```

When receiving a key as an argument, the underlying type of the interface is **`assets.Key`**, which is really convenient for us, since it will allow us to grab the key string easily. Then, the selector is assembled and sent to the search function. The empty string indicates that this asset is not part of any private collection. The **`true`** value passed as the last argument indicates to the search function that it should resolve all references before returning.

Transaction testing

CC-Tools supports a few different ways of writing tests for transactions, depending on the type of transactions implemented. These are mainly divided into two categories that we will call offline and online testing. Offline testing does not require a Fabric network to be up and running, while online testing does.

Offline testing

Offline testing is usually simpler and is effective for many transactions that do not rely on CouchDB queries or history queries. This type of testing takes advantage of the Go unit testing suite and a mock for the **Stub** object. It allows the developer to define the state of the blockchain, execute a transaction, and check its return while having code coverage and more. In the **hyperledger-labs/cc-tools-demo** repository, under the **chaincode** folder, the reader can find examples of unit tests written for some transactions.

Let us look at the file **txdefs_createNewLibrary_test.go**, as follows:

```
func TestCreateNewLibrary(t *testing.T) {
	stub := mock.NewMockStub("org3MSP", new(cc.CCDemo))

	expectedResponse := map[string]interface{}{
		"@key":         "library:3cab201f-9e2b-579d-b7b2-
72297ed17f49",
		"@lastTouchBy": "org3MSP",
		"@lastTx":      "createNewLibrary",
		"@assetType":   "library",
		"name":         "Maria's Library",
	}
	req := map[string]interface{}{
		"name": "Maria's Library",
	}
	reqBytes, err := json.Marshal(req)
	if err != nil {
		t.FailNow()
	}

	res := stub.MockInvoke("createNewLibrary", [][]byte{
		[]byte("createNewLibrary"),
		reqBytes,
	})

	expectedResponse["@lastUpdated"] = stub.TxTimestamp.AsTime().
Format(time.RFC3339)

	if res.GetStatus() != 200 {
		log.Println(res)
```

```
            t.FailNow()
      }

      var resPayload map[string]interface{}
      err = json.Unmarshal(res.GetPayload(), &resPayload)
      if err != nil {
            log.Println(err)
            t.FailNow()
      }

      if !reflect.DeepEqual(resPayload, expectedResponse) {
            log.Println("these should be equal")
            log.Printf("%#v\n", resPayload)
            log.Printf("%#v\n", expectedResponse)
            t.FailNow()
      }

      var state map[string]interface{}
      stateBytes := stub.State["library:3cab201f-9e2b-579d-b7b2-
72297ed17f49"]
      err = json.Unmarshal(stateBytes, &state)
      if err != nil {
            log.Println(err)
            t.FailNow()
      }

      if !reflect.DeepEqual(state, expectedResponse) {
            log.Println("these should be equal")
            log.Printf("%#v\n", state)
            log.Printf("%#v\n", expectedResponse)
            t.FailNow()
      }
}
```

In this code snippet, we are looking at a function named **`TestCreateNewLibrary`** which is a test case written in Go for testing a chaincode transaction in the demonstration repository. The purpose of this test is to verify the functionality of creating a new library entry in the blockchain.

The test begins by setting up a mock stub. This stub, **`mock.NewMockStub`**, is a simulated version of the blockchain environment, allowing the test to run without the need for an actual blockchain network. It is initialized with an identifier, *org3MSP*, and an instance of the chaincode, **`new(cc.CCDemo)`**.

Next, the expected response from the chaincode invocation is defined. This is a map representing the expected state of the newly created library entry. It includes metadata like the key, who last touched it, the last transaction, and the asset type, along with the name of the library *(Maria's Library)*.

The request for creating a new library is then prepared. It is a simple map containing the name of the library. This map is then serialized into JSON bytes, which is a necessary step since chaincode invocations in Hyperledger Fabric are done using byte arrays.

The actual invocation of the chaincode is done using **`stub.MockInvoke`**, simulating the chaincode call. It is passed the operation name, **`createNewLibrary`**, which is the tag of the transaction definition, and the request bytes. The chaincode's response is stored in **`res`**.

The test then updates the expected response with the transaction timestamp, formatted as per the RFC3339 standard. This is important because timestamps are generated at runtime and cannot be predetermined in the expected response.

Following this, the test checks if the response status is 200 (HTTP OK), which indicates success. If it is not, the test fails immediately. The payload of the response is then unmarshalled (converted from JSON bytes to a map) for comparison. If the unmarshalling fails, the test fails. The test asserts whether the unmarshalled response payload is deeply equal to the expected response. If they are not equal, it logs the discrepancy and fails.

Finally, the test retrieves the state directly from the mock stub's internal storage to ensure that the state in the ledger is as expected. It unmarshals the state and compares it with the expected response. If they do not match, the test logs the difference and fails.

The transaction tested by this test does not use CouchDB or history queries, for those we need the blockchain network to be up and running.

Let us now explore a test that reads something from the ledger. For that, we will explore, in the same repository, a file called **`txdefs_getNumberOfBooksFromLibrary_test.go`**, as follows:

```
func TestGetNumberOfBooksFromLibrary(t *testing.T) {
	stub, err := mock.NewMockStubWithCert("org2MSP", new(CCDemo), []
byte(clientUserOrg2Cert))
	if err != nil {
		t.FailNow()
	}

	// Setup state
	setupBook := map[string]interface{}{
		"@key":         "book:a36a2920-c405-51c3-b584-dcd758338cb5",
		"@lastTouchBy": "org2MSP",
		"@lastTx":      "createAsset",
		"@assetType":   "book",
```

```
		“title”:        “Meu Nome é Maria”,
		"author":       "Maria Viana",
		"genres":       []interface{}{"biography", "non-fiction"},
		"published":    "2019-05-06T22:12:41Z",
	}
	setupLibrary := map[string]interface{}{
		"@key":         "library:3cab201f-9e2b-579d-b7b2-
72297ed17f49",
		"@lastTouchBy": "org3MSP",
		"@lastTx":      "createNewLibrary",
		"@assetType":   "library",
		"name":         "Maria's Library",
		"books": []map[string]interface{}{
			{
				"@assetType": "book",
				"@key":       "book:a36a2920-c405-51c3-b584-
dcd758338cb5",
			},
		},
	}
	setupBookJSON, _ := json.Marshal(setupBook)
	setupLibraryJSON, _ := json.Marshal(setupLibrary)

	stub.MockTransactionStart("setupGetNumberOfBooksFromLibrary")
	stub.PutState("book:a36a2920-c405-51c3-b584-dcd758338cb5",
setupBookJSON)
	stub.PutState("library:3cab201f-9e2b-579d-b7b2-72297ed17f49",
setupLibraryJSON)
	refIdx, err := stub.CreateCompositeKey("book:a36a2920-c405-
51c3-b584-dcd758338cb5", []string{"library:3cab201f-9e2b-579d-b7b2-
72297ed17f49"})
	if err != nil {
		log.Println(err)
		t.FailNow()
	}
	stub.PutState(refIdx, []byte{0x00})
	stub.MockTransactionEnd("setupGetNumberOfBooksFromLibrary")

	expectedResponse := map[string]interface{}{
		"numberOfBooks": 1.0,
	}
	req := map[string]interface{}{
		"library": map[string]interface{}{
			"name": "Maria's Library",
```

```
		},
	}
	reqBytes, err := json.Marshal(req)
	if err != nil {
		t.FailNow()
	}

	res := stub.MockInvoke("getNumberOfBooksFromLibrary", [][]byte{
		[]byte("getNumberOfBooksFromLibrary"),
		reqBytes,
	})

	if res.GetStatus() != 200 {
		log.Println(res)
		t.FailNow()
	}

	var resPayload map[string]interface{}
	err = json.Unmarshal(res.GetPayload(), &resPayload)
	if err != nil {
		log.Println(err)
		t.FailNow()
	}

	if !reflect.DeepEqual(resPayload, expectedResponse) {
		log.Println("these should be equal")
		log.Printf("%#v\n", resPayload)
		log.Printf("%#v\n", expectedResponse)
		t.FailNow()
	}
}
```

As the function signature suggests, this test will run a transaction that gets the number of books from a library object. It naturally assumes that not only a library asset exists but that it has book references. A library can have zero books, but nonetheless, a setup must be done for the test to be able to run.

As a first step, it sets up the initial state by defining a book and a library with specific attributes and their relationships. These states are then stored in the mock ledger using **stub.PutState**. The function then initiates a composite key to link the book to the library and stores this reference, this is not used in this test, but since CC-Tools stores composite keys for references, this serves as an example of a true to life setup.

After setting up the initial state, the test constructs a request to get the number of books in *Maria's Library* and invokes the chaincode function **getNumberOfBooksFromLibrary**. The response is validated to ensure it matches the expected output, which indicates that the library contains one book. If the actual response deviates from the expected result, the test logs the discrepancies and fails the test case, ensuring the integrity of the function being tested. Running the tests shows the following output:

```
$ go test github.com/hyperledger-labs/cc-tools-demo/chaincode
-coverpkg=./... -v

main.go:147: 200 init 76.542µs
=== RUN   TestGetNumberOfBooksFromLibrary
main.go:147: 200 getNumberOfBooksFromLibrary 25.583µs
--- PASS: TestGetNumberOfBooksFromLibrary (0.00s)
=== RUN   TestUpdateBookTenant
main.go:147: 200 updateBookTenant 196.584µs
--- PASS: TestUpdateBookTenant (0.00s)
=== RUN   TestCreateNewLibrary
main.go:147: 200 createNewLibrary 13.917µs
--- PASS: TestCreateNewLibrary (0.00s)
PASS
coverage: 38.9% of statements in ./...
ok      github.com/hyperledger-labs/cc-tools-demo/chaincode     0.555s
coverage: 38.9% of statements in ./...
```

Online testing

In the **hyperledger-labs/cc-tools-demo** repository, the preferred method for performing online tests is the **behavior-driven development** (**BDD**) framework, *Godog*. This approach is particularly effective for testing transactions that are part of a sequence or flow. While the setup might be more time-consuming, it ensures the robustness and reliability of the chaincode logic, making it an invaluable tool for thorough and effective testing.

Godog is based on the *Cucumber* tool for running automated tests. They are written in plain language making it easy to understand and at the same time documenting code behavior. This framework utilizes the *Gherkin* syntax, which defines a structured way but still allows for plain text to be written.

Let us take a look at an example, as follows:

```
Feature: Create New Library
    In order to create a new library
    As an API client
    I want to make a request with the name of the desired library

    Scenario: Create a new library
        Given there is a running "" test network from scratch
```

```
        When I make a "POST" request to "/api/invoke/createNewLibrary" on
port 880 with:
            """
            {
                "name": "Elizabeth's Library"
            }
            """
        Then the response code should be 200
        And the response should have:
            """
            {
                "@key":             "library:9cf6726a-a327-568a-baf1-
5881393073bf",
                "@lastTouchBy": "orgMSP",
                "@lastTx":          "createNewLibrary",
                "@assetType":       "library",
                "name":             "Elizabeth's Library"
            }
            """

    Scenario: Try to create a new library with a name that already exists
        Given there is a running "" test network
        Given there is a library with name "John's Library"
        When I make a "POST" request to "/api/invoke/createNewLibrary" on
port 880 with:
            """
            {
                "name": "John's Library"
            }
            """
        Then the response code should be 409
```

Note that this example makes use of the chaincode API that will be further explained in *Chapter 10, Understanding the API.*

This code snippet outlines automated test scenarios for a feature that allows the creation of new libraries in the chaincode. The first scenario outlines the process for successfully creating a new library. It starts with the prerequisite of having a running test network. The test involves sending a POST request to a specific API endpoint with the name of the new library (*Elizabeth's Library*). The success of this operation is verified by checking for a 200 response code and the correct structure and content in the API response, which includes details like a unique library key, the name of the library, and other metadata.

The second scenario deals with an error case where an attempt is made to create a library with a name that already exists. Similar to the first, it begins with a running test network and the existence of a library named *John's Library*. The test then repeats the process of sending a POST request to create a new library, but this time using a name that already exists. The expected behavior in this scenario is to receive a 409 response code, indicating a conflict due to the library name already being in use. This approach to testing, using clear, descriptive scenarios, ensures that both successful operations and handling of error cases are verified in the application.

Now, let us explore a test for another transaction, as follows:

```
Feature: Get Books By Author
    In order to get all the books by an author
    As an API client
    I want to make a request to the getBooksByAuthor transaction
    And receive the appropriate books

    Scenario: Request an author with multiple books
        Given there is a running "" test network
        And there are 3 books with prefix "book" by author "Jack"
        When I make a "GET" request to "/api/query/getBooksByAuthor" on
port 880 with:
            """
            {
                "authorName": "Jack"
            }
            """
        Then the response code should be 200
        And the "result" field should have size 3

    Scenario: Request an author with no books
        Given there is a running "" test network
        When I make a "GET" request to "/api/query/getBooksByAuthor" on
port 880 with:
            """
            {
                "authorName": "Mary"
            }
            """
        Then the response code should be 200
        And the "result" field should have size 0
```

```
    Scenario: Request an author with 2 books while there are other authors
with more books
        Given there is a running "" test network
        Given there are 1 books with prefix "fantasy" by author "Missy"
        Given there are 2 books with prefix "cook" by author "John"
        When I make a "GET" request to "/api/query/getBooksByAuthor" on
port 880 with:
            """
            {
                "authorName": "John"
            }
            """
        Then the response code should be 200
        And the "result" field should have size 2
```

The first scenario, **Request an author with multiple books**, and set up a test environment with a running network and three books authored by *Jack*. The test involves sending a GET request to a specific API endpoint, requesting books by *Jack*. The expected outcome is a successful response (indicated by a 200 response code) and the result contains three books.

In the second scenario, **Request an author with no books**, the setup is similar, but in this case, the request is made for books by *Mary*, who has not authored any books. The test expects a successful response but with a result size of zero, indicating no books found.

The third scenario, **Request an author with 2 books while there are other authors with more books**, involves a more complex setup. The test environment includes books by different authors, specifically one by *Missy* and two by *John*. The test requests books by *John* and expects a successful response with exactly two books in the result, demonstrating the system's ability to correctly filter and return books by a specific author, irrespective of the presence of other authors with more books.

These scenarios ensure that the system accurately handles different cases, such as multiple books by an author, an author with no books, and correctly filtering books by a specific author in a mixed collection. The clarity and structure of BDD syntax make these tests comprehensible and useful for both developers and non-technical stakeholders in understanding the software's behavior.

Note that some text lines are similar between scenarios and features. For example, given there is a running, test network and when we make a METHOD request to endpoint on port 880 with. For each feature, these lines are implemented as functions that can be reused throughout the application. This makes it easy to write new tests and even for non-technical members of the team to outline behaviors and test them.

These functions are implemented, in out particular case, in the file **`tests/request_test.go`** of the **`hyperledger-labs/cc-tools-demo`** repository.

Following is an example:

```
func thereIsARunningTestNetworkFromScratch(arg1 string) error {
	// Start test network with 1 org only
	cmd := exec.Command("../../startDev.sh", "-n", "1")

	_, err := cmd.Output()

	if err != nil {
		fmt.Println(err.Error())
		return err
	}

	// Wait for ccapi
	err = waitForNetwork("880")
	if err != nil {
		fmt.Println(err.Error())
		return err
	}

	return nil
}
```

The function **thereIsARunningTestNetworkFromScratch** in the provided code snippet is directly related to the **given there is a running, test network** step in BDD scenarios. In BDD, **Given** statements are used to set up the context or the initial conditions for a scenario. They pre pare the environment in which the subsequent actions of the test will be performed.

Let us see how the chaincode is invoked by calling an API endpoint, as follows:

```
func iMakeARequestToOnPortWith(ctx context.Context, method, endpoint
string, port int, reqBody *godog.DocString) (context.Context, error) {
	var res *http.Response
	var req *http.Request
	var err error

	// Initialize http client
	client := &http.Client{}

	// Create request
	if method == "GET" {
		b64str := b64.StdEncoding.EncodeToString([]byte(reqBody.
Content))
		reqParam := "?@request=" + b64str
		req, err = http.NewRequest("GET", "http://localhost:"+strconv.
```

```
Itoa(port)+endpoint+reqParam, nil)
		if err != nil {
			return ctx, err
		}
	} else {
		dataAsBytes := bytes.NewBuffer([]byte(reqBody.Content))

		req, err = http.NewRequest(method, "http://
localhost:"+strconv.Itoa(port)+endpoint, dataAsBytes)
		if err != nil {
			return ctx, err
		}
	}

	// Set header and make request
	req.Header.Set("Content-Type", "application/json")
	res, err = client.Do(req)
	if err != nil {
		return ctx, err
	}

	// Get status code and response body
	statusCode := res.StatusCode
	resBody, err := ioutil.ReadAll(res.Body)

	if err != nil {
		return ctx, err
	}
	res.Body.Close()

	// Append status code and response body to context
	bodyCtx := context.WithValue(ctx, bodyCtxKey{}, resBody)
	statusCtx := context.WithValue(bodyCtx, statusCtxKey{}, statusCode)
	return statusCtx, nil
}
```

The function makes an HTTP request to a port and endpoint using a given HTTP method and request body, all in the context of a test scenario. It initializes an HTTP client and constructs the request accordingly. For GET requests, the request body is base64 encoded and appended as a query parameter. Note that, for other HTTP methods, the request body is included as a JSON payload. After executing the request, it captures the response's status code and body. These are then added to the context, allowing subsequent steps in the Godog test scenario to access and verify the response.

Functions are reutilized for many different scenarios, allowing the developer to assemble tests with already made building blocks. *Godog's* context is a mechanism that provides a way to share and manage data across different these steps in a test scenario. When you define your step definitions in *Godog*, you typically register them with a context. This context acts as a container for storing and retrieving data that needs to be shared between steps.

All functions are mapped by a scenario initializer, as follows:

```
func InitializeScenario(ctx *godog.ScenarioContext) {
	ctx.Step(`^I make a "([^"]*)" request to "([^"]*)" on port (\d+) with:$`, iMakeARequestToOnPortWith)
	ctx.Step(`^the response code should be (\d+)$`, theResponseCodeShouldBe)
	ctx.Step(`^the response should have:$`, theResponseShouldHave)
	ctx.Step(`^there is a running "([^"]*)" test network$`, thereIsARunningTestNetwork)
	ctx.Step(`^there is a running "([^"]*)" test network from scratch$`, thereIsARunningTestNetworkFromScratch)
	ctx.Step(`^there are (\d+) books with prefix "([^"]*)" by author "([^"]*)"$`, thereAreBooksWithPrefixByAuthor)
	ctx.Step(`^the "([^"]*)" field should have size (\d+)$`, theFieldShouldHaveSize)
	ctx.Step(`^there is a library with name "([^"]*)"$`, thereIsALibraryWithName)
}
```

It is highly recommended to read the official Godog material for further information on writing, generating and maintaining tests.

Conclusion

This chapter explored aspects of custom transactions using CC-Tools, a vital toolset for blockchain applications. Starting with the importance of custom transactions, we explained how they are fundamental to the flexibility and efficiency of blockchain systems. By dissecting a transaction's anatomy, we provided a clear blueprint of its structure, enhancing your understanding of how transactions are formulated and executed.

Our journey through the write functions: Put, Update, Delete, and their effective usage - offered practical insights into how data is added or modified on the ledger. These functions are the backbone of data management in blockchain, and understanding their details equips you with the tools to effectively interact with the ledger.

Equally important, we explored the read functions: Get, Search, History, and their application. These functions are crucial for retrieving data from the ledger, providing a comprehensive view of the ledger's state and history. This knowledge is vital for anyone looking to understand the current state and evolution of data within a blockchain system.

The reader also learned about implementing BDD in Golang using the Godog framework. They were introduced to the structure and execution of BDD scenarios, particularly the Given-When-Then format. This knowledge equipped readers with essential skills for writing and understanding BDD scenarios in Golang, focusing on test environment setup and validation.

By covering these topics, this chapter aimed to fulfill its objectives: providing a solid understanding of CC-Tools for creating and handling transactions in various blockchain applications. We not only explored how CC-Tools organizes transaction definitions but also uncovered the essential elements shared by the routines they encompass.

In the next chapter, readers will explore, using Fabric SDKs to build APIs for blockchain interaction, focusing on the CC-Tools development API and its translation of SDK calls into transactions, simplifying developer workflows.

CHAPTER 10
Understanding the API

Introduction

Previous chapters have dealt with a lot of information. Developing chaincodes is the core of what this book is about, however, chaincodes are developed to solve problems, and for that, they must be interacted with. There is more than one way to interact with a chaincode, where the two most used are running command-line interface commands or using one of the many SDKs to interact with a network.

The approach used in this book, in CC-Tools and, for that matter, in most production-grade applications is to use one of the Fabric SDKs to allow for interaction programmatically. More specifically, we advocate the creation of APIs that expose SDK functionality to interact with the blockchain.

In the CC-Tools demonstration repository, there is a development API that allows for full interaction with the chaincode. In this chapter, we will explore this implementation fully and touch on other implementations developers might want to try during their journey.

We will also understand how an SDK call is translated to a transaction call in CC-Tools and explore the generic aspect of the CC-Tools API, which vastly enhances and facilitates the work of a developer.

Structure

The chapter covers the following topics:

- Hyperledger Fabric SDK
- Endpoints

Objectives

By the end of this chapter, readers will have acquired a detailed understanding of the Hyperledger Fabric Gateway SDK and its function as a client for chaincode interaction. They will have learned the necessary skills to develop an API that interfaces effectively with their own chaincode. This knowledge encompasses a detailed exploration of the API development process, with a particular emphasis on the implementation techniques provided by CC-Tools.

Readers will be adept at customizing and extending these tools to meet their specific project needs. By the end of this chapter, readers will possess not just a theoretical understanding of the API's functionalities but also practical skills for crafting robust applications that interact seamlessly with chaincode.

Hyperledger Fabric SDK

The Fabric Gateway service, as we have seen in *Chapter 4, Fabric Concepts and Components,* is a service that runs in peer nodes of version v2.4 and greater and provides a simple API for transaction submission. One of the main characteristics of the gateway is its ability to perform the complete transaction flow on behalf of the client, thus allowing for simple handling of transactions on the client side. Legacy SDKs are now deprecated in favor of the gateway SDK, however, during your exploration of the CC-Tools API you may encounter legacy routes that use previous SDKs to ensure compatibility with Fabric networks of versions lower than v2.4. We will, consequently, focus on the more modern gateway model during this chapter.

Assuming the SDK is properly configured, handling a transaction call is as simple as calling a function as follows:

```
contract.SubmitTransaction(txName, args)
```

The SDK will connect to the right node and submit the transaction, which will then be handled by the gateway of the peer. This function calls returns only when the transaction is guaranteed to be on a finished block, thus ensuring that our transaction went through, or an error is returned. This means that all the transaction flow steps are done.

Following are the steps:

1. **Evaluate a transaction proposal**: The gateway initiates a chaincode function on a peer to query the ledger state without altering it, preferring a peer in its own

organization with the highest ledger block height, or else selecting one from another organization.

2. **Endorse a transaction proposal**: The gateway gathers enough endorsement responses to meet signature policies, then provides the client with a prepared transaction envelope for signing.
3. **Submit a transaction**: This phase involves the transmission of a signed transaction envelope to the ordering service.
4. **Wait for commit status events**: The client waits to confirm the transaction's commitment to the ledger, indicated by the commit status code's validation or invalidation.
5. **Receive chaincode events**: This mechanism allows client applications to react to events triggered by a smart contract function after a transaction is committed to the ledger.

Configuring the gateway SDK only requires passing correct identities and endpoints of connection during the GRPC connection. In the CC-Tools API, found in the **`hyperledger-labs/cc-tools-demo`** repository under the directory **`ccapi`**, environment variables control the configuration. You can find the call to get the gateway connection client, as follows:

```
client.Connect(
        gatewayId,
        client.WithSign(gatewaySign),
        client.WithClientConnection(grpcConn),

        // Default timeouts for different gRPC calls
        client.WithEvaluateTimeout(5*time.Second),
        client.WithEndorseTimeout(15*time.Second),
        client.WithSubmitTimeout(5*time.Second),
        client.WithCommitStatusTimeout(1*time.Minute),
)
```

The CC-Tools API also implements endpoints that use the legacy **`fabric-sdk-go`** package. The SDK allows for a single call by the developer to invoke a transaction, but it does not use the gateway service, thus making all the steps of the transaction flow on the client, behind the scenes. The configuration of the legacy SDK in Go is made with a configuration file usually called **`configsdk.yaml`**.

The most important section of this file can be seen as follows:

```
client:
  organization: org1
  logging:
```

```
    level: info
  cryptoconfig:
    path: "/fabric/organizations"
  credentialStore:
    path: "/tmp/examplestore"

  BCCSP:
    security:
      enabled: true
      default:
        provider: "SW"
      hashAlgorithm: "SHA2"
      softVerify: true
      level: 256

  tlsCerts:
    systemCertPool: true
    client:
      keyfile: /fabric/organizations/peerOrganizations/org1.example.com/
users/Admin@org1.example.com/tls/client.key
      certfile: /fabric/organizations/peerOrganizations/org1.example.com/
users/Admin@org1.example.com/tls/client.cert
      cacertfile: /fabric/organizations/peerOrganizations/org1.example.com/
users/Admin@org1.example.com/tls/ca.crt
```

We encourage further exploration by the reader of the lower-level functions of the gateway and the legacy SDK if more flexible customization of the API is required.

Endpoints

The API implemented in the repository aims to be a generic service that will allow any chaincode to be directly used. The API provides endpoints that use the gateway or the legacy Fabric SDK, intended to be used with older versions of Hyperledger Fabric.

The endpoints vary in that some will allow the request sender to send what channel and chaincode name they will be interacting with. While other endpoints will use the channel and chaincode configured as environment variables on the runtime environment. Let us present the endpoint definition to illustrate. You can check the following code under the **ccapi** directory in the **hyperledger-labs/cc-tools-demo** repository:

```
func addCCRoutes(rg *gin.RouterGroup) {
	// Gateway routes
	rg.POST("/gateway/:channelName/:chaincodeName/invoke/:txname",
```

```
handlers.InvokeGatewayCustom)
        rg.PUT("/gateway/:channelName/:chaincodeName/invoke/:txname",
handlers.InvokeGatewayCustom)
        rg.DELETE("/gateway/:channelName/:chaincodeName/invoke/:txname",
handlers.InvokeGatewayCustom)
        rg.POST("/gateway/:channelName/:chaincodeName/query/:txname",
handlers.QueryGatewayCustom)
        rg.GET("/gateway/:channelName/:chaincodeName/query/:txname",
handlers.QueryGatewayCustom)

        rg.POST("/gateway/invoke/:txname", handlers.InvokeGatewayDefault)
        rg.PUT("/gateway/invoke/:txname", handlers.InvokeGatewayDefault)
        rg.DELETE("/gateway/invoke/:txname", handlers.InvokeGatewayDefault)
        rg.POST("/gateway/query/:txname", handlers.QueryGatewayDefault)
        rg.GET("/gateway/query/:txname", handlers.QueryGatewayDefault)

        // Other
        rg.POST("/:channelName/:chaincodeName/invoke/:txname", handlers.
Invoke)
        rg.PUT("/:channelName/:chaincodeName/invoke/:txname", handlers.
Invoke)
        rg.DELETE("/:channelName/:chaincodeName/invoke/:txname", handlers.
Invoke)
        rg.POST("/:channelName/:chaincodeName/query/:txname", handlers.
Query)
        rg.GET("/:channelName/:chaincodeName/query/:txname", handlers.Query)

        rg.POST("/invoke/:txname/", handlers.InvokeV1)
        rg.POST("/invoke/:txname", handlers.InvokeV1)
        rg.PUT("/invoke/:txname/", handlers.InvokeV1)
        rg.PUT("/invoke/:txname", handlers.InvokeV1)
        rg.DELETE("/invoke/:txname/", handlers.InvokeV1)
        rg.DELETE("/invoke/:txname", handlers.InvokeV1)
        rg.POST("/query/:txname/", handlers.QueryV1)
        rg.POST("/query/:txname", handlers.QueryV1)
        rg.GET("/query/:txname/", handlers.QueryV1)
        rg.GET("/query/:txname", handlers.QueryV1)
}
```

All these endpoints are available to the developer as options for implementation. A developer may choose to remove some of these options and keep only what they think is necessary.

Note: All the endpoint depends on a txname URL parameter. This is the way that transactions are concretely called. If a user wants to call the createNewCar transaction, one of the possible URL paths would be /gateway/invoke/createNewCar.

Also, note that some endpoints are invokes and others are queries. This is relevant since transactions called **queries** are executed normally, but do not alter the state of the ledger (even if put calls are made). **Invokes** on the other hand generate new blocks, changing the state of the blockchain (even if no put calls are made).

Users of the generic API require comprehensive information about its features. CC-Tools addresses this need by offering built-in transactions, which provide a thorough understanding of the API's capabilities. We will treat them as endpoints since that is how an API user will see them.

Schema endpoint

The schema endpoint is multiple endpoints. This set of endpoints is aimed at informing the user of the API about the schema of data defined in the chaincode, that is, which assets are defined and what format they have.

In the chaincode, this is mapped to a transaction called **`getSchema`**, which is built into CC-Tools. Take a closer look at how this transaction is implemented in the following code:

```
var GetSchema = Transaction{
	Tag:         "getSchema",
	Label:       "Get Schema",
	Description: "",
	Method:      "GET",

	ReadOnly: true,
	MetaTx:   true,
	Args: ArgList{
		{
			Tag:         "assetType",
			DataType:    "string",
			Description: "The name of the asset type of which 
you want to fetch the definition. Leave empty to fetch a list of possible 
types.",
		},
	},
	Routine: func(stub *sw.StubWrapper, req map[string]interface{}) ([]
byte, errors.ICCError) {
		var assetTypeName string
		assetTypeInterface, ok := req["assetType"]
```

```
            if ok {
                  assetTypeName, ok = assetTypeInterface.(string)
                  if !ok {
                        return nil, errors.NewCCError("argument
'assetType' must be a string", 400)
                  }
            }

            // If user requested a specific asset type definition
            if assetTypeName != "" {
                  assetTypeDef := assets.FetchAssetType(assetTypeName)
                  if assetTypeDef == nil {
                        errMsg := fmt.Sprintf("asset type named %s does
not exist", assetTypeName)
                        return nil, errors.NewCCError(errMsg, 404)
                  }
                  assetDefBytes, err := json.Marshal(assetTypeDef)
                  if err != nil {
                        errMsg := fmt.Sprintf("error marshaling asset
definition: %s", err)
                        return nil, errors.NewCCError(errMsg, 500)
                  }
                  return assetDefBytes, nil
            }

            assetTypeList := assets.AssetTypeList()
            // If user requested asset list
            type assetListElem struct {
                  Tag         string   `json:"tag"`
                  Label       string   `json:"label"`
                  Description string   `json:"description"`
                  Readers     []string `json:"readers,omitempty"`
                  Writers     []string `json:"writers"`
                  Dynamic     bool     `json:"dynamic"`
            }
            var assetList []assetListElem
            for _, assetTypeDef := range assetTypeList {
                  assetList = append(assetList, assetListElem{
                        Tag:         assetTypeDef.Tag,
                        Label:       assetTypeDef.Label,
                        Description: assetTypeDef.Description,
```

```
                    Readers:     assetTypeDef.Readers,
                    Dynamic:     assetTypeDef.Dynamic,
                })
            }

            assetListBytes, err := json.Marshal(assetList)
            if err != nil {
                return nil, errors.WrapErrorWithStatus(err, "error
marshaling asset list", 500)
            }
            return assetListBytes, nil
    },
}
```

The transaction is marked as **ReadOnly** and **MetaTx**, signifying that it does not alter the state of the ledger and pertains to metadata transactions.

The primary purpose of **GetSchema** is to fetch schema information about various asset types. It takes one argument, **assetType**, which is a string specifying the asset type whose definition is to be retrieved. If this argument is left empty, the function returns a list of all available asset types.

Inside the **Routine** block, the function first verifies the provided **assetType** argument, ensuring it is a string. If a specific asset type is requested and it exists, the function retrieves its definition and returns it in JSON format. If the requested asset type is not found, it generates an error message.

In cases where no specific asset type is requested, **GetSchema** compiles and returns a list of all available asset types. This list includes comprehensive details for each asset type, such as tags, labels, descriptions, and information about who can read or write these assets. The function is equipped with robust error handling mechanisms, returning appropriate error messages and statuses for issues like invalid arguments or problems in JSON serialization.

An API call for this transaction is as follows:

```
curl -X 'GET' \
  'http://localhost/api/gateway/query/getSchema' \
  -H 'accept: */*'
```

In the demo repository of CC-Tools, a response body will be as follows:

```
[
  {
    "description": "Personal data of someone",
    "dynamic": false,
    "label": "Person",
    "tag": "person",
```

```
    "writers": null
  },
  {
    "description": "Book",
    "dynamic": false,
    "label": "Book",
    "tag": "book",
    "writers": null
  },
  {
    "description": "Library as a collection of books",
    "dynamic": false,
    "label": "Library",
    "tag": "library",
    "writers": null
  },
  {
    "description": "Secret between Org2 and Org3",
    "dynamic": false,
    "label": "Secret",
    "readers": [
      "org2MSP",
      "org3MSP",
      "orgMSP"
    ],
    "tag": "secret",
    "writers": null
  },
  {
    "description": "AssetTypeListData",
    "dynamic": false,
    "label": "AssetTypeListData",
    "tag": "assetTypeListData",
    "writers": null
  }
]
```


Note that a list of all defined assets without their properties was returned. To get details on a specific asset, we can tweak the call to include the **assetType** parameter in the body, as follows:

```
curl -X 'POST' \
  'http://localhost/api/gateway/query/getSchema' \
  -H 'accept: */*' \
  -H 'Content-Type: application/json' \
  -d '{
  "assetType": "person"
}'
```

The endpoint is the same but making it a **POST** request with the required body allows us to get details for a particular asset.

The response body in this case is as follows:

```
  "description": "Personal data of someone",
  "label": "Person",
  "props": [
    {
      "dataType": "cpf",
      "description": "",
      "isKey": true,
      "label": "CPF (Brazilian ID)",
      "readOnly": false,
      "required": true,
      "tag": "id",
      "writers": [
        "org1MSP",
        "orgMSP"
      ]
    },
    {
      "dataType": "string",
      "description": "",
      "isKey": false,
      "label": "Name of the person",
      "readOnly": false,
      "required": true,
      "tag": "name",
      "writers": null
    },
    {
      "dataType": "datetime",
      "description": "",
```

```
      "isKey": false,
      "label": "Date of Birth",
      "readOnly": false,
      "required": false,
      "tag": "dateOfBirth",
      "writers": null
    },
    {
      "dataType": "number",
      "defaultValue": 0,
      "description": "",
      "isKey": false,
      "label": "Person's height",
      "readOnly": false,
      "required": false,
      "tag": "height",
      "writers": null
    }
  ],
  "tag": "person"
}
```

Transactions endpoint

For transaction details, another set of endpoints can be used. This, in turn, will inform the API user of which transactions are defined and what arguments they expect. Take a look at how the **getTx** implements the return of a specific transaction in the following code:

```
// getTx returns a specific tx definition or a list of all configured txs
var getTx = Transaction{
      Tag:         "getTx",
      Label:       "Get Tx",
      Description: "",
      Method:      "GET",

      ReadOnly: true,
      MetaTx:   true,
      Args: ArgList{
            {
                  Tag:         "txName",
                  DataType:    "string",
```

```
                Description: "The name of the transaction of which
you want to fetch the definition. Leave empty to fetch a list of possible
transactions.",
            },
        },
        Routine: func(stub *sw.StubWrapper, req map[string]interface{}) ([]
byte, errors.ICCError) {
            var txName string

            txNameInterface, ok := req["txName"]
            if ok {
                txName = txNameInterface.(string)
            }

            txList := TxList()

            // If user requested a specific transaction definition
            if txName != "" {
                txDef := FetchTx(txName)
                if txDef == nil {
                    errMsg := fmt.Sprintf("transaction named %s does
not exist", txName)
                    return nil, errors.NewCCError(errMsg, 404)
                }
                txDefBytes, err := json.Marshal(txDef)
                if err != nil {
                    return nil, errors.WrapErrorWithStatus(err,
"error marshaling transaction definition", 400)
                }
                return txDefBytes, nil
            }

            // If user requested asset list
            type txListElem struct {
                Tag         string   `json:"tag"`
                Label       string   `json:"label"`
                Description string   `json:"description"`
                Callers     []string `json:"callers,omitempty"`
            }
            var txRetList []txListElem
            for _, tx := range txList {
```

```
                txRetList = append(txRetList, txListElem{
                      Tag:         tx.Tag,
                      Label:       tx.Label,
                      Description: tx.Description,
                      Callers:     tx.Callers,
                })
          }

          txListBytes, err := json.Marshal(txRetList)
          if err != nil {
                return nil, errors.WrapErrorWithStatus(err, "error
marshaling transaction list", 500)
          }
          return txListBytes, nil
     },
}
```

Functionally, **getTx** takes one argument, **txName**. This argument specifies the name of the transaction definition to be retrieved. If this argument is left empty, the function returns a list of all possible transactions in the system.

Let us take a look at two API calls for this endpoint, as follows:

```
curl -X 'GET' \
  'http://localhost/api/gateway/query/getTx' \
  -H 'accept: */*'
```

This will retrieve, as one might expect, the list of transactions supported by the system.

Following is an example of a response to the call above:

```
[
  {
    "callers": [
      "$org3MSP",
      "$orgMSP"
    ],
    "description": "Create a New Library",
    "label": "Create New Library",
    "tag": "createNewLibrary"
  },
  {
    "callers": [
      "$org2MSP",
```

```
      "$orgMSP"
    ],
    "description": "Return the number of books of a library",
    "label": "Get Number Of Books From Library",
    "tag": "getNumberOfBooksFromLibrary"
  },
  {
    "callers": [
      "$org\\dMSP",
      "orgMSP"
    ],
    "description": "Change the tenant of a book",
    "label": "Update Book Tenant",
    "tag": "updateBookTenant"
  },
  {
    "callers": [
      "$org1MSP",
      "$org2MSP",
      "$orgMSP"
    ],
    "description": "Return all the books from an author",
    "label": "Get Books by the Author Name",
    "tag": "getBooksByAuthor"
  },
  {
    "description": "",
    "label": "Get Schema",
    "tag": "getSchema"
  }
  ...
]
```

This response was shortened as not to be too extensive. However, not only custom-defined transactions are returned, but also all CC-Tools built-in transactions, as well.

In order to get more information about a specific transaction, the following call is used:

```
curl -X 'POST' \
  'http://localhost/api/gateway/query/getTx' \
  -H 'accept: */*' \
  -H 'Content-Type: application/json' \
```

```
  -d '{
  "txName": "createNewLibrary"
}'
```

This call returns the transaction metadata and list of expected arguments, as follows

```
{
  "args": [
    {
      "dataType": "string",
      "description": "Name of the library",
      "label": "Name",
      "private": false,
      "required": true,
      "tag": "name"
    }
  ],
  "callers": [
    "$org3MSP",
    "$orgMSP"
  ],
  "description": "Create a New Library",
  "label": "Create New Library",
  "metaTx": false,
  "method": "POST",
  "readOnly": false,
  "tag": "createNewLibrary"
}
```

Query endpoint

As we have seen, transaction calls follow a similar standard where the transaction tag is added to the last part of the endpoint path, such as **/api/gateway/query/getSchema** or **/api/gateway/invoke/createNewCar**. Transactions can be executed as queries or invokes, defined, also, in the endpoint path. Let us explore how a query call is translated into a transaction call when using the gateway endpoints.

After handling the parameters received in the request, the chaincode API implements a query function that uses the gateway to make the transaction call, as follows:

```
func QueryGateway(channelName, chaincodeName, txName, args string) ([]byte,
error) {
	// Gateway endpoint
	endpoint := os.Getenv("FABRIC_GATEWAY_ENDPOINT")
```

```
        // Create client grpc connection
        grpcConn, err := common.CreateGrpcConnection(endpoint)
        if err != nil {
                return nil, errors.Wrap(err, "failed to create grpc
connection")
        }
        defer grpcConn.Close()

        // Create gateway connection
        gw, err := common.CreateGatewayConnection(grpcConn)
        if err != nil {
                return nil, errors.Wrap(err, "failed to create gateway
connection")
        }
        defer gw.Close()

        // Obtain smart contract deployed on the network.
        network := gw.GetNetwork(channelName)
        contract := network.GetContract(chaincodeName)

        // Query transaction
        if len(args) == 0 {
                return contract.EvaluateTransaction(txName)
        }

        return contract.EvaluateTransaction(txName, args)
}
```

This function accepts four string parameters: **channelName**, **chaincodeName**, **txName**, and **args**, which are treated by the handler and come from the request. Initially, the function retrieves the Fabric Gateway endpoint from an environment variable. Using this endpoint, it establishes a GRPC connection to the network.

Upon successfully creating the GRPC connection, the function proceeds to establish a gateway connection, providing a higher-level API for interacting with the network. The next step involves accessing the specified smart contract by obtaining the network object corresponding to the given channel name and retrieving the contract object using the chaincode name.

If the **args** string is empty, the function calls **EvaluateTransaction** using only the transaction name. If **args** is not empty, it includes these arguments in the call. The **EvaluateTransaction** method is used for querying the ledger, without making any changes to it.

Invoke endpoint

Invoke calls alter the state of the ledger, and although the function call with the gateway SDK is just as simple, there are some differences. Let us see the invoke function as implemented by the chaincode API, as follows:

```
func InvokeGateway(channelName, chaincodeName, txName, args string,
transientArgs []byte, endorsingOrgs []string) ([]byte, error) {
	// Gateway endpoint
	endpoint := os.Getenv("FABRIC_GATEWAY_ENDPOINT")

	// Create client grpc connection
	grpcConn, err := common.CreateGrpcConnection(endpoint)
	if err != nil {
		return nil, errors.Wrap(err, "failed to create grpc
connection")
	}
	defer grpcConn.Close()

	// Create gateway connection
	gw, err := common.CreateGatewayConnection(grpcConn)
	if err != nil {
		return nil, errors.Wrap(err, "failed to create gateway
connection")
	}
	defer gw.Close()

	// Obtain smart contract deployed on the network.
	network := gw.GetNetwork(channelName)
	contract := network.GetContract(chaincodeName)

	// Make transient request
	transientMap := make(map[string][]byte)
	transientMap["@request"] = transientArgs

	// Invoke transaction
	if transientArgs != nil && len(endorsingOrgs) > 0 {
		return contract.Submit(txName,
			client.WithArguments(args),
			client.WithTransient(transientMap),
			client.WithEndorsingOrganizations(endorsingOrgs...),
		)
```

```
	}

	if transientArgs != nil {
		return contract.Submit(txName,
			client.WithArguments(args),
			client.WithTransient(transientMap),
		)
	}

	if len(endorsingOrgs) > 0 {
		return contract.Submit(txName,
			client.WithArguments(args),
			client.WithEndorsingOrganizations(endorsingOrgs...),
		)
	}

	return contract.SubmitTransaction(txName, args)
}
```

This function is more complex than a simple query as it potentially alters the state of the ledger. It accepts several parameters: **`channelName`**, **`chaincodeName`**, **`txName`**, **`args`**, **`transientArgs`**, and **`endorsingOrgs`**. These parameters specify the channel, chaincode, transaction name, arguments for the transaction, transient arguments (confidential data), and the endorsing organizations, respectively.

Just like the query function, the invoke function creates a GRPC connection to the Fabric network using this endpoint. After successfully establishing the GRPC connection, the function sets up a gateway connection and defines the necessary objects that will allow interaction.

The function then prepares for the transaction invocation. It creates a **`transientMap`** for holding the transient arguments, which are typically used for sensitive data that should not be stored on the ledger but are required for transaction processing.

The invocation of the transaction depends on the provided arguments and endorsing organizations. The function checks various conditions: if both transient arguments and endorsing organizations are provided, if only transient arguments are provided, and if only endorsing organizations are provided. Depending on these conditions, it calls the **`Submit`** method on the contract object with appropriate options like arguments, transient data, and endorsing organizations.

If none of the special conditions apply (no transient arguments or specific endorsing organizations), the function simply invokes the **`SubmitTransaction`** method with the transaction name and arguments. This method is used to submit a transaction to the ledger, potentially altering its state.

Conclusion

In this chapter, we have provided a thorough exploration of the Hyperledger Fabric Gateway SDK, emphasizing its significance as a client interface for chaincode interactions. We detailed the transition from legacy SDKs to the more efficient Fabric Gateway service, particularly for peer nodes in version v2.4 and beyond. The reader learned about various API endpoints such as schema, transactions, query, and invoke, each serving distinct roles in the interaction with the chaincode. The differences between query and invoke endpoints were highlighted, illustrating how they uniquely affect the ledger's state.

Additionally, we discussed the functionalities of CC-Tools, showcasing their utility in developing and customizing APIs for specific chaincode applications. This chapter aimed to not only impart theoretical knowledge about the SDK and its endpoints but also to provide practical insights and skills for effective API development. Now, readers are well-equipped with a comprehensive understanding of the Hyperledger Fabric Gateway SDK, enabling them to proficiently develop and implement APIs for diverse blockchain applications.

In the next chapter, we will cover the use of private data collections to keep data secret in a Hyperledger Fabric network.

CHAPTER 11
Using Private Data Collections

Introduction

In the evolving landscape of blockchain technology, the aspects of security and privacy stand at the forefront, driving innovation and adoption across various applications. The advantage of blockchain, particularly for enterprises, lies in its robust security features and the promise of enhanced privacy. Hyperledger Fabric distinguishes itself through its channel architecture, offering a foundational step toward the effective segregation of data among participating entities. This architecture not only facilitates the creation of isolated information containers, channels to which only authorized organizations have access but also addresses the need for data privacy within these shared spaces.

As discussed in *Chapter 4, Fabric Concepts and Components*, Hyperledger Fabric introduces a solution to this challenge through the mechanism of **private data collections** (**PDCs**). These PDCs are designed to safeguard sensitive information from other parties, enabling organizations to selectively share data within a confined subset of participants while ensuring the utmost confidentiality of other pieces of information. This chapter aims to explore the practicalities of PDCs, elucidating their significance, operational mechanisms, and implementation with CC-Tools.

By expanding on the concepts introduced earlier, this chapter will provide readers with a comprehensive understanding of how to leverage PDCs to enhance data privacy and security within the Hyperledger Fabric ecosystem. Through detailed exploration and practical guidance, we will navigate the intricacies of implementing these private data constructs, thereby empowering organizations to achieve a balance between transparency and privacy in their blockchain endeavors.

Structure

The chapter covers the following topics:

- Understanding private data
- Using private data
- Learning to use private data

Objectives

By the end of this chapter, readers will understand the concept of private data within Hyperledger Fabric, its role, how it is organized into collections, and its storage mechanisms. This section aims to provide a foundation for understanding secure and selective information sharing in a blockchain network. By exploring PDCs and storage, readers will grasp the architecture that protects sensitive information, ensuring data confidentiality.

Furthermore, the chapter will guide readers through scenarios that necessitate the use of private data, highlighting relevant use cases. By the end of this chapter, readers will know when to implement PDCs effectively, improving their blockchain solution planning. The chapter concludes with a guide on defining PDCs, making transaction calls, and managing data privacy. By the end, readers will have the skills to use PDCs, enhancing the security and privacy of their blockchain applications.

Understanding private data

In the realm of Hyperledger Fabric, a key innovation lies in its approach to handling confidential information through the concept of private data. This mechanism is pivotal for organizations that seek to leverage blockchain technology while ensuring the utmost confidentiality and privacy of their transactions. Private data in Hyperledger Fabric is not merely a feature; it represents a shift towards more secure and private blockchain networks.

Private data is stored distinctly from the channel ledger, in a private database accessible only to authorized peers. This separation is crucial for maintaining the confidentiality of sensitive information, as it restricts data access to a select group of organizations within a channel, known as PDC. These collections specify which organizations are entitled to store and interact with the private data, effectively isolating it from those not authorized. While unauthorized organizations can observe a hash of the private data on the channel ledger, the actual content remains inaccessible to them, ensuring that confidentiality is not compromised. The ingenuity of this system lies in its ability to balance privacy with transparency, allowing for the verification of transactions by all channel participants through the presence of hashes, without exposing the underlying private data.

PDCs address a critical challenge in blockchain privacy, eliminating the need for multiple channels to maintain data confidentiality among different organizational participants. This feature simplifies network architecture and reduces the administrative burden associated with managing separate channels for privacy purposes. PDCs enable a wide array of use cases, from GDPR compliance to the selective sharing of sensitive healthcare information. By facilitating efficient management of confidential transactions within a single channel, PDCs represent a significant advancement in blockchain technology, offering a scalable and flexible solution for privacy-focused applications.

Collections

PDCs in Hyperledger Fabric serve as a robust mechanism for managing confidential data within a blockchain network, allowing specific data to be shared among a subset of organizations while keeping it hidden from others. These collections are defined in a JSON format and include policies that specify which members of the network can access and transact with the private data. For instance, an **`Org1Org2PrivateCollection`** may allow only members of **`Org1`** and **`Org2`** to access its private data, ensuring that sensitive information is accessible only to those with the necessary permissions. Similarly, an **`Org2Org3PrivateCollection`** would restrict access to members of **`Org2`** and **`Org3`**. This setup allows for the segregation of data, where each organization controls its own private data, yet can interact within the broader network for transactions that require consensus across all nodes.

Each collection is configured with a JSON file containing the following parameters:

- **Name**: It identifier of the collection.
- **Policy**: It describes the private data distribution policy, detailing which organization's peers can access and store the collection data. It requires a broader set of organizations than the endorsement policy for supporting read/write transactions and outlines conditions under which non-members can endorse transactions.
- **RequiredPeerCount**: The minimum number of peers needed to disseminate private data before endorsing a transaction. A count of zero indicates no obligatory distribution, but some level of distribution is recommended for data availability.
- **MaxPeerCount**: The maximum number of peers to which data will be disseminated for redundancy. If set to zero, it implies reliance on data pulls from endorsing peers at commit time.

- **BlockToLive**: Defines the duration data will remain in the private database, measured in blocks. A setting of zero means data is never purged.
- **MemberOnlyRead**: It ensures that only clients from member organizations can read private data. A setting of false allows for customized access control.
- **MemberOnlyWrite**: It ensures that only clients from member organizations can write to the private data. A setting of false enables specific non-member clients to write.
- **EndorsementPolicy**: This is optional and allows for a collection-specific endorsement policy, which may differ from the general chaincode level policy. It can be tailored to match the distribution policy or incorporate a different organizational mix.

In the CC-Tools-Demo, under the file **`chaincode/collections.json`** we can see an example JSON defining a collection. It will become clearer how this definition is used in the context of the demo project.

Refer to the following code:

```
[
    {
        "name": "secret",
        "requiredPeerCount": 0,
        "maxPeerCount": 3,
        "blockToLive": 1000000,
        "memberOnlyRead": true,
        "policy": "OR('org2MSP.member', 'org3MSP.member')"
    }
]
```

Hyperledger Fabric introduces implicit PDCs for every chaincode, allowing organizations to store their private data without the need for explicit definitions. These collections, specific to each organization, manage data endorsement and dissemination policies internally, facilitating secure, organization-specific data storage and sharing in multi-party business processes. Unlike explicit collections, implicit ones do not support properties like **`memberOnlyRead`** or **`blockToLive`**, requiring access control to be managed through chaincode logic. This simplifies private data handling in blockchain applications, promoting efficient and confidential data exchange among participating organizations.

In essence, PDCs and their implicit counterparts are foundational to creating secure, efficient, and privacy-preserving blockchain applications within the Hyperledger Fabric ecosystem. They provide a flexible framework for data privacy that can be tailored to the specific needs of various applications, ensuring that sensitive information remains confidential while still benefiting from the decentralized and immutable nature of blockchain technology.

When using PDCs in chaincode, the transaction process is adapted to maintain data secrecy. The transaction flow is adapted: a client application sends a proposal to invoke a chaincode operation concerning private data to a selected peer. This peer, using the gateway service, picks appropriate endorsers based on the data's collection policy. The proposal contains private data in a temporary, secure manner. Endorsers evaluate the proposal, temporarily storing and distributing the private data as needed, without revealing it outside authorized circles. They respond with an endorsement that includes a hash of the private data, ensuring confidentiality. The transaction, now with endorsements, is signed by the client and sent through the network to be recorded, with only the hash of the private data included in the ledger. Authorized peers later access the actual private data, verify it against the hash, and store it securely, ensuring both privacy and integrity.

Figure 11.1 provides an example of how organizations can arrange themselves in different PDCs:

Figure 11.1: *Private collections in Hyperledger Fabric*

Storage

In Hyperledger Fabric, the storage of private data is a critical feature that enables participants in a blockchain network to share sensitive information securely and selectively. Private data is stored in a separate, private database associated with each peer, LevelDB or CouchDB, distinct from the ledger that records the transactions and the world state. This architecture ensures that private data is accessible only to authorized parties, maintaining confidentiality while allowing transactions that depend on this data to be verified by all participants. The mechanism for defining and managing access to private data is through collections, which specify the policies governing the distribution and accessibility of the data among the network's organizations.

Purging of private data in Fabric plays a vital role in managing the lifecycle and confidentiality of sensitive information. The **BlockToLive** property of a collection defines how long (in terms of the number of blocks added to the ledger) private data should remain accessible before it is automatically purged from the private database. This feature is crucial for compliance with data retention policies and regulations, as it allows organizations to ensure that sensitive data does not persist indefinitely on the network. Once the specified **BlockToLive** period has elapsed, the data is purged, meaning it is deleted from the private database and cannot be accessed or recovered by peers. However, the proof of the transaction involving private data remains on the blockchain, ensuring the integrity and auditability of the network's transaction history.

The purging process underscores Fabric's commitment to privacy and security, providing a systematic method for the removal of outdated or no longer necessary private data. It also highlights the platform's flexibility in handling the diverse requirements of enterprise applications, where the ability to enforce data governance and comply with privacy laws is paramount. By allowing organizations to define custom retention periods for private data, Fabric ensures that blockchain networks can adapt to various industry standards and regulatory environments, making it a robust solution for building secure, compliant, and efficient enterprise blockchain applications.

Using private data

Private data collection should be used whenever a subset of registries needs to be hidden from a group of organizations that are members of a channel. However, when complete transactions and data should be kept private for a group of organizations, a channel should be used.

It is important to remember that private data is composed of the actual data, stored on the peer database and shared peer-to-peer with gossip, and the hash of the data, which is endorsed, ordered, and committed to the ledger. A consequence of this architecture is that only the history of the hash is kept whenever the key changes.

Use cases

Let us see with a couple of examples when we might choose to use PDCs. Imagine a supply chain environment where five organizations partner to get products from origin to consumers. These organizations are as follows:

- Farmer
- Distributor
- Shipper
- Wholesaler
- Retailer

The farmer produces their goods and sells them abroad, the distributor works with the farmer to make that happen. The shipper takes care of transporting those goods and fulfilling the wholesaler and retailer orders.

In this scenario, the distributor seeks to maintain the confidentiality of transaction terms with the farmer and shipper, aiming to shield the markup prices from the wholesaler and retailer. This requirement emerges from the distributor's intent to safeguard competitive pricing strategies and prevent disclosure of financial margins.

Furthermore, the distributor is inclined to establish a distinct, private data relationship with the wholesaler, attributed to the preferential pricing offered to the wholesaler compared to the retailer. This strategy is designed to sustain differentiated pricing models while preserving transaction confidentiality.

Additionally, the wholesaler expresses an interest in forming private data connections with both the retailer and the shipper. This inclination stems from a desire to manage pricing and supply chain information discreetly, ensuring competitive advantage and operational efficiency.

In order to address these requirements without resorting to the creation of numerous, isolated channels for each pairwise relationship, which would significantly complicate network topology and management, a strategic approach leveraging multiple PDCs is adopted.

This methodology enables the selective sharing of confidential data among specified parties, thus, the following:

- **PDC1** is configured exclusively for the distributor and wholesaler, enabling a private data exchange that reflects the special pricing agreement.
- **PDC2** is established between the distributor, farmer, and shipper, facilitating the confidential exchange of transaction details among them.
- **PDC3** encompasses the wholesaler, retailer, and shipper, designed to allow the discreet sharing of information pertinent to their transactions.

This configuration efficiently utilizes the capabilities of Hyperledger Fabric's PDCs to meet the organizations' privacy requirements. It ensures that sensitive information, such as pricing and terms of trade, remains confidential within the specified subsets of network participants, thereby maintaining the integrity and confidentiality of business transactions within the consortium.

Figure 11.2 illustrates an example of how PDCs can be structured in a supply-chain context:

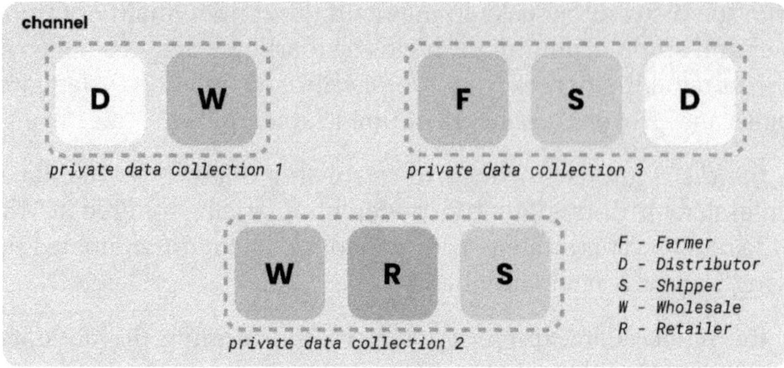

***Figure 11.2:** Example of private collections for supply-chain*

Imagine a different scenario, a private **Central Bank Digital Currency** (**CBDC**). Although CBDCs are currently a research topic encompassing multiple areas, let us focus on the privacy aspect of what might constitute the implementation of a wholesale CBDC, that is, a CBDC aimed at banks and not the general public. In blockchain terms, it can be represented by a token.

The objective is to configure a system within a Hyperledger Fabric channel where each bank, acting as an organization, can access only its own tokens, while the Central Bank, serving as the regulatory body, has visibility into the tokens of all banks. This is achievable through a specific setup of PDCs.

Figure 11.3 illustrates how PDCs can be arranged in this context:

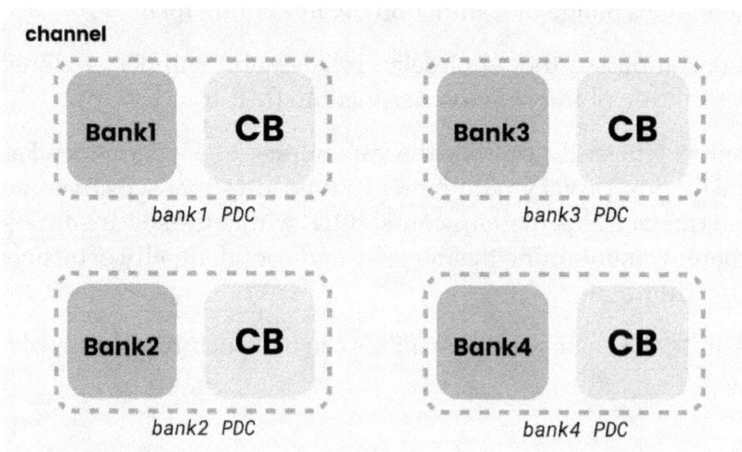

***Figure 11.3:** Example for private collections for a private token*

This setup ensures that a token, once registered, is accessible solely by the owner bank and the Central Bank, addressing the issue of read permissions. Additionally, banks must transfer tokens amongst themselves. The **MemberOnlyWrite** policy in Fabric allows collections to be writable by external members without granting read access. Consequently, a chaincode transaction for transferring tokens can be designed to adhere to the appropriate rules for recording the transaction in the intended collection. By including it in every PDC, the Central Bank can monitor transactions to maintain accurate balance records, which is essential for managing private tokens.

This approach is a common practice in Hyperledger Fabric for managing the transfer of private assets between collections and is part of a broader set of strategies for handling private data within the network.

Other patterns for private data are as follows:

- **Leveraging public keys for state tracking:** Utilize public keys to monitor public states like asset attributes and ownership, alongside private keys/values in each organization's private data collection for authorized access to private data.
- **Access control via Chaincode:** Implement access controls within chaincode to define client permissions for querying private data, utilizing client credentials and potentially a passphrase for data access verification.
- **Out-of-band private data sharing:** Share private data directly with other organizations, allowing them to verify authenticity through on-chain hash comparisons using the `GetPrivateDataHash()` API.
- **On-chain private data sharing and transferring:** Enable sharing and transferring of private data across organizations' collections via chaincode, with verification through `GetPrivateDataHash()` and conditional on additional endorsements for transaction integrity.
- **Transaction approval using private data:** Use private data for transaction pre-approval, employing the `GetPrivateDataHash()` for consent verification. Fabric v2.0 supports enhanced security with collection-level endorsement policies.
- **Maintaining transaction participant anonymity:** Keep transaction participants' identities confidential by recording agreements in private collections and using hashed references on-chain, with the option for participants to reveal pre-images for verification if needed.

Learning to use private data

Collections are specified at the time of chaincode development and deployment, serving a crucial role in transactions. To effectively manage private data, chaincodes need to be designed to interact with these collections directly. When initiating a transaction, whether through a **command line interface** (**CLI**) or a client application, it is essential to employ the transient map for passing parameters. This approach safeguards against potential data exposure within the blockchain ledger.

CC-Tools offers an enhanced method for handling PDCs, streamlining their integration by abstracting operations such as **PutPrivateData**. This simplification facilitates a more straightforward interaction with PDCs, while still maintaining the integrity and confidentiality of the underlying data. The forthcoming discussion will delve into the utilization of PDCs, comparing the conventional methodology with the refined process offered by CC-Tools.

Define collections

Whether using PDCs conventionally or through CC-Tools, collections, as we have seen, should be defined in JSON files, that are passed as parameters of the chaincode lifecycle. For example, let us define the collections for our CBDC scenario, as follows:

```
[
    {
        "name": "bank1MSPfunds",
        "requiredPeerCount": 0,
        "maxPeerCount": 3,
        "blockToLive": 0,
        "memberOnlyRead": true,
        "memberOnlyWrite": false,
        "policy": "OR('bank1MSP.member', 'centralBankMSP.member')"
    },
    {
        "name": "bank2MSPfunds",
        "requiredPeerCount": 0,
        "maxPeerCount": 3,
        "blockToLive": 0,
        "memberOnlyRead": true,
        "memberOnlyWrite": false,
        "policy": "OR('bank2MSP.member', 'centralBankMSP.member')"
    },
    {
        "name": "bank3MSPfunds",
        "requiredPeerCount": 0,
        "maxPeerCount": 3,
        "blockToLive": 0,
        "memberOnlyRead": true,
        "memberOnlyWrite": false,
        "policy": "OR('bank3MSP.member', 'centralBankMSP.member')"
    },
    {
```

```
        "name": "bank4MSPfunds",
        "requiredPeerCount": 0,
        "maxPeerCount": 3,
        "blockToLive": 0,
        "memberOnlyRead": true,
        "memberOnlyWrite": false,
        "policy": "OR('bank4MSP.member', 'centralBankMSP.member')"
    }
]
```

Next, let us define an asset in CC-Tools that will represent a token object, as follows:

```
var Token = assets.AssetType{
      Tag:          "token",
      Label:        "Token",
      Description: "Token representation. Following the UTXO model.",

      Props: []assets.AssetProp{
            {
                  // Primary key
                  Required: true,
                  IsKey:    true,
                  Tag:      "txId",
                  Label:    "Transaction ID",
                  DataType: "string",
            },
            {
                  Required: true,
                  IsKey:    true,
                  Tag:      "owner",
                  Label:    "Owner (Org’s MSPID)",
                  DataType: "string",
            },
            {
                  Required: true,
                  IsKey:    true,
                  Tag:      “quantity”,
                  Label:    “Quantity”,
                  DataType: “number”,
            },
            {
```

```
                    Required: true,
                    Tag:      "spent",
                    Label:    "Spent?",
                    DataType: "boolean",
                },
        },
}
```

This token is implemented in the **unspent transaction output (UTXO)** model, a fundamental concept used in blockchain technology, particularly known for its use in the Bitcoin blockchain. In the UTXO model, transactions are structured around the idea of inputs and outputs, where each output from one transaction can become an input in another.

A UTXO represents an unspent output from a blockchain transaction, essentially indicating the amount of digital currency available for a user to spend. Unlike account-based models that track the balance of each account, the UTXO model tracks individual pieces of currency. This model enhances privacy by making it more challenging to trace the flow of funds and improves scalability by allowing transactions to be processed in parallel.

The implementation of a token within this framework means that each movement of the token is recorded as a discrete transaction output, awaiting to be spent by the new owner, thereby contributing to a secure and transparent ledger of ownership and transaction history.

The remaining part of our private token chaincode is a transaction that will make issuing tokens and transferring them possible. Those transactions will make use of the following code, where the collection can be assembled from parameters received by the transaction and will reference the respective collection defined in the previous JSON:

```
err = stub.PutPrivateData(collection, assetKey, assetBytes)
if err != nil {
        return errors.WrapError(err, "failed to write asset to ledger")
}
```

CC-Tools takes a novel approach when defining private data. Each asset type can have a **`Readers`** property, which encodes for private data collection for that asset type. That means that organizations can share private definitions of assets and their respective registries. In CC-Tools-Demo, an example is fully implemented, and the asset secret is located in **`chaincode/assettypes/secret.go`**. Check the implementation of a secret asset in the code, as follows:

```
// Secret is and information available only for org2 and org3
// Collections.json configuration is necessary
var Secret = assets.AssetType{
        Tag:        "secret",
```

```
        Label:        "Secret",
        Description: "Secret between Org2 and Org3",

        Readers: []string{"org2MSP", "org3MSP"},
        Props: []assets.AssetProp{
              {
                    // Primary Key
                    IsKey:    true,
                    Tag:      "secretName",
                    Label:    "Secret Name",
                    DataType: "string",
                    Writers:  []string{`org2MSP`}, // This means only org2
can create the asset (org3 can edit)
              },
              {
                    // Mandatory Property
                    Required: true,
                    Tag:      "secret",
                    Label:    "Secret",
                    DataType: "string",
              },
        },
}
```

The configuration of a collection is required, and in this case, the name of the collection is important, as it must be the same as the **asset** tag. Beyond that, the readers defined in the chaincode must be the same as the **orgs** defined in the collection policy to keep the logic consistent.

The following code defines the contents of the collection configuration file:

```
[
    {
        "name": "secret",
        "requiredPeerCount": 0,
        "maxPeerCount": 3,
        "blockToLive": 1000000,
        "memberOnlyRead": true,
        "policy": "OR('org2MSP.member', 'org3MSP.member')"
    }
]
```

Once this is set up and the chaincode is up and running, every write made to this asset type will automatically be to its collections, regardless of which write function of CC-

Tools is being used. This is achieved through many verifications that CC-Tools does on the data that are being registered and their validations. Let us see what happens when a **PutNew** function is called for a private asset. All the code shown is available at the CC-Tools repository.

At first, nothing particularly specific is done. The asset is checked against the state of the ledger, to ensure that it does not exist.

Refer to the following code for a better understanding:

```
// PutNew inserts asset in blockchain and returns error if asset exists.
func (a *Asset) PutNew(stub *sw.StubWrapper) (map[string]interface{},
errors.ICCError) {
	// Check if asset already exists
	exists, err := a.ExistsInLedger(stub)
	if err != nil {
		return nil, errors.WrapError(err, "failed to verify if asset
already exists")
	}
	if exists {
		return nil, errors.NewCCError("asset already exists", 409)
	}

	// Marshal asset back to JSON format
	res, err := a.Put(stub)
	if err != nil {
		return nil, errors.WrapError(err, "failed to write asset to
ledger")
	}

	return res, nil
}
```

Then, the **Put** function is called, which checks allowed writers, injects metadata, and validates references, before calling the private **put** function, as follows:

```
// Put inserts asset in blockchain
func (a *Asset) Put(stub *sw.StubWrapper) (map[string]interface{}, errors.
ICCError) {
	// Check if org has write permission
	err := a.CheckWriters(stub)
	if err != nil {
		return nil, errors.WrapError(err, "failed write permission
check")
```

```
	}

	err = a.injectMetadata(stub)
	if err != nil {
		return nil, errors.WrapError(err, "failed injecting asset
metadata")
	}

	err = a.validateRefs(stub)
	if err != nil {
		return nil, errors.WrapError(err, "failed reference
validation")
	}
	return a.put(stub)
}
```

The **put** function processes the asset some more and checks if the asset is private with the **IsPrivate** function, and if so, it calls **PutPrivateData** instead of **PutState**, as follows:

```
func (a *Asset) put(stub *sw.StubWrapper) (map[string]interface{}, errors.
ICCError) {
	var err error

	// Clean asset of any nil entries
	a.clean()

	// Write index of references this asset points to
	err = a.putRefs(stub)
	if err != nil {
		return nil, errors.WrapError(err, "failed writing reference
index")
	}

	// Marshal asset back to JSON format
	assetJSON, err := json.Marshal(a)
	if err != nil {
		return nil, errors.WrapError(err, "failed to encode asset to
JSON format")
	}

	// Write asset to blockchain
	if a.IsPrivate() {
```

```
		err = stub.PutPrivateData(a.TypeTag(), a.Key(), assetJSON)
		if err != nil {
			return nil, errors.WrapError(err, "failed to write 
asset to ledger")
		}
		assetKeyOnly := map[string]interface{}{
			"@key":       a.Key(),
			"@assetType": a.TypeTag(),
		}
		return assetKeyOnly, nil
	}

	err = stub.PutState(a.Key(), assetJSON)
	if err != nil {
		return nil, errors.WrapError(err, "failed to write asset to 
ledger")
	}
	return *a, nil
}
```

The **IsPrivate** function does something very straightforward, checking if there are readers defined. This is why it is important to keep collection configuration and asset definition consistent.

Refer to the implementation as follows:

```
func (t AssetType) IsPrivate() bool {
	return len(t.Readers) > 0
}
```

Transaction call

In chaincode proposals, it is critical to ensure that private data is not embedded within the main content of the proposal that gets recorded on the blockchain. To address this concern, a designated area known as the transient field within the chaincode proposal is utilized for transmitting private data from the client, or for passing data that the chaincode will subsequently use to produce private data, to the chaincode execution on the peer. The chaincode accesses this data through the **GetTransient** call. Notably, the transient field is specifically designed to be omitted from the transaction records on the channel, thereby safeguarding the confidentiality of the data.

The importance of the transient map in blockchain applications cannot be overstated. This feature plays a crucial role in maintaining the privacy and security of sensitive information during transactions. By providing a secure mechanism for transmitting private data that is excluded from the permanent transaction ledger, the transient map ensures that confidential data remains protected from unauthorized access and visibility. This is especially vital in applications requiring high levels of data privacy, such as financial transactions, identity management, and confidential agreements. The transient map, therefore, is a fundamental aspect of designing and implementing blockchain solutions that require the handling of sensitive information, enabling developers to build systems that are both transparent and secure.

In the chaincode API provided by the **CC-Tools-Demo**, invoke functions implement the use of transient arguments. One such function is the **`InvokeGateway`** found under **`ccapi/chaincode/invokeGatway.go`**.

Refer to the implementation, as follows:

```
func InvokeGateway(channelName, chaincodeName, txName, args string,
transientArgs []byte, endorsingOrgs []string) ([]byte, error) {
	// Gateway endpoint
	endpoint := os.Getenv("FABRIC_GATEWAY_ENDPOINT")

	// Create client grpc connection
	grpcConn, err := common.CreateGrpcConnection(endpoint)
	if err != nil {
		return nil, errors.Wrap(err, "failed to create grpc
connection")
	}
	defer grpcConn.Close()

	// Create gateway connection
	gw, err := common.CreateGatewayConnection(grpcConn)
	if err != nil {
		return nil, errors.Wrap(err, "failed to create gateway
connection")
	}
	defer gw.Close()

	// Obtain smart contract deployed on the network.
	network := gw.GetNetwork(channelName)
	contract := network.GetContract(chaincodeName)

	// Make transient request
	transientMap := make(map[string][]byte)
	transientMap["@request"] = transientArgs

	// Invoke transaction
	if transientArgs != nil && len(endorsingOrgs) > 0 {
```

```
            return contract.Submit(txName,
                client.WithArguments(args),
                client.WithTransient(transientMap),
                client.WithEndorsingOrganizations(endorsingOrgs...),
            )
        }

        if transientArgs != nil {
            return contract.Submit(txName,
                client.WithArguments(args),
                client.WithTransient(transientMap),
            )
        }

        if len(endorsingOrgs) > 0 {
            return contract.Submit(txName,
                client.WithArguments(args),
                client.WithEndorsingOrganizations(endorsingOrgs...),
            )
        }

        return contract.SubmitTransaction(txName, args)
}
```

Following the establishment of the gateway connection, the function accesses the desired smart contract by specifying the channel and chaincode names, enabling the invocation of transactions defined within the smart contract. It handles transient data by populating a transient map with the provided **transientArgs**. This ensures that sensitive data is passed securely and is not persisted in the blockchain ledger.

The function checks submission options, accommodating scenarios with or without transient data and endorsing organizations. Depending on the presence of **transientArgs** and **endorsingOrgs**, it can submit transactions with transient data and specific endorsement policies, only with transient data, only with specific endorsement policies, or perform a standard transaction submission when neither is provided.

Finally, CC-Tools accesses the data passed as transient in transparent form. The complete function can be found in the CC-Tools repository under **transactions/getArgs.go**.

Refer to the implementation, as follows:

```
// Unmarshal private args
transientMap, _ := stub.GetTransient()
var transientArgs []byte
if transientMap != nil {
```

```
        var transientExists bool
        transientArgs, transientExists = transientMap["@request"]
        if transientExists && transientArgs != nil {
              err = json.Unmarshal(transientArgs, &transientReq)
              if err != nil {
                    return nil, errors.WrapErrorWithStatus(err, "failed to
unmarshal transient args", 400)
              }
        }
}
```

Transient arguments play a crucial role in maintaining privacy and security in Hyperledger Fabric blockchain transactions. They allow sensitive data to be passed securely without being permanently recorded on the blockchain ledger, ensuring confidentiality. This feature is essential for transactions that require discretion, enabling only relevant data to be stored permanently. In summary, transient arguments are key to balancing transparency with privacy and security needs in blockchain applications.

Conclusion

In this chapter, the reader gained a comprehensive understanding of the critical importance of security and privacy within the blockchain ecosystem, focusing on Hyperledger Fabric's unique solutions. You have learned about channel architecture and PDCs, which are instrumental in ensuring data privacy and selective information sharing among network participants. The discussion on the operational mechanisms and the use of CC-Tools for managing PDCs has highlighted how to balance transparency and privacy effectively.

You have understood the concept of private data, its organization into collections, and the scenarios that necessitate the use of PDCs, thereby enhancing your blockchain application's security and privacy. The exploration of implicit PDCs and real-world applications, including agricultural distributions and the potential of a private CBDC, has illustrated the practical importance of these concepts in maintaining transaction confidentiality.

This chapter has equipped you with essential knowledge on securing private data in Hyperledger Fabric, preparing you to apply these insights to real-world blockchain solutions confidently.

In the next chapter, we will address the deployment of Hyperledger Fabric networks in a production environment, focusing on governance, security, and operational scalability. It explores the integration of multiple organizations, policy enforcement, and the maintenance of network stability. Transitioning from development to production requires both technical precision and strategic planning, which will be examined in detail.

Join our book's Discord space

Join the book's Discord Workspace for Latest updates, Offers, Tech happenings around the world, New Release and Sessions with the Authors:

https://discord.bpbonline.com

CHAPTER 12
Production Networks

Introduction

This book has encompassed a range of subjects, beginning with the foundational aspects of blockchain technology, advancing through the specifics of Hyperledger Fabric, and detailing the process of developing applications with CC-Tools. The subsequent phase involves deploying these applications within the real business environment. This necessitates the establishment of networks that are created for actual use by various organizations in a collaborative manner.

The creation of networks ready for business application is a topic with numerous approaches. This chapter serves as a guide for transitioning applications from a developmental stage to a fully operational environment. Although the subject of preparing networks for business use is extensive enough to merit its discussion, the focus here is on essential considerations.

The preparation of networks for business entails a broad spectrum of considerations, including deployment on cloud platforms, understanding network configurations, and mastering the requisite technical skills for maintaining operational stability.

This chapter will cover the fundamentals of configuring and managing a Hyperledger Fabric network for business purposes. Emphasis will be placed on utilizing cloud services to establish a resilient, secure, and efficiently functioning network. It will outline the requirements for a network to be deemed ready for business, such as continuous availability, reliability, and security. Additionally, the chapter will discuss the infrastructure components necessary for constructing such a network and the advantages of cloud deployment, highlighting its adaptability, scalability, and cost-effectiveness.

This chapter will also touch upon Fabric-specific configurations to consider when structuring and deploying a production network, such as channel block formation rules, certificate rotation, node optimization, monitoring options, and more.

By the conclusion of this chapter, the groundwork for understanding how to prepare a network for real-world business applications will have been laid.

Structure

The chapter covers the following topics:

- Characteristics of production network
- Production infrastructure
- Fabric configuration
- Deploying in production

Objectives

By the end of this chapter, readers will be equipped with a general understanding of production networks, starting from defining their key characteristics to outlining the most important requirements to consider for their deployment. By its conclusion, readers will have gained the ability to identify aspects of production networks that are essential and comprehend the basic requirements necessary for successful deployment. The text discusses some available methodologies of deploying in varied environments, emphasizing the processes involved with **virtual machines** (**VMs**), Docker, and Kubernetes, ensuring readers are prepared to independently navigate each deployment scenario. Additionally, it extends the discussion towards deploying Hyperledger Fabric using cloud infrastructure. More importantly, this chapter will deal with Fabric configurations to consider when deploying production environments. The chapter concludes with an introduction to production deployment tools, covering technical-oriented solutions like Hyperledger Bevel and Fabric Operator and less-technical ones like *GoFabric*, an orchestration platform.

Characteristics of production network

In previous chapters we have focused on application development, and, generally, when an application is ready, the next step is to bring it to the real world with a production-grade network. Hyperledger Fabric is a framework that is agnostic to deployment and management methods and can be deployed in multiple ways. However, there are general guidelines that a network administrator is advised to follow to create a network with best practices.

Fabric is made of binaries that run a continuous program. The peer binary can be run on a laptop and be part of a fully functional Fabric network, even though that will not be the best of practices when deploying a production network. Fabric, also, does not impede that two peers are run on the same environment, be it a VM or physical server, but that would mean that one outage could take out two nodes at the same time. Decentralization is paramount in blockchain, so that would not be advisable, as well. This illustrates how important it is to correctly choose the infrastructure of the network as well as the actual network structure that will be deployed.

When talking about production networks, generally, the infrastructure that comes to mind is either VM or cluster-based. Those can be on public or private clouds as well as on-premises. During the discussions in this chapter, we will attempt to show the advantages, disadvantages, and caveats of the types of deployment that can be done.

Deploying a Fabric network involves setting up nodes in a distributed manner, most of the time, collaboratively, while generating and setting up digital certificates that will authenticate those nodes in the network. It is important to ensure node security on the infrastructure level, with firewall rules or even VPNs, and on the network level with TLS communication enabled between nodes, setting up correct channel policies, or setting up **Hardware Security Modules** (**HSMs**) to protect the private key of the nodes. On an application level, Fabric even supports the execution of chaincode in secure Intel SGX environments with the Fabric Private Chaincode module.

Refer to the following figure for a schematic of TLS communication:

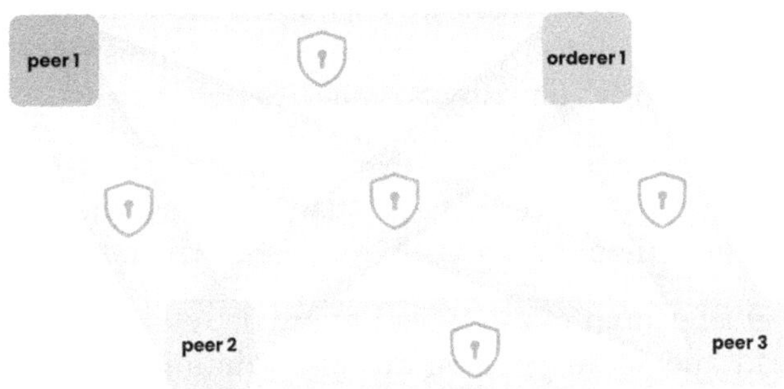

Figure 12.1: *TLS ensures secure communication within the network*

Depending on the situation, a Hyperledger Fabric network administrator will have a set of tasks that, in many cases, will encompass managing one organization, for example, for their own company, and working with others to ensure a successful deployment. The network administrator must, then, consider privacy in the network. That can take many forms, from working with application developers to establish if the application will have multiple channels, and which organizations should be part of each channel, to establishing ways of interaction with the blockchain that use certificates with the correct permissions, such as client certificates. Additionally, it requires coordinating with the chaincode developer to correctly configure private data collections throughout the chaincode lifecycle.

The topics of security and privacy are tightly related to channel configuration and policies. At this point, you have a solid knowledge of how aspects of the channel might influence the security and privacy aspects of a network. The channel configuration block is the sole place where organizations are defined for the channel, that is, it is the structure that will allow a particular organization to be a part of the channel or not, be it as an application organization or an orderer organization. The channel will hold the public certificate of the **certificate authority** (**CA**) of the organization, and even how that CA is managed will influence security.

Network administrators have many options for CAs in an organization. They could simply generate a self-signed certificate and private key pair using a **command line interface (CLI)** tool like OpenSSL. Although, technically, that would work, it would require that administrator to do many manual things, such as issuing new identities for the nodes, tracking those identities and even tracking revocations and providing **certificate revocation lists (CRLs)** when needed. Hyperledger Fabric provides a binary called **cryptogen** that serves that very purpose in development environments, but never for production.

The next level would be deploying, for example, a CA implementation that will have all the tools needed for the correct management of certificates. One implementation, the Fabric CA, generates its own self-signed certificate when deployed from scratch. These CA can be deployed in a secure environment, used for certificate issuance, and even turned off when it is not needed.

The Fabric CA can also receive a certificate and key from the external world, which allows it to be an intermediate CA in a certificate chain, just like **Secure Sockets Layer (SSL)** certificates for web pages. And of course, the network administrator can choose to use a completely external CA, if their company has one.

Still on the topic of CAs, the Fabric CA, together with the peers and orderers, can be altered to support HSMs. This means that certificate issuance will use the HSM to generate, store, and then sign data, maintaining the private key always private.

It is also on the channel configuration where many network policies are defined. These encompass from read and write policies, but also administration policies. Governance is a widely discussed topic in blockchain, and administration policies will determine the governance aspect of the network, such as which combinations of organizations are needed for a configuration change to happen, such as adding new members, changing the ordering service, or even changing block formation rules.

Refer to *Figure 12.2*, where we can see how channel policies can be customized, as an example:

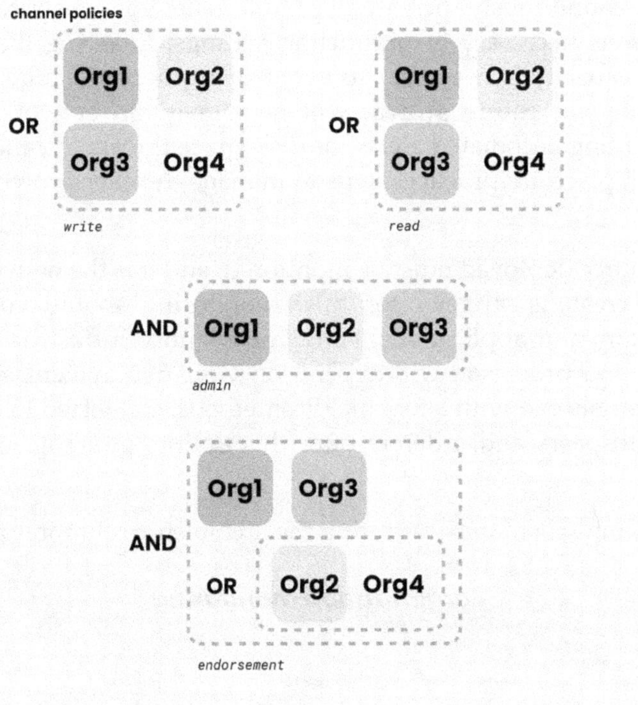

***Figure 12.2:** Channel policies will vary depending on the business case*

Scalability is key for a production-grade Fabric network. A network is a live entity that must adapt to business requirements across time. As the network grows, it must handle increased loads efficiently. Fabric boosts scalability by adding more peers, orderers, and channels. Horizontal scalability distributes transaction loads across multiple peers, preventing bottlenecks. The ordering service can also scale horizontally with additional nodes using distributed services like the standard Raft protocol, which improves scalability and fault tolerance. Channels segment the network, increasing throughput by allowing parallel transaction processing.

Another aspect that must be decided in the very planning of the network is whether to use CouchDB or LevelDB. They can influence transaction execution performance. LevelDB, the default state database, is lightweight, using an embedded key-value system ideal for simplicity and performance. It checks the box for basic read and write operations with lower resource consumption, but its limited query capabilities make it less suitable for applications needing complex queries. CouchDB, an optional state database, supports rich JSON-based queries, making it ideal for complex data retrieval needs. It provides a RESTful API and can store complex data structures but requires more resources and is slightly more complex to manage.

Storage is also an aspect that must be a focus of a network administrator. A blockchain is a database that only ever grows. Each transaction adds a new block to the ledger, making the storage needs continuously increase over time. Therefore, a strategy to monitor and expand disk space is necessary in production settings. Ensuring that the network has sufficient storage capacity is necessary to avoid disruptions. Regularly tracking storage usage and planning for future growth will help maintain network performance and stability. Implementing automated alerts for disk space thresholds and having a scalable storage solution in place are practical steps to manage the ever-growing blockchain data effectively.

Finally, every resource deployed must be monitored, and it is the network administrator's responsibility to create a strategy for this. Monitoring should cover infrastructure, network, blockchain, and applications. How you monitor infrastructure usage, such as storage, memory, and processor, will depend on your deployment. At the Fabric level, nodes should be monitored with a tool like Prometheus, connected to the operations port of each node. Both peers and orderers offer this option, guaranteeing visibility of the network's health.

Refer to the following schematic illustrating the architecture of monitoring tools:

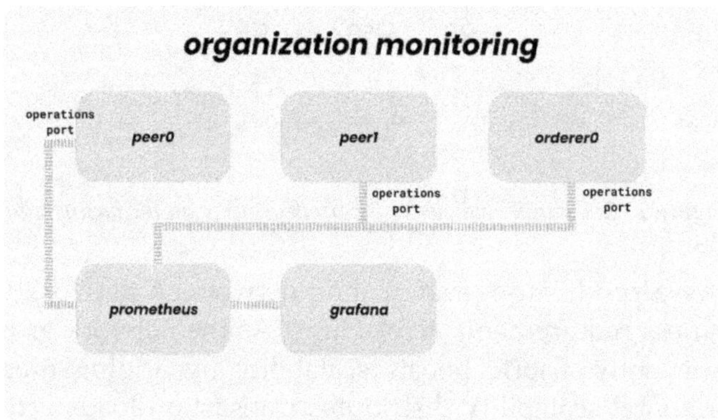

Figure 12.3: Fabric supports peer and orderer monitoring with Prometheus and Grafana

Production infrastructure

One of the first decisions is where to deploy your Fabric resources. Fabric is flexible with deployment methods, allowing the network administrator to choose. While we will discuss a few methods and infrastructures, these are not the only options. The options we cover tend to become more automated and reliable, but also more complex, which is not always positive.

First, we will explore the basic element of our deployments: the compute resource that will host the network's components, typically a VM. We will begin by examining the simplest deployment method, which involves using Fabric binaries directly on the VM. This approach means manually setting up the Fabric environment and running it on the system, providing a straightforward yet basic deployment strategy.

Next, we will cover more advanced techniques by introducing Docker and containerization. Containers offer an efficient and consistent way to manage and deploy applications, including Fabric. We will discuss various containerization strategies, highlighting their advantages in terms of scalability, portability, and ease of management. By using Docker, we can create isolated environments that ensure consistent performance across different stages of development and production.

Finally, we will address Kubernetes deployments, which allow for the dynamic scaling, management, and orchestration of containers. We will explore how Kubernetes can be used to deploy Fabric networks, discussing its benefits in maintaining high availability, resilience, and seamless updates. However, it is important to note that Kubernetes can also introduce unnecessary complexity, which may not be suitable for all deployment scenarios.

By the end of this discussion, you will have a clear understanding of the different deployment methods for Fabric networks, ranging from simple VM setups to more complex Kubernetes orchestrations, enabling you to choose the best approach for your specific needs.

Virtual machines

Deploying on servers, be it bare metal or VMs, requires similar approaches. We will assume VMs since many production deployments will be done on cloud providers using compute services that employ VMs. You should be aware of the many possibilities and take everything here as general guidelines, not strict requirements.

Not always a network administrator has the power to decide where their company's organization resources will be deployed. That will depend on what type of infrastructure the company already uses. Perhaps the company has on-premises servers, uses AWS, Google Cloud, Azure, or operates in a hybrid environment. This should not matter if the infrastructure is sound, can be scaled to the desired computing and networking requirements, and provides the prerequisites to run Fabric. One important thing to note is that each organization should provide its own hardware to host its own organization's resources.

The fabric should be a distributed network and, as with every blockchain network, the more distributed the better, meaning it will span different environments for different organizations. Communication between nodes is vital, for that reason a high-speed network should be used. The official documentation of Fabric suggests a minimum of 1 Gbps between all nodes and organizations for a production setting.

On the matter of the underlying VM resources, it is necessary to talk about storage, CPU, and memory. Remember that Fabric, as a blockchain network, writes and reads a high volume of data to the disk. Official documentation suggests always using the fastest disk storage available. This will vary if you are using a cloud provider with network-attached storage or on-premises with a physically attached disk to the server. Storage size will vary, and you should monitor it to scale accordingly. A general guideline is to use the 70 to 80% threshold to trigger a resource scaling.

CPU affects network performance on peers, so allocating as much as possible will improve network performance. Orderer nodes should have 1 CPU with 2GB of memory as a general guideline.

Non-technical requirements should also be considered when deploying resources, depending on the usage. For example, some applications have geographical restrictions for regulatory purposes, which may impede the network administrator from using resources on different cloud regions, and this may impact cost and security. The location of the deployment should also be easily scalable. A location that checks all the initial boxes for deployment but does not allow for resource scaling will only go so far.

Note that, so far, the things we talked about do not cover deployment methods, but rather infrastructure requirements that will be the same for VMs, Docker, Kubernetes, or any other deployment method.

Using VMs without any additional layers of resources will provide a straightforward deployment method. In this case, the network administrator will perform a fully manual deployment, albeit auxiliary code and scripts can be developed to automate deployment. Later, we intend to build upon this by adding additional layers with Docker and Kubernetes.

Before deployment begins, the network administrator must be sure that their infrastructure is ready to run Fabric and its binaries. Downloading and installing the binaries with proper versions for the operating system should be the first step. These binaries will be run directly on the machine. Specific Fabric configurations to consider will be covered in the following section.

Depending on the network set-up, as the network admin, you should make sure that your VM hosts are accessible via private IP (for network deployment behind a VPN), public IP, or a configured domain, with the proper ports open. Fabric resources can be configured to run on any port of your choice.

Docker

Running binaries directly on machines can pose problems that are well known in modern application development. Running the same application on different systems may require different setups, dependencies, and binary compilations. Containerization is then used to allow for different environments to run the same applications with minimal changes. Containerization will also allow more control over the applications being run, like scaling, health monitoring, and self-healing.

Deploying a Fabric network with Docker works the same way as any other deployment, with the difference that now applications are running inside Docker containers. For that reason, additional details on networking and storage must be considered. As a network admin, you should make sure that your container is reachable and that volumes are correctly mounted onto the container to make sure that persistent storage is being used. Fabric provides official Docker images for every resource needed, meaning that our pre-requisite for running Docker is now only a Docker installation.

Using Docker will allow many configurations to be saved and reused on other deployments or even shared with business partners by using Docker Compose files.

Refer to the following illustration on the hierarchy of Docker and containers in a VM:

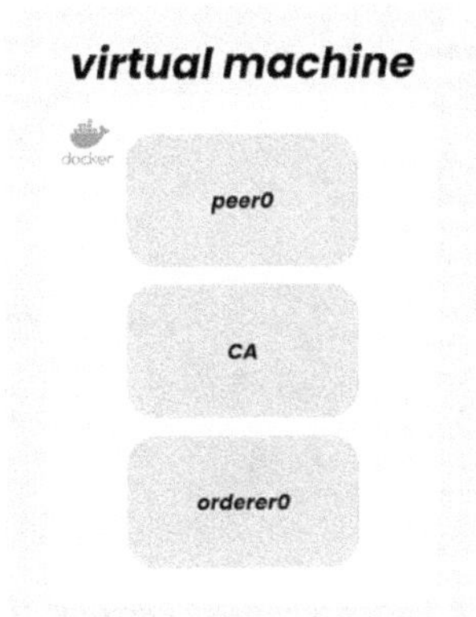

Figure 12.4: Fabric resources deployed on a simple Docker environment

Kubernetes

Kubernetes is widely known in the world of modern development, but if you have never heard of it, it is a platform designed for automating the deployment and management of containerized applications. You can think of Kubernetes as one level higher than Docker based management. Kubernetes orchestrates clusters in VMs and schedules containers to run on those machines. It is commonly used to provide a consistent environment for development, testing, and production, enhancing the reliability and efficiency of deploying and managing applications at scale. It is important to underscore that a Kubernetes cluster setup can be significantly more time-consuming and complex than using Docker.

Deploying Hyperledger Fabric on Kubernetes offers several advantages, including dynamic scaling, high availability, resilience, and seamless updates. To set up Kubernetes, you need to install it on your VM or server, ensuring the installation is verified for proper functionality. Creating Kubernetes manifests for Fabric involves defining deployments for peer nodes, orderers, and CAs, as well as services to expose these components.

Proper network configuration is essential, which involves setting up Kubernetes networking for inter-container communication and configuring Ingress controllers for external access. Persistent storage must be handled by creating **Persistent Volume Claims**

(**PVCs**) and **Persistent Volumes** (**PVs**) to ensure data persistence across pod restarts and deployments. However, it is important to evaluate the complexity Kubernetes introduces, as it may not be suitable for all deployment scenarios, particularly for simpler or smaller-scale setups, and many of the Kubernetes advantages can be easily achieved with Docker as well.

Refer to the following schematic illustrating Kubernetes architecture for an example network:

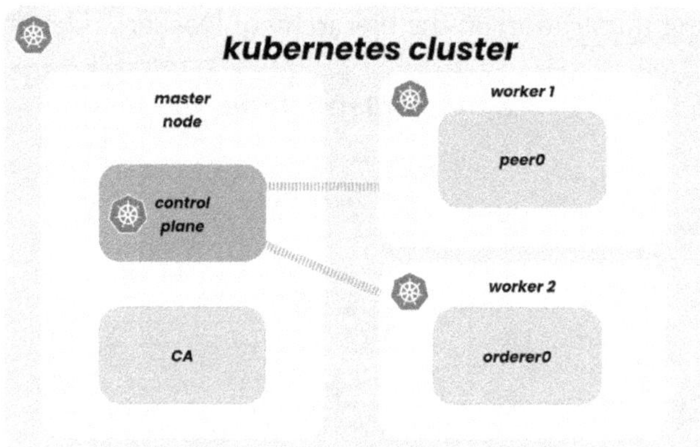

Figure 12.5: Kubernetes diagram example

Fabric configuration

Hyperledger Fabric networks are extremely flexible and customizable. In conjunction with the infrastructure choice, the network configuration itself must be decided following best practices, requirements, and possible infrastructure limitations.

In this section, we will cover production considerations for Fabric resources, their setup, and how to optimize performance.

Certificate authority

As you are aware, organizational resources require an identity known by the network represented by a public certificate and a private key. This identity can be issued in many ways, from standard OpenSSL commands to certificate authorities.

Fabric provides its own CA implementation, called Fabric CA, which is the recommendation made in the official documentation. However, you can use external CAs and even deploy a Fabric CA as an intermediate CA. Here, we outline considerations for Fabric CA.

The topology of CAs can vary. To increase security in the overall network, it is recommended that identity certificates be issued separately from certificates that secure TLS communication. That means two CAs per organization are suggested, an organization

CA and a **Transport Layer Security (TLS)** CA. Different CAs will ensure that these two layers of the network are secured by different root certificates.

Fabric provides an option to configure two CAs in one, which combines an organization's organization CA and a TLS CA within a single CA. They operate on the same node and port but are identified by different CA names. This allows each CA to have its configuration while sharing the same runtime and database.

There is also the choice to deploy intermediate CAs, establishing a chain of trust for added security. Although this is optional it is useful when an organization already has its own root CA, allowing the Fabric CA to work as an intermediate CA for the blockchain network. Another reason for an intermediate CA is when a company has many departments that will be separate organizations in a Fabric network.

Finally, Fabric CA can be integrated with a **Lightweight Directory Access Protocol** (**LDAP**) server by providing connection details during configuration.

Before we go through other resources, it is important to touch upon the matter of certificate rotation. Every single identity issued will have an expiry date, defaulting, generally, one year after the issuance date. The network administrator must be attentive to the expiry date and consider rotating certificates before the expiry. Many production projects in the past went live only to completely break after one year because peers and orderers could not communicate and sign messages anymore. To make matters worse, rotating certificates after expiration is a hard feat because orderers do not recognize updates to the configuration block anymore, since signatures are made by expired certificates, meaning the block certificates cannot be updated. This causes the administrator to have to time-shift orderer to a time when the certificates were not expired.

Peers

Peers will have their identity issued by the CA of their respective organization; with all the considerations we made in the previous subsection. The peer needs not only its own certificates, singing, and TLS but also a set of certificates of the organization, with root CA and intermediate CA certificates when needed. Thus, the network administrator must manage a directory structure that is organized. Fabric CA can automatically generate and output files in a folder structure in the expected standard when using the **`fabric-ca-client`** command with the **`--mspdir`** flag.

In a production setting peers should have TLS communications enabled, to prevent attacks and secure communications between nodes. Meaning, those certificates should also be issued by the CA.

One thing to consider is the peer count for the organization. Increasing peer count can improve network performance since transaction endorsements can be done by different peers at the same time. However, beware that performance gains can be hindered by the way client applications deal with peer selection when sending requests.

The number of channels in a peer can also influence performance. The official Fabric documentation states that a single channel in a peer cannot drive the peer's CPU usage beyond 70%, which means that multiple channels will consume the available resources, and if channel loads are not correlated, multiple channels are a good option for increased performance. As a general guideline, it is important to ensure that there is one CPU core available to the peer for each channel running at maximum load.

Peers have a companion database to store world data, and we have seen that it can be a LevelDB or a CouchDB. LevelDB is more lightweight and faster in some instances but does not support rich queries as CouchDB does. Although the state database choice must be done when deploying peers, it can directly influence chaincode usage, especially if the chaincode requires rich queries to be made. Most of the chaincodes created with CC-Tools will do rich queries, so have that in mind when selecting the state database.

Peers can be configured with some parameters that can restrict the number of **transactions per second** (**TPS**), such as the concurrency limit. This ensures the peer is not flooded with client requests. As a default, the endorser and delivery service has a value of 2500 concurrent requests. The gateway service has a default limit of 500 requests, and this will be the main limiter for client application requests and TPS, so it is worth tinkering with this value for your network configuration.

Orderers

Orderers will have their identity issued by the CA, just like peers. The considerations made for peers are also applicable here. One good practice regarding orderers is that orderers are deployed as nodes of an organization-specific for orderering. Using an organization as an application and orderer organization should only be done if the **BlockValidation** policy in channel configuration is set to allow only the subset of identities responsible for ordering.

One critical aspect to consider is the number of orderer nodes in the network. Increasing the number of orderers can improve fault tolerance and ensure high availability. The type of consensus mechanism used by the orderers significantly influences the network's performance and scalability. Raft is used for production environments due to its decentralization and fault tolerance capabilities. For example, an ordering service with 5 nodes will allow crash fault tolerance for two nodes. The network administrator should consider that more nodes increase communication complexity for the leader of the cluster. Generally, clusters with more than 20 to 30 members start to see performance problems. The official Fabric documentation states that once it reaches 100 nodes, they have problems maintaining quorum. Clusters with five, seven, or nine nodes with no more than 50 channels per orderer are the most popular configurations. Other models for ordering services have since been deprecated and will not be covered.

Refer to the following figure illustrating a Raft cluster:

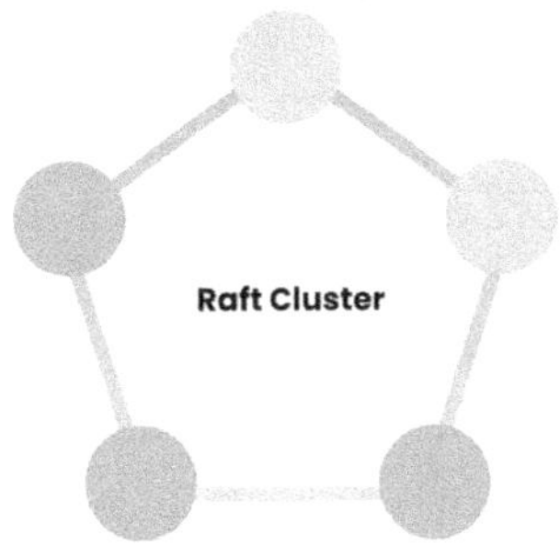

Figure 12.6: A Raft cluster with five members can tolerate two being unavailable

Orderers also handle channel management, and the number of channels can impact overall performance. Each channel will require resources, and if a set of orderers becomes a bottleneck, you should consider deploying a separate set for each channel

Orderers can be configured with parameters that influence performance, such as batch size and batch timeout. These settings help control the orderer's workload and ensure the stability of the network. The default values can be adjusted based on the specific needs of the network to optimize performance. We will cover this in more detail in the channel's subsection.

Channels

Channel configuration is one of the core parts that a network administrator will need to deal with and, as opposed to the organization's resources, channel configuration must be decided jointly with other participants, as it involves network-wide configuration and policies that determine governance.

Channel participants and their policies will vary widely between networks, because of different application requirements. However, other parameters can be tuned to improve throughput in any network, determining the ordering service block-cutting parameters.

The **`BatchTimeout`** parameter is set to the time in seconds to wait before cutting a block after the first transaction arrives. If it is too low, you will risk the block not being filled to the preferred size, and if it is too high, it will cause the orderer to wait too long to cut a new block. A good rule outlined in the official docker is maximum message count divided by maximum TPS for optimal performance.

The **`MaxMessageCount`** is the number of transactions per block. **`AbsoluteMaxBytes`** is the largest block size in bytes, typically two-ten times the **`PreferredMaxBytes`**, with a maximum recommended size of 49 MB. The **`PreferredMaxBytes`** determines the ideal block size. Usually, a transaction is around 3-4 KB. Blocks will not exceed this size unless a single transaction causes the block to exceed the absolute max bytes, in which case the block is cut, and the transaction starts a new block.

A network architecture with multiple channels is also possible. Multiple channels should be used when different scopes of data or participants are needed. Naturally, this will allow participants to be part of one channel, but not others, creating a web-like topology. If for a single application purpose data separation is not a problem, multiple channels can improve performance, as we have seen with peer resource usage for channels. For orderers, however, each channel will create a separate Raft instance, which means that an orderer that is part of ten channels does ten times more work than one in a single channel.

Refer to the following figure that shows the architecture for a multi-channel network:

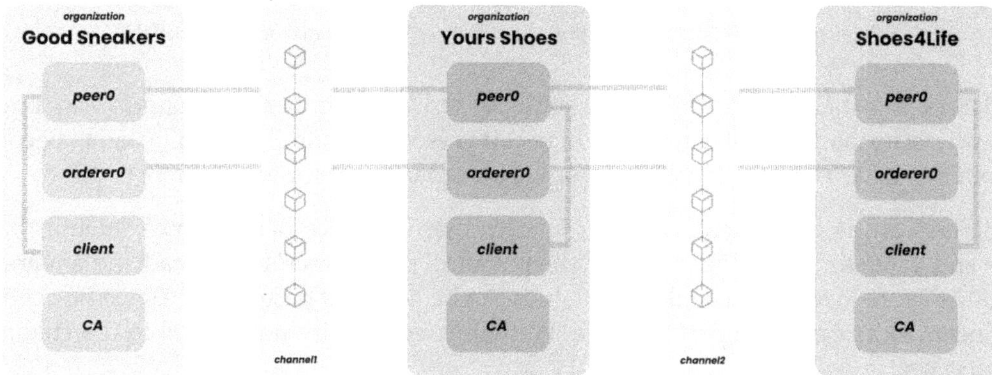

Figure 12.7: *Simple multi-channel architecture example*

In *Figure 12.6*, note that in this network architecture, we have Your Shoes being part of two channels, with both their peer and orderer being part of the two channels. The other organizations are part of only one channel each.

Chaincodes

Chaincode guidelines for production networks are related to peers and channels in some capacity. As we have mentioned, the peer choice of the state database may influence the way a chaincode is developed and used. When choosing CouchDB, indexes can and should be used to improve read performance during chaincode execution, and they should be part of the development of the application. Chaincodes can package CouchDB indexes and during chaincode lifecycle, they will automatically apply to CouchDB.

Although indexes are essential for more performant chaincodes, some queries require a full scan of the database, such as the one that uses **or** operators. These should be avoided, and large amounts of data may cause a timeout during chaincode execution.

During the course of this book, we exclusively dealt with Go chaincodes, which are known to be more efficient and use concurrency, CPUs available without any tuning. However, if you plan to deploy chaincodes in other languages, you should become aware that Java chaincodes are the least performant and that Node chaincodes are self-limiting and additional CPUs may not improve performance.

Chaincode endorsement, as you know, is a core part of the transaction flow. Endorsement policies, which determine how many peers must endorse a transaction, will affect performance depending on the policy. It is easy to imagine that a policy that requires one endorsement from any peer to faster than one that requires all peers to endorse the transaction proposal. The peer gateway service is responsible for sending the transaction only to the peers deemed enough for the policy to be satisfied.

On the same note, private data collection will significantly affect performance, reaching approximately half the TPS if it was using the world state to store an asset.

Channels can host multiple chaincodes and the choice of having separate chaincodes instantiated lies in business rules, maintenance of code, and scope of each one. Importantly, they will share the same ledger, as shown in *Figure 12.8:*

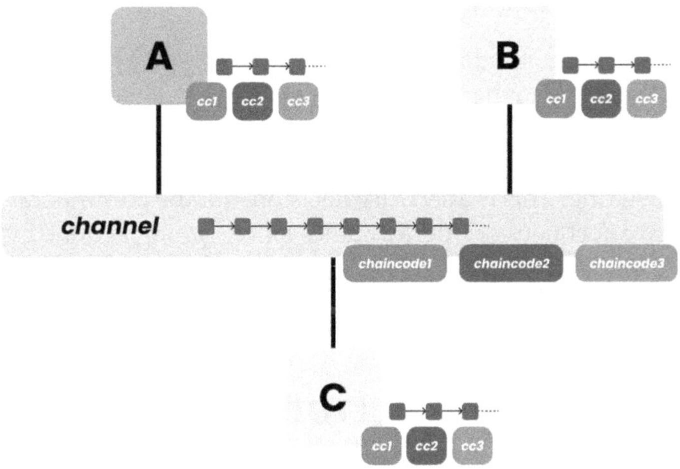

Figure 12.8: *Multiple chaincode in a channel share the same ledger*

Finally, the peer can have a custom builder and launcher for chaincodes, which enables more possibilities for the way chaincodes are run. If running the chaincode in a separate environment is important for your application, consider configuring an external builder and using the chaincode-as-a-service model.

Client applications

Client applications should use the gateway service introduced in Fabric 2.4 by leveraging the Fabric-Gateway SDK, which improves many characteristics when compared with the legacy SDKs.

The gateway service provides better throughput and avoids unnecessary complexity when writing code. Additionally, this improved service gets the necessary endorsements depending on chaincode, collection, and state-level policies, making the life of the application developer much easier.

Client applications can vary in implementation and facilitate integration with diverse systems, leveraging the blockchain for various use cases. In addition to using the gateway service introduced in Fabric 2.4, client applications should implement robust error handling and retry mechanisms where necessary. Strong authentication and authorization should be ensured by leveraging Fabric's identity management system, with client certificates.

Using HSMs

Fabric can be configured to use HSMs. They are dedicated devices used to enhance the security of cryptographic operations by safeguarding and managing digital keys. They are essential for protecting sensitive data and ensuring the integrity of cryptographic processes. HSMs generate, store, and manage encryption keys within a secure, tamper-resistant environment, preventing unauthorized access.

By reconfiguring the Fabric standard images, certificates, and private keys can be generated and connected to an HSM, where the identities' private keys are stored and the nodes offload signing to the HSM. This has big security improvements since node compromise will not expose private keys. Certain production use cases are strongly recommended to use HSMs in their setting. This is a security decision, but the administrator must know that using HSMs might affect network performance since signing is done by another resource.

Using HSMs requires more work since it is required to rebuild Fabric images enabling PKCS11 for HSM communication, which does not come enabled by default.

Deploying in production

Many tools are available to deploy Fabric production networks more easily. Automating deployment is no easy feat and it may be the case that the developer or network administrator does not have enough time on their hands to deploy a network manually. Maybe a chaincode developer merely wants to test their developed chaincode in a production-like environment.

Tools for deployment range from more technically oriented solutions, like the Fabric Operator Hyperledger Labs project and Hyperledger Bevel to less technical solutions that can increase productivity and solve support, like software-as-a-service or cloud solutions, such as *Amazon Managed Blockchain, Kaleido, Catalyst,* and the now extinct IBM Blockchain Platform.

We will briefly talk about some of the solutions available, so the reader can have a grasp of the choices available to them.

Fabric Operator

Fabric Operator is a Hyperledger Labs project and an open-source, cloud-native operator for managing Hyperledger Fabric networks on Kubernetes. It automates the detailed and repetitive configuration tasks typically required for managing Fabric networks.

Using Fabric Operator, a Fabric network is set up in a declarative manner by applying CA, Peer, Orderer, and Console resources to the Kubernetes API. The controller orchestrates containers, storage, and configurations to achieve the specified target state.

This approach reduces manual intervention and ensures a more streamlined and efficient setup and management of Hyperledger Fabric networks, allowing administrators to focus on strategic objectives while the operator handles the execution of routine tasks.

Fabric Operator configures Fabric networks on any Kubernetes environment, including local setups on your laptop. It leverages Kubernetes APIs, and supporting tools like kubectl, kustomize, helm, and SDK clients for configuration. Additionally, it allows network configuration through a web browser and integrates with Ansible and native Fabric CLI binaries.

Figure 12.9 shows an overview of Fabric Operator's architecture:

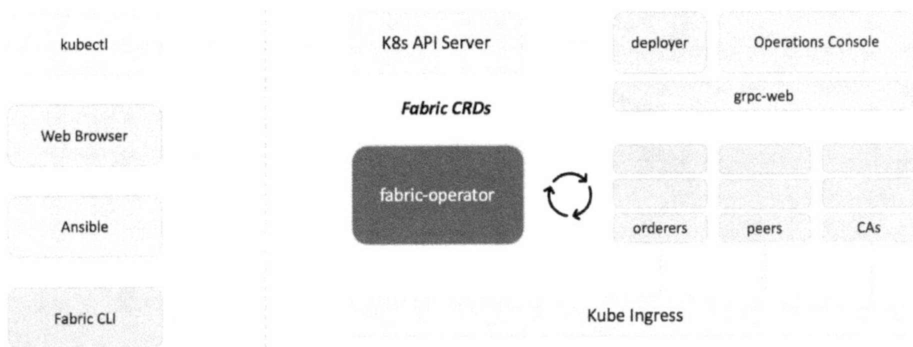

Figure 12.9: *Fabric Operator architecture*

One of its standout features is its support for CI/CD, enabling streamlined and automated deployments. It also facilitates immediate chaincode deployment with integrated chaincode-as-a-service and Kubernetes external builders.

The operator automatically detects and re-enrolls TLS certificates, ensuring continuous security. It supports hybrid cloud, multi-organization, and multi-cluster Fabric networks. It is backed by enterprise-grade support from IBM, ensuring reliability and long-term support for future migrations and revisions.

This comprehensive tool simplifies the setup and management of Hyperledger Fabric networks, allowing administrators to leverage Kubernetes' full potential and focus on strategic goals.

Hyperledger Bevel

Bevel, another project under the Hyperledger Foundation umbrella, facilitates the deployment of DLT networks like Fabric Operator. It supports Hyperledger Fabric, Hyperledger Besu, Hyperledger Indy, R3 Corda, and more, utilizing Kubernetes for container orchestration. Bevel manages networks in multi-cloud and multi-cluster environments using Ansible playbooks and Helm charts, ensuring repeatability.

It can be deployed on various enterprise cloud providers, including AWS, GCP, Azure, DigitalOcean, and OpenShift. Bevel provides Helm charts for deploying Hyperledger Cacti connectors for Fabric, Quorum, and Besu networks, enabling interoperable blockchain networks. It also offers modular role definitions to automate the deployment of Hyperledger Fabric using the bevel-operator-fabric, a Kubernetes operator for managing Hyperledger Fabric networks.

Following figure shows Bevel's architecture:

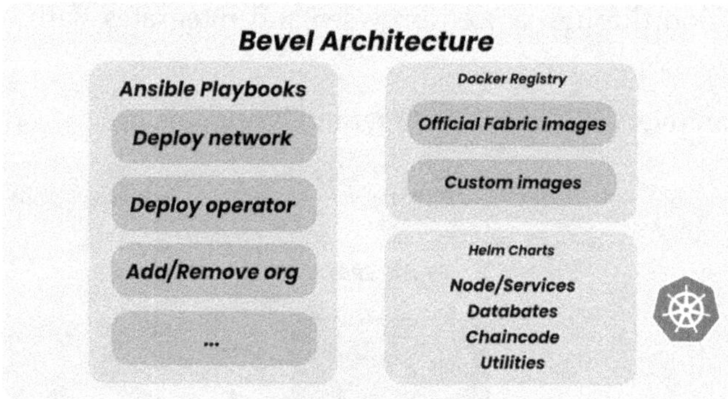

Figure 12.10: Hyperledger Bevel architecture [1]

GoFabric

GoFabric is designed to simplify the orchestration of permissioned blockchain networks using Hyperledger Fabric. It tackles the challenges of managing a growing corporate blockchain, including adding new nodes, organizations, and smart contracts, while emphasizing efficient and consistent network governance. GoFabric provides a comprehensive solution for creating a fully-fledged production blockchain network offering all the necessary artifacts for seamless network orchestration.

GoFabric deploys resources in the user's infrastructure, meaning you own the resources. It is available free of charge for starter organizations and it is a great way to deploy and test the chaincodes you learned to develop in a production-like setting.

The following figure shows GoFabric's main organization dashboard:

1. based on source: https://github.com/hyperledger/bevel

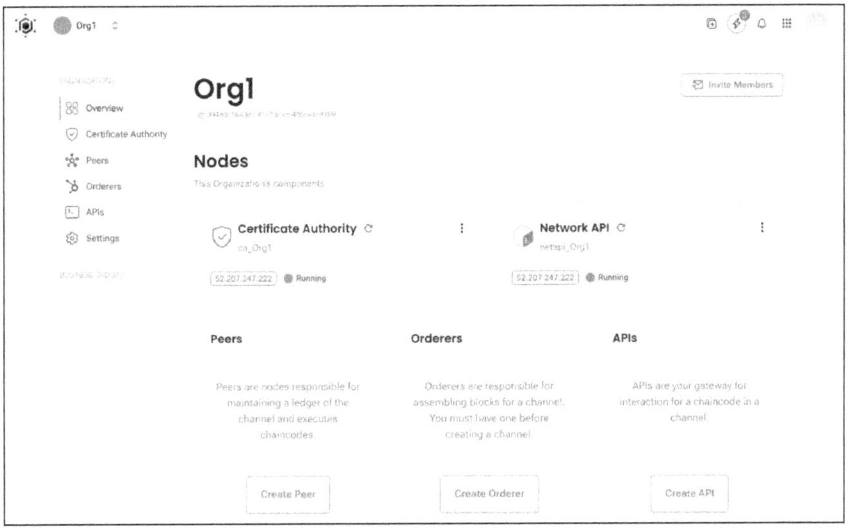

Figure 12.11: Organization dashboard allows for resource creation

It supports the creation of organizations, peers, orderer, and client applications with ease while providing the creation of business groups managed with other member organizations with a big focus on network governance. It provides also full monitoring of resources' containers, with logs and environment variable views.

Refer to the following figure for a monitoring screen example:

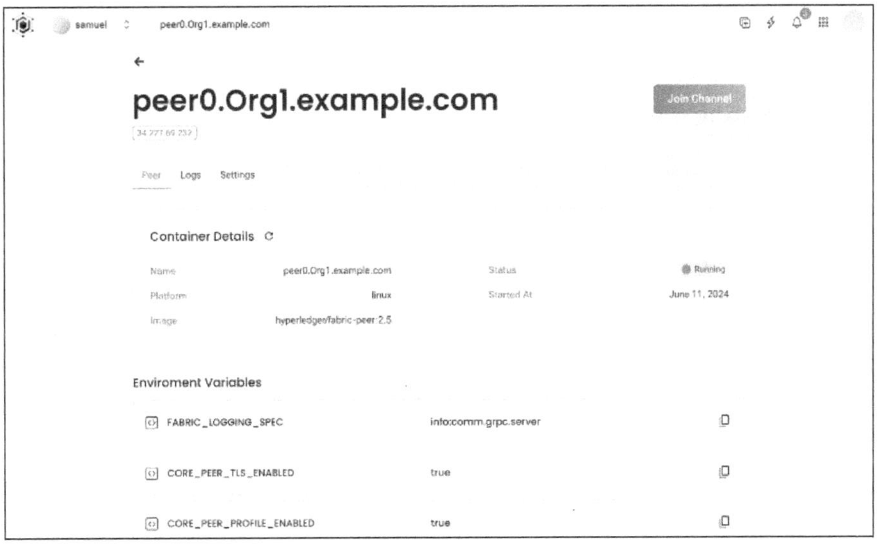

Figure 12.12: Containers can be monitored in real time

GoFabric's network management is based on proposals for changes that must be approved according to the network's governance policy.

Following figure shows an example of a proposal that must be approved:

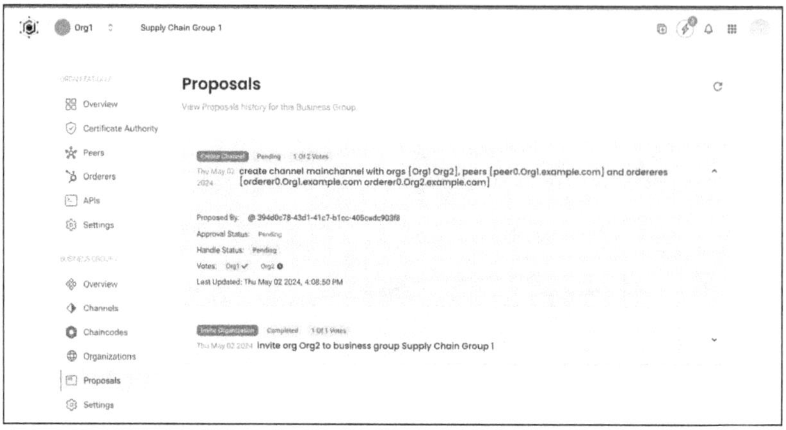

Figure 12.13: *Proposals govern how the network is managed between organizations*

Conclusion

In this chapter, we learned the essential characteristics of a production network and the critical components required for its deployment. We explored various production infrastructure options, including VMs, Docker, and Kubernetes, and delved into the detailed configuration of Hyperledger Fabric, covering CAs, peers, orderers, channels, chaincodes, client applications, and the use of HSMs.

We covered good practices when setting up CAs for an organization, covering CA and TLS CA as well as intermediate CAs. We also covered the importance of tracking certificate expiration and rotating them.

We covered how peer and orderer quantity impact network availability, crash tolerance, and performance, requiring a thoughtful decision based on real-world requirements.

The chapter provided a comprehensive overview of deploying Hyperledger Fabric in production environments, highlighting tools like Fabric Operator, Hyperledger Bevel, and GoFabric. By understanding these elements, the reader is now equipped with the knowledge to identify key aspects of production networks, comprehend their basic requirements, and navigate different deployment scenarios using a variety of tools and methodologies.

In the next chapter, readers will reflect on the broader implications of blockchain adoption, moving beyond technical implementation to examine its transformative impact on digital ecosystems. It explores how blockchain redefines trust, decentralization, and system integration, contrasting these advancements with traditional client-server architectures. This final discussion highlights the fundamental shifts blockchain introduces to digital infrastructure and its role in shaping the future of technology and society.

CHAPTER 13
Web3 Society

Introduction

By reading all the chapters, we covered how to develop and deploy business blockchain networks using the Hyperledger Fabric framework. This is the last chapter, and by now, you already know the main principles of one of the most critical digital distributed technologies available. However, as important as technical knowledge is understanding the goals and changes that blockchain will provide to enhance digital systems capabilities, evolve society, and create a neatly integrated environment.

Blockchain offers several artifacts for registering programmable and auditable data with tamper-resistant capabilities. As more processes are integrated with distributed technologies, society stands to gain from the digital trust and innovation they provide. This underscores the significant role of blockchain in our digital future. Hyperledger Fabric is one of these distributed technologies.

This final chapter will not contain technical details or exercises. The focus will be on the transformative impact of the growing adoption of blockchain technologies and how they differ fundamentally from traditional digital projects, particularly concerning client-server architectures.

Structure

The chapter covers the following topics:

- Web3 revolution
- Importance to our society

Objectives

By the end of this chapter, readers will know the possibilities of blockchain innovation in our society. After the book explains how to create Hyperledger Fabric networks, it is time to assess the consequences of applying such technology in real-world processes.

The history of digital platforms from Web 1.0 to Web 3.0 will be discussed, especially to create a deeper understanding of the differentials regarding the use of distributed technologies. The primary aim of this chapter is to equip you with the right mindset to contribute to the creation of more resilient, secure, and efficient networks. By bridging technical knowledge with practical application, we can drive the evolution of digital transformation processes.

Knowledge acquired during the chapter studies will meet real case-turning key usages that will be pursued in the reader's professional future.

Web3 revolution

For the past decades, technology has evolved at a fast pace, providing more ways to benefit the population and provide the best artifacts for them to connect. Sharing information was key to navigating the path to a better life in modern society.

Trust has always been a fundamental requirement in systems development. The pursuit of reliable digital systems has been reflected throughout computer programming history, but until recently, most of the effort has been done using centralized approaches.

Web 1.0

With *Tim Berners-Lee's* advent of the **World Wide Web** (**WWW**) in the late 1980s, a large number of new possibilities have arrived in the digital world.

The first era of WWW, or Web 1.0, was characterized by static, read-only web pages that provided information but offered limited interactivity with HTML programming. The population began to use web browsers to access static sites around cyberspace.

The quest for making the web accessible, usable, and especially reliable had begun.

Web 2.0

Web 2.0 marks the achievement of usability standards that reflect the user experience when accessing the WWW, especially through new website platforms and mobile applications.

Regarding the client-server approach, backend technology evolved several times, from databases to application servers, but the population could notice greater improvements at the presentation layers, with a large set of mobile applications that changed the digital society forever.

It is not an exaggeration to say that Web 2.0 was a revolutionary period for front-end technologies, even though some back-end techniques had evolved significantly.

Web 2.0 technological upgrades reached greater usability and accessibility levels that the users could easily perceive. However, most of the architecture was still centralized, and this approach did not fulfill some goals regarding security and trust.

Web 3.0

Maybe readers have already heard about the expression Web 3.0, but it is important to notice what really changes with the arrival of Web 3.0 in digital development and processes.

Web 3.0 speeds up the pursuit of the achievement of some important requirements for our digital society, like trust, data ownership, interoperability, and privacy.

These requirements could be obtained up to a point using traditional and centralized techniques, but these techniques were not enough for a satisfactory offering.

Web 3.0 approach has some key characteristics, as follows:

- **Decentralization:** It emphasizes distributed networks and blockchain technology.
- **Interoperability and data integration:** It connects information across different platforms and databases.
- **User control and privacy:** It enhanced user control over data and digital identities.
- **Programmability and automation:** Allows autonomous processes to be executed flawlessly with certain parameters.
- **Reliability:** Ensures trust over digital data.

Web 3.0 marks a significant shift from the current web paradigm, introducing new methodologies and structures that transform how we interact with digital systems and manage information.

Web 3.0 speeds up the pursuit of achieving some essential requirements for our digital society, such as trust, data ownership, interoperability, and privacy. These elements are crucial for creating a more secure and user-centric internet experience. Trust is essential for online transactions and interactions, ensuring data integrity and authenticity are maintained.

Data ownership empowers users, giving them control over their personal information and the processes designed to use this data.

Interoperability is another critical requirement, as it allows different systems and platforms to communicate seamlessly, fostering a more connected and efficient digital environment. Interoperability and data integration enable the connection of information across different platforms and databases, facilitating a more cohesive digital ecosystem.

Privacy is increasingly vital in today's digital age, ensuring users' information protection against unauthorized access and misuse. While traditional and centralized techniques could achieve these requirements, they often failed to provide a satisfactory solution.

User control and privacy are significantly enhanced in Web 3.0, providing individuals with greater control over their data and digital identities. This control is crucial for building trust and ensuring the correct and appropriate usage of personal information. Programmability and automation are also fundamental aspects, allowing autonomous processes to be executed flawlessly with predetermined parameters, increasing efficiency, and reducing human error.

The Web 3.0 approach introduces several vital characteristics that address these shortcomings. Decentralization, which emphasizes distributed networks and blockchain technology, is at the core of Web 3.0. This structure eliminates single points of failure and reduces the risk of data breaches.

Reliability, a critical factor in digital interactions, ensures trust in digital data. Users can rely on the integrity and authenticity of the information they encounter online. Web 3.0 strongly relies on blockchain technology, although it may use other innovations, such as *AI, Big Data, or IoT*. These technologies complement each other, enhancing the capabilities and functionalities of Web 3.0 systems.

As Web 2.0 was a frontend revolution focusing on user interface and interactivity, Web 3.0 has arrived as a backend revolution.

It fundamentally changes the underlying structures and processes of the web, creating a more secure, efficient, and user-centric digital environment. This shift promises to transform digital development and processes, paving the way for a more advanced and integrated internet experience.

Refer to the following figure, that illustrates the different interactions from Web 1.0 to Web 3.0:

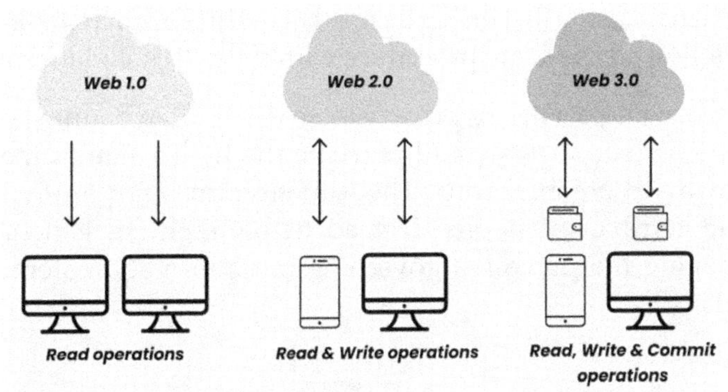

Figure 13.1: Web 1.0, Web 2.0, and Web 3.0

Importance to our society

Our society has become increasingly dependent on digital services provided by different institutions and this situation requires several requirements for each service provided. For a long time, several free or low-cost digital services were offered with a secret tradeoff: user personal data.

Social networks, media entertainment, and navigation services are some examples of platforms that users can initially access without having to spend any financial amount. At first glance, this is perceived as a great deal for most users.

Life has become more accessible, especially since the smartphone has become the most used personal device in many communities worldwide. Civilization changed, and it seemed to be for the best of all, people could communicate with each other, ask for food or supplies, and arrange trips and travels, and transportation services evolved incredibly.

Several questions were asked about how digital providers that offer so many free services could profit, as the development, implementation, maintenance, and evolution of such platforms are usually expensive. The answer became clear rather quickly, user personal data holds significant value.

Saving, processing, and selling personal data has become one of the most profitable segments of our time. Companies like *Meta* (*Facebook*) or *Alphabet* (*Google*) have arrived at the top, turning out to be among the most valuable organizations in the world. They provide a wide range of free digital services while commercializing digital propaganda for customized audiences.

At first glance, free or low-cost services seem to be an excellent way to deliver to the people. Still, soon, some noticed that all these offerings came with a price, as data privacy and digital ownership were requirements that were often put aside. Digital data silos are still a reality, saving the personal data of millions of people inside privately owned data centers, and little or nothing is known about governance for this information.

However, rather than focusing just on big tech, other entities, from regular service providers to governments, followed the same procedure with their digital platforms.

Security breaches, hacking events, or privacy losses have often haunted centralized digital silos. As bad news arrived, users could perceive the high value of the digital personal data they gave away to organizations. This situation does not imply that any of these organizations had terrible intentions. Instead, it highlights a general need for more diligence in managing the processes governing the information stored in data centers worldwide, as follows:

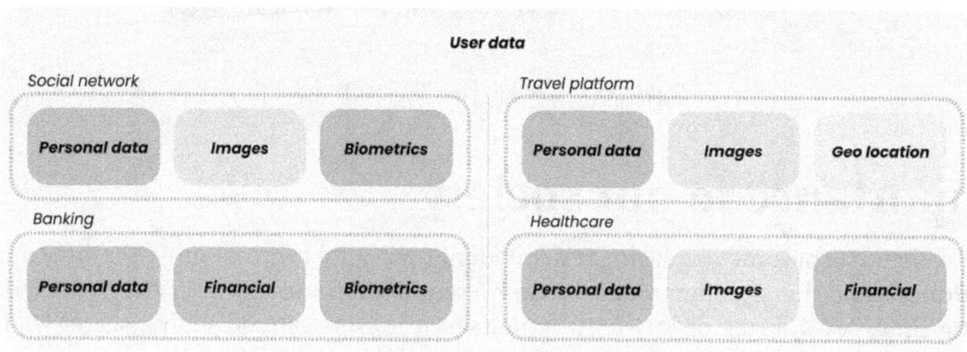

Figure 13.2: *Data Silos*

Some pillars of security governance reside in best practices like real-time auditability, anti-tampering procedures, and user data privacy measures. Still, the centralized approach adds many hurdles to proper digital process management.

Society and regulators have highlighted some of these erratic situations, and digital platform companies are increasingly pressed to provide the correct tools to tackle them.

The pressure regarding the usage of more reliable digital platforms has naturally found a comfort zone at **decentralized ledger technologis (DLT)** and blockchain-based systems as they provide several important features necessary for evolving the client/server paradigm and offering better-governed solutions to society. The emphasis will be on changes that will happen with the growing adoption of blockchain technologies, and how it differs from traditional digital projects, especially regarding client-server schemes.

The emphasis will be on evolutionary changes with the growing adoption of blockchain technologies and how they differ from traditional digital projects, especially regarding conventional digital approaches.

Web3 approach versus client/server architecture

Client/server architecture is widely used by technical teams worldwide, so it is normal for most of them not to consider innovation to solve digital challenges. Not all leaders push their teams to think outside the box to find new solutions for old problems.

The distributed approach of Web3 offers new and exciting possibilities that should be considered to achieve the benefits of blockchain technology. Being open to new ideas and knowing when to use one scheme or another is key to a successful digital process.

The emphasis will be on the changes that will occur with the growing adoption of blockchain technologies and how these differ from traditional digital projects, particularly client-server schemes.

For example, let us consider a regional aircraft control process, as follows:

- **Stakeholders**: Flight companies, fight regulation agency
- **Information**: Aircraft registration, maintenance, fight steps
- **Workflow**: Transactions for aircrew registration, flight logbooks, aircraft maintenance, and aircraft ownership changes

This process has the following characteristics that should make the decision-makers consider using blockchain technology for platform development:

- Several stakeholders
- Several legacy systems
- Valuable unique information among systems
- Transaction-driven process
- Digital trust and audibility

Regarding this example, it is easy to perceive the value of information. Correctly controlling aircraft and flight data results in more efficiency and safety for the sector. In the dread case of a flight crash, it is not acceptable to have inconsistencies around the legacy systems. All information should be the same, no matter where to look. More than that, a signed audit trail is important to reach the proper conclusions and take the necessary precautions to improve safety and trust between passengers and aircrew.

Blockchain technology should be used when the technical team knows how innovation may improve processes and reach the necessary acceptance levels for modern society. The Web3 society is keen to receive new solutions that will help them tackle the problems regarding the evolving relationships worldwide.

Traditional client/server architectures constantly fall on a lack of data integrity or workflow tampering, especially when dealing with distributed information and processing. It is usual to find integration system robots with the only task of receiving data from a database and passing it to another with little or no intelligence. Unfortunately, finding flaws, bugs, or security issues regarding these same robots is also common. Working with distributed data was never easy, and that is why blockchain solutions are spreading around, providing more and more reliability for digital platforms.

The Web 3.0 perspective is crucial for digital architects and developers to achieve satisfactory results and offer top-notch solutions that users will consume.

Blockchain platforms versus blockchain interfaces

After making the crucial decision to leverage blockchain benefits in their projects and systems, organizations are faced with the pivotal task of selecting the most suitable approach to creating Web3 platforms. This decision will significantly shape the evolution of their processes and services.

The first approach (mostly chosen) is to create new digital blockchain layers that will connect and interoperate with existing legacy systems, adding new trust features to old platforms. This approach requires a change in the workflow of legacy systems, creating new paths for blockchain registration schemes. After a deeper analysis, the legacy system will need to be modified to accommodate new read or write transitions that will take place outside the traditional registration data layers.

Following figure illustrates some blockchain interfaces seen in the industry:

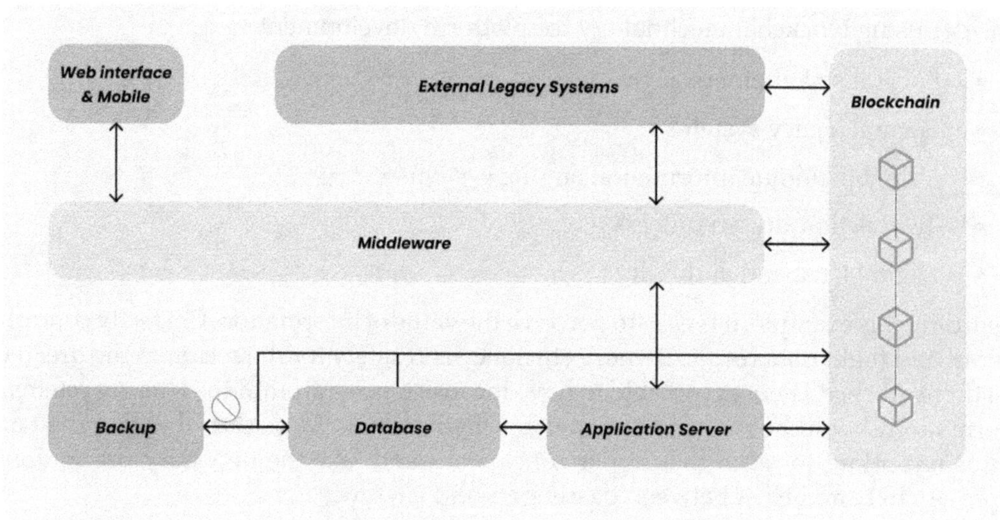

Figure 13.3: Blockchain interfaces

The figure illustrates an example of an architecture for blockchain interfaces. This example uses the following integration possibilities:

- The application server calls the blockchain directly for specific procedures.
- Database uses triggers to share data with the blockchain layer for synchronization.
- Middleware APIs read and write within the blockchain network for consistent transactions.
- External organizations may consume the blockchain directly for reliable information.
- Blockchain distributed ledger may substitute the backup server.

This approach is typically straightforward, as it often involves a relatively simple revamping of existing systems to incorporate blockchain registration into the process workflow without the need for complete system substitution.

Achieving the described result usually takes little technical effort, as it can be done by upgrading part of the application server source code, redirecting the middleware, or, even so, by creating triggers and stored procedures in the main database. The risk of adding new digital Web 3.0 artifacts as blockchain interfaces is primarily low, and the necessary development time spent creating such layers is tiny compared to substituting digital modules from the legacy platforms.

The second approach is to change the whole platform architecture to become dependent on the blockchain network. Sometimes, it is better to recreate the platform from the ground and migrate the old data afterward.

Creating a nato-blockchain platform is the best path to achieving what technology offers the best regarding processing, registering, and auditing the digital process.

Following figure illustrates integration where blockchain is the central entity in the system:

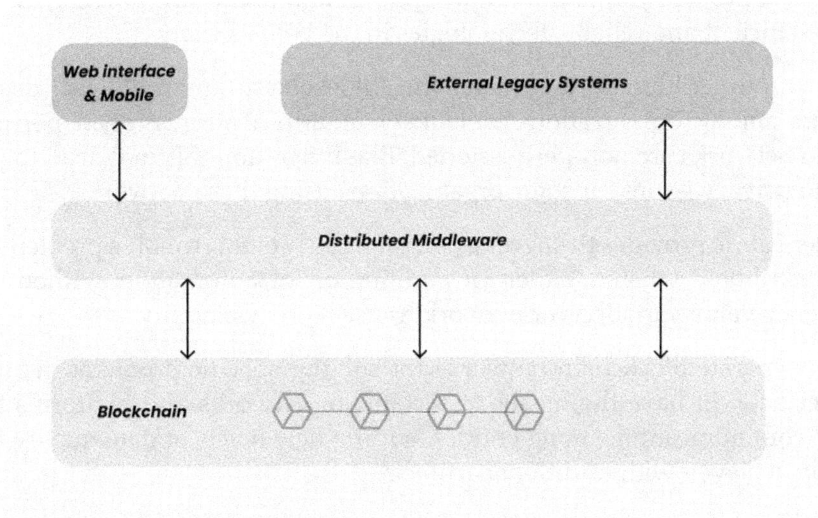

Figure 13.4: *Blockchain platforms*

The figure shown above is an example of a blockchain platform that relies almost uniquely on the technical feature which provides the following:

- Smart contract execution instead of application servers.
- Signed distributed ledgers instead of centralized databases and backup platforms.
- APIs integrated directly into the blockchain nodes.
- Wallets as the credentials for transaction committing.

Substituting old legacy systems for complete blockchain platforms is time-consuming and cost-consuming, as the development team will likely solve new technical challenges, but there is no doubt about the great advantages this approach offers regarding scalability, audibility, and automation.

Choosing between these two options is a decision that should be made with a clear understanding of the team's knowledge about blockchain and the resources available for the project. This understanding will be crucial in making an informed decision.

Hyperledger Fabric solutions

This book aims to provide the proper knowledge to create solutions that may solve problems regarding integration, processing, verifying, and tracing transactions sent and received from different stakeholders.

Blockchain technologies offer a world of potential, each offering unique features to achieve reliable data registration. The future is bright and full of exciting opportunities. As a digital architect, being well-informed about the development tools available is crucial. This knowledge will prepare you to build new systems and platforms, meeting the increasing demand for efficient and reliable technologies in the Web3 society.

Although crypto solutions dominate the blockchain environment, dealing with relationships among organizations will likely require a permissioned perspective. As most crypto networks are non-permissioned, like Ethereum, this may lead to prohibitive security and privacy issues for some organizations using these networks.

Hyperledger Fabric provides the necessary development tools to solve problems requiring trust in a distributed scheme, either for auditing or for automation, without relying on cryptocurrency value variations or network transaction availability.

By creating separate blockchain networks for solving specific problems, a Hyperledger Fabric specialist will have the means to instantiate networks and platforms for reliable transaction communication among entities, adding new levels of data quality that would not be easily achieved with traditional artifacts.

The permissioned approach raises the levels of security and privacy around the information registered within a Hyperledger Fabric network, and reliable automation can be reached, ensuring the correct processing and recording of data.

By creating different blockchain network structures, the Web 3 society goals become closer to reality, as interoperability, privacy, data ownership, and trust may be achieved by offering the necessary digital quality to the end users.

Several production-level Hyperledger Fabric use cases are already available as functional platforms enabling organizations to provide digital services to other organizations or end-users. The reliable technical concept provided by Hyperledger Fabric is widely used for different purposes at projects all around the world.

Some examples are easily found in segments as follows:

- Supply chain
- Manufacturing
- Retail/Wholesale
- Financial
- **Central Bank Digital Currency (CBDC)**
- Transportation
- Healthcare
- Cloud computing

Following figure shows the dominance Hyperledger Fabric has in the enterprise space:

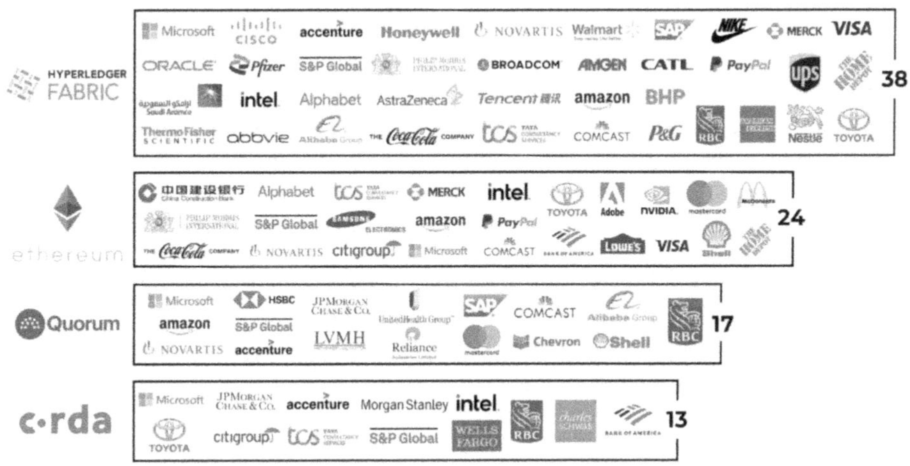

Figure 13.5: *Top blockchain technologies used by the top 100 institutions. (Source: Blockdata. tech, October 2022)*

The adoption of Hyperledger Fabric-based platforms has increased as long as the technology itself has evolved constantly. Those who have been working with Hyperledger Fabric for the past years have experienced a fast-paced evolution as new features are released to solve technical gaps and obtain state-of-the-art solutions for the market.

Two considerations are worth mentioning for Hyperledger Fabric, as follows:

- Open-source approach
- Active development community

These characteristics allow tech managers to trust the continuity and sustainability of their projects, as the open-source artifacts will help development teams create and upgrade their systems, and the community will support them actively, helping to solve bugs or plan new features.

This environment is constantly evolving not only from a technical perspective but also at institutional and organizational levels. On the release date of this book, the Linux Foundation announced the formation of the **Linux Foundation Decentralized Trust** (**LF Decentralized Trust**), aiming to support the expanding market for decentralized technologies.

This initiative will wrap up the Hyperledger Foundation, which is looking forward to fostering the growing portfolio of Hyperledger projects and supporting new initiatives critical to the emerging landscape of distributed trust. It marks a significant expansion of the foundation's commitment to open-source innovation and developing a digital-first global economy.

Conclusion

Digital platforms are substituting old processes, removing human assessment from workflows, and leaving digital machines the main tasks of processing information that was previously done by people. Trust is fundamental for society to function around relationships among people and organizations. Blockchain technology offers the means to achieve reliable services and those who know how to develop such innovative solutions will be able to enhance the services consumed by our society, therefore making it easier for users to reach their daily goals, either from business or personal life.

Reaching the end of this book, the authors would like to send you a message to readers and students who made it through the last chapter of the book. Right now, you should be able to think, design, develop, and install new programs using the development tools provided by the Hyperledger Fabric project.

Blockchain projects allowed people and organizations to better interact with each other but also offered the opportunity to many developers to increase their technical skills and capabilities and some of them have just stirred their careers, either being hired by organizations that need Web3 benefits or by creating their projects and companies that use blockchain as a tool to add value to their services.

The authors of this book are perfect examples of professionals who changed their professional lives completely by learning and applying Web3 techniques around their projects and ultimately led to a company dedicated specifically to blockchain-based platforms. After several years of learning, developing, and installing blockchain networks, we have worked for important companies in segments like supply chain, oil and gas, financial, aviation, tokenization, and more. Feel free to contact us on our social networks, not only to ask for technical information but also to share some of the projects and platforms created after studying this book.

Blockchain technology is always evolving, and Hyperledger Fabric is only one of several available options, so do not stop searching for new possibilities that may appear in the Web3 environment. This is just the beginning.

Index

F

G

H

I

K

L

T

U

W

X